AF480782

The Future:
A New Paradigm

Pathways for averting collapse

Sesh Velamoor

Published by Seshadri Velamoor

Bellevue,Washington, USA

seshvelamoor@gmail.com

Velamoor, S. (2022). *The Future: A New Paradigm - Pathways for averting collapse*.

ISBN: 979-8-9857721-0-4 (hardcover)

979-8-9857721-1-1 (paperback)

979-8-9857721-2-8 (e-book)

United States Library of Congress Catalogue Entry

Library of Congress Control Number: 2022903317 (hardcover)

Library of Congress Control Number: 2022903726 (paperback)

Library of Congress Control Number: 2022903724 (e-book)

Cover Artwork and Book Design © Lynda Sampson

Cover created using stock photography from Adobe Stock.

"Man has lost the capacity to foresee and forestall. He will end by destroying the Earth"

- Albert Schweitzer.

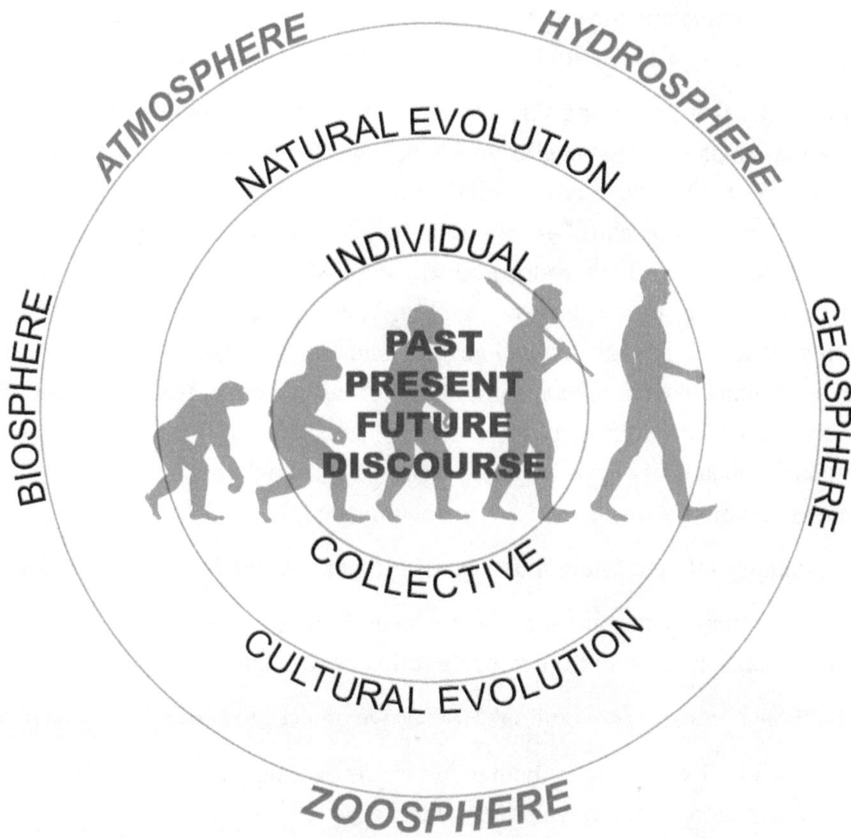

Figure 1. The Human-Earth System

Foreword

We cannot know the long-term future, but can we conceive what the future may look like over the long term? The really long term? Can exploration of human possibilities over the long term be epistemologically and cognitively justified? And what can we learn from such an exercise? These questions are somewhat similar to questions that interrogate the deep past. What was it like at the moment of the "Big Bang" or when the dinosaurs ruled the earth, or when "man" first learned to stand erect and walk? Thinking about what we might become is just as important in trying to understand what we were a thousand, ten thousand or even a million years ago. But in what respect is the dim and distant past a function of the long-range future? How many contemporary inventions and innovations, developments, and digressions—from globalization to global warming, increasing global populations, and the advent of the World Wide Web, to genetic engineering and the merging of biology and information—could have a direct bearing on the shape of humanity at the dawn of the third millennium?

The purpose in presenting this compilation of essays, talks and interviews that follow is not to provide easy, glib answers, but specifically to present the canvas upon which to explore these issues within a framework of larger totalities—such as "humankind" and "planet earth"—within the scope of an evolutionary time frame. The evolutionary perspective is there to produce subtle shifts in our mind sets, forcing a humbling capitulation to the unknown and an openness to all varieties of pluralism. Addressing issues of human survival in this framework also forces us to recognize that we, as humans, have a responsibility; not just as current custodians of the planet, but also as shapers of long-range futures: viable futures, with meaningful legacies for generations far ahead. Disregarding this responsibility would be tantamount to leaving the future generations a wasteland as their inheritance.

Any enquiry into the future must necessarily address the following questions.

1. Can humans design and obtain ideal futures, or are they mere "active" participants in an evolutionary process that creates outcomes?

2. What is conscious evolution? How do we proceed to participate in the process?

3. What will it mean to be human, given the evolutionary advances taking place in information technology and genetics?

4. Can we evolve a system of global ethics that will become the basis for our actions and supersede our current constraints and boundaries of nation-states, religious orientations and cultures?

5. How will we define and manage the role of science and technology, inclusive of social responsibility in a multi-disciplinary, pluralistic framework?

6. Will we be able to ensure global participation in the shaping of the future in an inclusive, co-equal framework?

Given all the uncertainties of the terrain, can we discern any basic principles or underlying patterns, the understanding of which could enable breaking out of the paradigmatic prisons we have been locked up in?

Of course, such questions cannot be easily answered. Indeed, they could have different answers in different world views. But they do simultaneously tax the imagination as well as give it absolutely full reign. At the very least, they force us to examine our common assumptions and widely-held premises on which we have built our modern and postmodern world.

All of this means that we need to transcend history in an imaginative and bold manner. As Francisco Sagasti[1] suggests, in his grand and sweeping essay, the unique character of this current period of history was the "articulation and implementation" of what we may call the "Baconian Program", whose main architect was the philosopher Frances Bacon, firmly rooted in the foundational ideas of the Abrahamic religions. The main driving force of this program was the belief in the unending, linear and steady advance of humanity: the idea of progress. That linear notion of progress now lies in tatters. A whole range of new discoveries and theories, from chaos to complexity, from string theories to postmodern notions of truth and reality, are forcing us to question, indeed abandon, the legacy of the Baconian Age and interrogate the very idea that "humans" are the center, sum and substance of the world!

The central idea in what follows is that the long-term future is a product of a complex set of interacting factors, forces and processes wherein humans have an active role, but do not, and cannot, determine the outcomes.

End Notes

1. Sagasti, F. (1997). *The Twilight of the Baconian Age: Background paper for a book of Essays on Knowledge, Progress and Development*. [S.N.]

This foreword used excerpts from the essay:

Velamoor, S. & Heydon, P. (2000). Exploring the next thousand years. *Futures*, 32(6). 509-512. https://doi.org/10.1016/S0016-3287(00)00003-3

Acknowledgement

A life changing journey that began in 1997, at the Foundation For the Future, extricated me from the prison of conventional thinking about the "Past, Present and Future" of our civilization.

For my re-education, I owe a deep debt of gratitude to the late Walter Kistler, the founding benefactor of the Foundation, and over three hundred scholars of world renown whose work and participation in the programs of the Foundation For the Future made a profound difference.

This brief section precludes naming them all but a few: Professor Eric Chaisson of Harvard, whose classic *Epic of Evolution* was a profound eye opener; Dr. Dawkins and his concept of "memes" to enable understanding "cultural evolution'; Dr. Sohail Inayatullah for his work on Causal Layered Analysis in explaining how to get to the causal roots of civilizational ideas; Dr. Brian Fagan for his masterful story telling in cultural anthropology; and Dr. Spencer Wells for his genetic approach in *Journey of Man*.

A deep debt of gratitude is also owed to the staff at the Foundation For the Future, especially Bob Citron, Donna Hines, Jean Gilbertson, Kevan Rayne and Tom Price, without whose support the almost flawless planning, design and implementation of the programs would have been all but impossible.

I am thankful most of all to family and friends, particularly my siblings, my wife Shobana, my children Gautam and Priya, and their spouses Mina and Jarrod for their incessant prods and taunts that motivated me to finally get it done!

Last but not least, I am thankful to Dr. Kuo Hua Chen of Tamkang University, Taiwan, for introducing me to young Ricardo Schnug, to help with putting this book together. Ricardo has been extraordinarily competent, thorough, and professional. I will be eternally grateful for his invaluable assistance throughout the writing of this book.

A debt of gratitude is also owed to Lynda Sampson for her creative endeavors in the design of the cover and the preparation of the print ready file.

References have been made throughout the book to the work of literally hundreds of scholars in support of my writings, but I am solely responsible for any and all errors, misrepresentations and or misinterpretations of their work.

Sesh Velamoor

2021.

Table of Contents

CHAPTER 1

Future as Emergence: Paradigms, Patterns and Processes

There is general agreement among scholars that humans are now in what is defined as the *Anthropocene*, best described in The Encyclopedia of Earth[1] as follows:

> The Anthropocene defines Earth's most recent geologic time period as being human-influenced, or anthropogenic, based on overwhelming global evidence that atmospheric, geologic, hydrologic, and other earth system processes are now altered by humans. The word combines the root anthropo, meaning "human" with the root -cene, the standard suffix for "epoch" in geologic time. The Anthropocene is distinguished as a new period either after or within the Holocene, the current epoch, which began approximately 10,000 years ago (about 8000 BC) with the end of the last glacial period.

The Anthropocene is a starting point in terms of a major revolution, wherein humans moved away from being hunter-gatherers and toward farming and agriculture, and for all intents and purposes, there was an onset of evolution of what can be described as "civilization" and "societies", inclusive of varieties of politics, economics, religion, and culture based on philosophies, concepts, and ideas, or operant paradigms. These operant paradigms can be traced to human attempts to understand, define and act on three major relationships, that is: humans and divinity; humans and nature, and humans *vis-à-vis* humans.

Civilizations—Eastern and Western—have, in a broad sense, operated on two such paradigms or philosophies, describing the nature of the three relationships named above. The first one, namely the polytheistic Eastern civilization, which predates the monotheistic Western paradigm by millennia, is based on the ideas that humans and the divine are inseparable: humans are part and parcel of nature, inextricably connected and interdependent, and all life, including human life, is one and the same. This philosophy is best articulated, and is synonymous with what is, in Hindu philosophy, termed as the *Sanatana Dharma*[2]. In contrast, the ideas of Western civilization postulate that humans and the divine are wholly separate: God has given humans dominion over nature to understand and use for human progress and human life is sanctity personified, over and above all other life.

Both of these paradigms are operating to this day, even though the Eastern paradigm is steadily receding into the background. Despite this, recent realizations seem to be forcing humans to reconsider returning to an Eastern paradigm, notwithstanding the fact that the Western paradigm has emerged, over the last two millennia, as the dominant one. A major difference in these two paradigms is that the Eastern template pursued knowledge for knowledge's sake, and in the process obtained profound understandings of the external world, whilst primarily being preoccupied with knowing the inner human self, based on inner-directed explorations to obtain release from the human condition (as in *Moksha*, or *Nirvana* etc.).

The Western paradigm moved forward within the framework of what is best described as the "Baconian Method". It was directed at the external world (including using the ones discovered by the East), thus obtaining discoveries and inventions to apply and use for human progress. Progress was deemed to be limitless and based on understanding and exploiting nature for meeting human material needs.

An important distinction needs to be made with respect to the inherent nature of the two paradigms. The distinction comes in respect to the scope and extent of human "agency" in obtaining desired outcomes and futures. Implied in the Western paradigm is the assumption that human agency, as ordained by the divine, is the sole determinant of desired outcomes and futures. The Eastern paradigm, on the other hand, while not eliminating human agency, is much more fatalistic and demands human agency be used within the framework of broader ideas and values described above.

Given this background, it will now be appropriate to assess the state of the planet and the general condition of humans on it, and more importantly, to examine whether the idea of human agency, as the sole determinant of desired outcomes and futures, is valid and sustainable.

The dominant paradigm operating for the last two millennia, based on human agency as the sole determinant of desired outcomes, has developed and implemented a plethora of ideas to create "Utopia". While it is important to acknowledge that the accomplishments are fantastic by way of improving the material condition of humans, uneven as it is, it would be fair to expect that Utopia would have manifested long ago. Needless to say, however, anyone looking dispassionately at the human condition and the state of the planet today, one would have to conclude that Utopia is nowhere near to being achieved and actually, in many respects, we are confronted with the stark reality of "dystopia" and unintended consequences. Human populations have burgeoned, from hundreds of millions to billions, and poverty, disease (pandemics), war, destruction of the natural world, extinction of species, climate change and impending exhaustion of natural resources etc., is there for all to see.

At this critical juncture, it is therefore imperative that we take a second look at how the future comes about. In order to get to such an understanding, it is necessary to first attempt to describe a model—a construct—that will best illustrate the process in action that causes the future to come about. It is important to first acknowledge that the paradigms and models we have used thus far have failed to be predictable, because our models for managing our futures, and the structure of the model of the real world in use, have been completely unrealistic and do not come close to reflecting the structure of the real world. As noted in 1998 by James Gleick in his book *Chaos*: "The degree to which the model (our current models!) reflects reality then, depends entirely on how the logical structure of the model and logical structure of the real-world observable match".

The following is an attempt to outline the framework of a model that more closely approximates the logical structure of the real world. The model can be described as follows.

It is a three-dimensional matrix. The first axis represents humans as participants, individually and collectively, concurrently functioning, as agents at eight different levels of identity, continuously attempting to optimize their multiple interests with respect to individual, family, neighborhood, city, state, region, nation, the planet. The second axis represents the world around them in the natural realm—that is, the hydrosphere, the biosphere, the zoosphere, the atmosphere and space and beyond—all in a constant state of flux, naturally and otherwise. The third axis represents the varieties of systems that humans have initiated and have then evolved into current forms: social, economic, political, religious, cultural et al., similarly in a state of constant flux. This complex, three-dimensional matrix, mathematically speaking, equates to a mind bogglingly huge number of dynamic interactions taking place sequentially and simultaneously every second, every minute, every hour, every day and so on. Humans act as agents between themselves, interacting with elements of the second and third dimensions. Similarly, interactions occur within and between the elements of the second and third dimension. All result in outcomes and consequences that, one can reasonably argue, would be beyond any currently known means of managing toward a desired outcome, and destroys the smug and misplaced notion of humans managing and obtaining desired outcomes and futures. The evidence to support this conclusion abounds all around us.

Scholars around the world currently suggest that humans are at a critical juncture as to their future, and that survival of the species is at risk if course corrections are not taken.

As it relates to course corrections, recent scholarship has given rise to ideas and concepts that enable a better understanding of how the future comes about, human agency notwithstanding. A complete and comprehensive presentation of them is beyond the scope of this book, but a list of them with brief definitions is as follows, along with a comprehensive reading list. The idea that the "Earth is a being" or "Gaia."

1. The Gaia Hypothesis, also known as *The Gaia Paradigm*, or *The Gaia Principle*:

> [P]roposes that living organisms interact with their inorganic surroundings on Earth to form a synergistic and self-regulating complex system that helps to maintain and perpetuate the conditions for life on the planet (Lovelock, 2005).

2. The seven principles underlying all life, as outlined by Murchie in 1981 are as follows:

> *a.   The principle of abstraction.* There is something intangible behind the life in physical bodies—indeed behind all matter. The immateriality (energy, if you will) is revealed by the flow of time, which literally makes things into events. All forms of this mysterious noumenon is abstraction.

> *b.   The principle of interrelatedness.* Geneticists tell us interrelatedness is a measurable fact among all members of a species (including humanity in all its races) and on deeper investigation, turns out to apply as well to whole kingdoms of creatures; not to mention interrelations between kingdom and kingdom, or between world and world, without end. (Also see Vital Dust: Life as a Cosmic Imperative by Christian De Duve.)

> *c.   The principle of Omniscience of life,* which denies that an impervious boundary has ever been found between any of the kingdoms, or for that matter, between life and non-life, leading to the inescapable conclusion that all rocks

and seas and worlds, and consequently the entire universe must, in a sense, be alive.

d.   The polarity principle, which recognizes the balance and mutuality of the opposites that we see everywhere: light and darkness; good and evil; male and female; predator and prey; matter and energy—all of which, by their contrast, give definition to life and make it work.

e.   The principle of Transcendence, which refers to the development of our perspectives on time and space as we grow older, as well as the progressive absorption of self into a wider awareness as one matures spiritually. All such factors ultimately reveal themselves to be, in effect, tools of learning in the inexorable drift from our ever-present earthly finitude toward some sort of infinitude far beyond.

f.   The germination of worlds. A critical event that seems to happen once to every celestial organism. After billions of years of slow evolution, this is occurring right now on Earth, as evidenced by many fundamental changes during this period we call modern times; things that, as far as we know, never happened before and can never happen again on our planet.

g.   The greatest mystery of all. The ultimate mystery of divinity—or whatever you choose to call the unknowable essence—that leading thinkers have long believed somehow exists beyond creation and maintenance of all body, mind and spirit, not to mention behind every other known or unknown wonder of the universe.

3. The Future as Emergence: Based on the description of the complex model given above, it should be easy to see that the Future "emerges" out of interaction, with human inputs as "active walkers" (as opposed to "passive walkers") (Lui Lam 2005). Some processes that are inherent in the emergence are the elements of complexity, the "butterfly effect", catastrophes, tipping points, self-organization etc. All of these have become relatively new fields of study and are producing critical insights that should be availed. A retroactive look at how things have evolved over the millennia will show close links to the above-mentioned processes at work.

A brief look at each of the processes is warranted.

1. Complexity: Simply defined as the study of the phenomena that emerge from a collection of interacting objects. Neil Johnson (2007) defines it as such:

Complexity characterizes the behavior of a system or model whose components interact in multiple ways and follow local rules, meaning there is no reasonable higher instruction to define the various possible interactions. The term is generally used to characterize something with many parts where those parts interact with each other in multiple ways, culminating in a higher order of emergence greater than the sum of its parts.

2. *Catastrophes*: Gleick (1998) notes that:

Catastrophes occur when, as we move in a continuous way through the family of parameters, usually by smoothly changing [incrementally—my word] parameters describing the system, a stable fixed point of the family loses its stability. This change of stability forces the system to move abruptly to the region of a new stable fixed point.

3. *The "butterfly effect"*: According to Edward Lorenz, in chaos theory:

The butterfly effect is the sensitive dependence on initial conditions in which a small change in one state of a deterministic non-linear system can result in large differences in a later state. (Wikipedia)[3]

4. *Tipping points*: Gladwell (2001) notes: "The critical point in a situation, process, or system beyond which a significant and often unstoppable effect or change takes place."

5. *Self-organization*: According to Yates (1987):

Self-organization, also called spontaneous order, is a process where some form of overall order from local interactions between parts of an initially disordered system. The process can be spontaneous when sufficient energy is available not needing control by an external agent.

The totality of what has been presented in the following by way of models, concepts and ideas are essentials for new approaches to the study and understanding of ourselves and the world around us. As such, humans as agents—as active walkers—play a role as an enlightened participant in the emergence of the future, with thought and respectful consideration given to the idea of the planet as our only home; a system inclusive of the biosphere, the zoosphere, the oceans, the atmosphere and space; aware of the concepts and processes described above and cognizant of the fact, as documented by evolution, that we are not exempt from extinction.

What follows in this book is a collection of works by the author penned with the specific purpose of elaborating on the idea that a desirable future that emerges will essentially be because of human agency employed in an educated, informed, bottom-up process of inputs to the complex system described above. What it requires is a shift in what is described as the *Overton Window*; the current operant paradigm and the approaches that are circumscribed by it. Named after the American policy analyst who first laid it out, Joseph P. Overton (1960-2003), this approach identifies the ideas that define the spectrum of acceptability of government policies. Politicians can act only within that acceptable range. Shifting the Overton Window involves the proponents of policies outside of the window persuading the public to expand the window. The "public" here is the human agents.

REFERENCES

Bak, P. (1996). *How Nature Works: The Science of Self-Organized Criticality.* Springer-Verlag.

Gladwell, M. (2001). *Tipping Point. How Little Things can Make a big Difference.* Little Brown and Company.

Gleick, J. (1998). *Chaos: The amazing science of the unpredictable.* Vintage

Johnson, N.F. (2007). *Two's Company, Three's Complexity.* Oneworld.

Lovelock, J. (2005). *Gaia: Medicine for an Ailing Planet.* Gaia Books.

Lui Lam, (2005). Active Walks: The First Twelve years (Part 1). *International Journal of Bifurcation and Chaos, 15*(8) 2317-2348

Murchie, G. (1981) The Seven Mysteries of Life. Houghton Mifflin.

Yates, F.E. (1987). *Self-Organizing Systems. The Emergence of Order.* Springer.

RECOMMENDATIONS FOR FURTHER READING

Ball, P. (2005). *Critical Mass.* Arrow.

De Duve, C. (1995) *Vital Dust. Life as a Cosmic Imperative.* Basic Books.

END NOTES

[1] The Anthropocene. (n.d.). *Anthropocene.info*. Retrieved, from https://www.anthropocene.info/

[2] Sanatana Dharma. (n.d.). *Encyclopedia Britannica*. Retrieved from https://www.britannica.com/topic/sanatana-dharma

[3] Wikipedia: Used extensively as reference for definitions wherever needed.

Human Futures: An Eternal Play

"Although with this phrase, I refer in general to the account of our emergence out of the fireball and into galaxies and stars and earth's life, I also think of the cosmic story as something that has not yet emerged... so too with our moment we have nothing compared to the massive accumulation of hate, fear, arrogance that the inter-continental ballistic missiles, the third world debt and the chemical toxins represent. But we are in the midst of a revelatory experience of the universe that must be compared in magnitude with those of the great religious revelations. And we need only to wander about telling this new story to ignite a transformation of humanity."

- Brian Swimme (1992)

Current Frameworks

The consideration of humanity's future in one-thousand-year time frames can be a daunting task. There are no precedents, frameworks, or structures available that can be utilized. There are, of course, many treatises available that study the past covering some or all of human civilization over, either some, or all periods of time, covering some or all aspects of human civilization. There are also those who have articulated the grand all-encompassing patterns. Nonetheless, in the final analysis they are at best incomplete and more importantly reflective of worldviews, mindsets, ideologies. The human story, the Earth's story however is all that and more. There are three broad frameworks which have until now attempted to encompass the cosmic and human story with implications for the past, present and the future.

- The Evolutionary

- The Divine Creation

- The Anthropocentric

The Evolutionary Framework:

This framework of conventional evolutionary theory has been used to encompass the totality of the cosmos in terms of time and more important in terms of a process that is more complete than any other with perhaps the exception of the idea of divine creation. This conventional notion of evolution described as "a tinkerer who during millions of years has slowly modified his products, touching, retouching, cutting, lengthening, using all opportunities to transform and create." (Jacob, 1982) It should be noted though that this framework is itself evolving and is now much expanded and inclusive of several new elements. This extended framework of evolution will be described in detail later.

The Divine Creation Framework:

This framework to think about the past, present and the future is steadily losing its appeal and there are many reasons.

It will soon be impossible for an intelligent educated man or woman to believe in a God as it is now to believe that the earth is flat, that flies can be spontaneously generated, that disease is divine punishment or that death is always due to witchcraft. Gods will doubtless survive, sometimes under the protection of the vested interests, or in the shelter of lazy minds or as puppets used by politicians, or as refuge for unhappy and ignorant souls. But the God type will have ceased to be dominant in man's ideological evolution. (Huxley, 1957)

In so far as we are interested in considering human futures — or more apropos, human destiny — the religions of the world, some two hundred of them, by last estimation, have been competing for establishing primacy of their brand of the human story, past present and future with little or no success. They are themselves locked in an unprecedented evolutionary struggle for survival, pitted one against the other. For the first time in human history, with geographic and communication barriers being dismantled they are interacting with each other on an unprecedented scale. A war of attrition is what is likely with each ending up spent as knowledge and the accumulation of it through science will erode most, if not all of their content with perhaps the exception of a theology about the "first cause" that brought the cosmos into existence and science will never completely explain." As science proceeds to dismantle ancient mythic stories one by one, theology retreats to the final redoubt from which it can never be driven. This is the idea of God in the creation myth. "God remains a viable hypothesis as the prime mover, however undefinable and untestable that conception may be." (Wilson, 1978)

The Anthropocentric Framework:

This framework gives preeminence to humans and human agency. This by far has dominated the civilizational stage for the last 2000 years and is largely an outgrowth of the divine creation myths of the Judeo-Christian traditions, but now has a life of its own in a secular cocoon. This framework dominates the current stage in human affairs. Combined with science, it is squarely positioned in the convictions of progress, control, direction, objectives, and vision as it pertains to almost any issue. It is inclusive of utopian ideas and systems such as communism, capitalism, democracy, egalitarianism, and so on. It squarely places the problems and opportunities with regard to the future at humanity's doorstep and too the capabilities to solve any problem or achieve any future. This approach is variously characterized as secular humanism, scientific humanism, and so on, with appropriate and presumably satisfactory modifications to the original and unadulterated versions of both divine creation and natural evolution. The champions and stalwarts for this have been many in the past and so too today. Here is a sampling:

> To us in our brief span of life falls the honor and good fortune of coinciding with a critical change of the noosphere. In these confused and restless zones, in which the present blends with future in a world of upheaval, we stand face to face with all the grandeur, the unprecedented grandeur of the phenomenon of man. (Teilhard De Chardin, 1959)

Barbara Marx Hubbard defines it by saying "what we are seeking is a world view that will call forth our creative action and direct our immense powers toward life-oriented and evolutionary purposes. That guiding worldview is, I believe, conscious evolution" (Hubbard, 1997).

As we stand in the present with multiple panoramic views of the past and on the threshold of a new millennial future, what do we make of it all? The present does indeed represent a critical juncture. In a civilizational sense, we seem to be at the crossroads of many interacting opposites. The frameworks discussed above, all seem to have relevance and yet all appear to be in need of profound modifications. This is manifest everywhere and the problems are many. In the fields of governance, in cultural and religious systems, in science and technology, in the area of population, resources, the environment and in respect of the very meaning of what it means to be human. All this should raise enough doubt in our minds about the anthropocentric framework and reconcile to a lesser role for human agency.

The New Framework

A new framework for considering the long-term future is akin to developing what John Barrow calls "new algorithmic compressions" (Barrow, 1991). An algorithmic compression that admits to the idea of progress in the strict evolutionary sense "as a noxious culturally embedded, untestable, non-operational idea that that must be replaced if we wish to understand the pattern of history" (Gould, 1977), and yet allows for human intervention in evolution because we already are and must continue to do so; a kind of intensive evolution articulated by Ervin László:

> I am suggesting there is a possibility for continuing the evolutionary adventure of humanity which is not the extensive mode (conquest, colonization, consumption) assumption. Instead, it is building on a tremendous momentum, which is already occurring in our lives during this present lifetime of ours and continues to gain momentum, and thus is becoming ever stronger. That is a kind of evolution which is not centered toward extensive conquest, colonization and consumption, but communication connection and comprehension. (László, 2000)

This new framework has three significant components to it. These are:

- Extended Evolution

- Gaia

- Self-Organization.

One might argue about whether it is really a new framework. There is plenty of evidence to show that earlier non-western intuitions had a good grasp of the same and "it is not that the eastern approach was misguided, it was simply premature." (Barrow 1991) These new "old" intuitions have not received wide acclaim from the scientific world but there are inklings that with more and more being understood, the validation of these major concepts is most likely a question of not "if" but "when". The following is a brief description of these components.

1. Extended Evolution. Evolution and the understanding of it has been changing over the years since Darwin. Modification through Descent, survival and adaptation have remained the cornerstones but is also now inclusive of "bricolage", stasis, punctuation, altruism, cooperation, memetics, directed evolution and so on, such that not any of them explain anything completely but together they form a more coherent paradigm for comprehension. "Enough is known, enough is suggestive to give a hint that Monod and Teilhard may both be right and that Dawkins and Lovelock too, may have a finger on the pulse of the universe" (Barlow & Waldrop, 1991). A brief description of the key new elements of the concept of extended evolution are in order.

> *b.   System.* This framework views humanity and Earth as major constituents of a hierarchical system comprised of sub systems and sub-sub systems that are interacting continuously, both vertically and horizontally.

> *c.   Control.* An underlying principle of such a system is that "No part of an internally interactive system can have unilateral control over the remainder of any other part"(Bateson, 1994).

> *d.   Symbiosis.* "Symbiosis has shaped the features of many an organism, and represents the union of two or more organisms yielding what is in essence a new organism" (McMenamin & Margulis, 1990).

> *e.   Stability.* The tendency in evolution has been to establish stratified stability. "The stratification of stability is fundamental in living systems, and it explains why evolution has a consistent direction in time" (Bronowski, 1973), meaning it never regresses.

> *f.   Punctuated Equilibrium.* The possibilities of viewing evolution and more in terms of punctuated equilibrium is yet another aspect in this new inventory of understanding. "In its barest essentials punctuated equilibria is stasis interrupted by brief bursts of evolutionary change" (Eldredge, 1995).

> *g.   Non-Linearity.* It has been very convenient and comfortable to use linearity, locality and immediate cause and effect as the fundamental assumptions in pursuing reductionist science to date, explaining the remaining unexplainable as "chance". Barrow (1991) asserts that in modern terms, the western perspective has regarded nature as linear phenomenon in which what happens at a given place and time is determined exclusively by what has occurred in nearby places immediately beforehand. The holistic view assumed nature to be non-linear so that non-local influences

predominate and interact with one another to form a complicated whole.

2. Gaia. With increasing concerns about governance, global ethics, the future of science and technology in respect of defining what it means to be human, the nagging questions of population and sustainability, the extinction of bio-diversity, an over-arching realization is dawning on us, even as it has always been there in our deep mythic past. The realization of Earth as "Mother Goddess", Gaia. While in earlier times it might have been divination or intuition, it is now emerging as a reality, though not a scientific fact beyond a reasonable doubt. This too appears to be a case of not if, but when. Gaia is the biggest complex adaptive system.

> What does it mean to say that the Earth is one living organism? A single organism is a structure in which the various parts are interconnected or functionally integrated so that failure at one part may cause the rest of the structure to die too. (Barlow & Waldrop, 1991)

3. Self-Organizing Criticality. By far the most important concept to have emerged is that of "self-organizing criticality." If there is one operant process that captures the movement in time, the interrelationships of things, the pathways of evolution, allows for human agency and intervention, and yet disallows the notion of absolute control by humans over their evolution, and does not stand in opposition to different epistemes, even as it allows for the impossibility of complete knowledge, it is the idea of "self-organizing criticality."

> *A word of warning is essential at this point. It should be noted that the pioneers of this concept do not attribute the all-encompassing applicability to this concept that the author does.*

What is self-organizing criticality? The term self-organizing criticality has been used by physicist Per Bak (1996) and others in studying physical systems such as sand piles, having certain characteristics in common.

These systems are observed to evolve out of an initial state (addition of sand to a pile) accompanied by discrete events which change the configuration of the system (avalanches of varying quantity of sand) finally reaching a critical state where a balance has been reached and the dynamic events redistributing energy through the system (avalanches carrying gravitational energy away from sand added to the edge of the pile) become stable in a statistical sense over time.

(Donnelly, 2000)

It is, in this author's view, self-organizing criticality as a process that offers meaning and purpose to human activity within the larger context of being a participant, a variable in Gaia. The Earth as organism; it has a sense of eternity to it. A pile of sand is the net totality of humans and human civilization on the planet and inclusive of it. It is the equivalent of a document or a time capsule of the planet and our traverse on it. We are the grains of sand being added or subtracted from the pile, not only in the physical sense but also in the metaphoric sense, our ideas and our actions. We affect the future, each one of us, good bad or indifferent. These actions achieve connectedness and accumulate to cause effects over time, in turn affecting the pile itself. The essence of this is best captured by James Burke in his important work, *Connections* (1995): "In some way each one of us affects the course of history. Because of the extraordinarily serendipitous way change happens, something you do during the course of today may eventually change the world."

The Future as Process: An Outline

The foregoing has been an attempt to set the stage for describing an approach to studying the future. An approach therefore that is cognizant of the evolutionary perspective, acknowledges the notion of Gaia and accepts self-organizing criticality as the operant process. The perfect metaphor for the methodology is the sand pile and the addition of grains to it. It is an ongoing event!

What is being described as an approach to the future is actually the facilitation of a process that:

- enables participation by all those who actually affect and create the future;

- increases and diffuses knowledge on issues concerning the long-term future of humanity, so as to enable informed involvement;

- requires that the knowledge and the information that is generated is not organized in the sense of providing preferred or desirable interpretations, summaries, or abstracts. Rather it is to present, as is, with all of the inherent polarities; and

- allows the recipients of such information to decide to extract whatever meaning and substance they wish. The knowledge and the information are in the raw.

An important premise in this approach is that "the ease with which information can be spread is critical to the rate at which change occurs" (Burke, 1995). Whichever alternative we choose, "the key to success will be in the use of what is undoubtedly the vital commodity of the future, information." A second important premise in this approach is that "there is a point at which if only one more person tunes into a new awareness, a field is strengthened, so that, this awareness reaches almost everyone" (Burke, 1995).

To the practitioners of "futures studies" this would be an entirely unsatisfactory approach. However, it is unlikely that any methodology can or will completely contain all that will be needed to meaningfully study something so immense as humanity's long-term future! The consolation lies in the fact that the field of futures studies, with its structured and rigorous approaches, will stay that way and proceed, in that such studies are also meaningful and become needed inputs to the process of self-organizing criticality. The approaches are not mutually exclusive. The latter becomes subsumed by the former.

The process for a study of the long-term future of humanity then, is akin to a "play" that takes place on a continuous basis, forever, with continuously changing plots and themes appropriate for that time as determined by the players, and the larger audience of humanity. In essence, this is a play that never ends, and therefore a future that no one will ever see.

There is comfort and satisfaction in knowing there is a play, we do play a part, and thus our actions make a difference. This is indeed a worthless process if we remain obsessed with our centrality to Gaia, but completely meaningful if we let go of that illusion and return to our true identities as nothing more than grains of sand (Keyes, 1993).

Reprinted with permission from the Journal of Futures Studies.

Journal of Futures Studies, May 2001, 5(4): 181-189.

References

Bak, P. (1996). *How Nature Works: The Science of Self-Organized Criticality*. Springer-Verlag.

Barlow, C. & Waldrop, M. Beyond the Binary, passages extracted from "From Gaia to Selfish Genes" (MIT: Boston (1991) (Ed), found in *Evolution Extended: Biological Debates on the Meaning of Life* (Ed) MIT: Boston (1994): 214.

Barrow, J. (1991). *Theories of Everything: The Quest for Ultimate Explanation*. Fawcett.

Bateson, G. (1994). Governors, Tinkerers, and the Role of Synergy, passages extracted from "Steps to an Ecology of Mind", found in *Evolution Extended: Biological Debates on the Meaning of Life* (Ed) MIT: Boston, MA (1994): 99.

Bronowski, J. (1973). Ratchets, Uroboros, and the Role of Initiative, passages extracted from "The Ascent of Man" (Little & Brown 1973) and "Nature and Knowledge" (Oregon State System of Higher Education 1969), found in *Evolution Extended: Biological Debates on the Meaning of Life* (Ed) MIT: Boston, MA (1994): 119.

Burke, J. (1995). *Connections*. Little, Brown & Co..

De Chardin, T. (1959). Cosmic Visions, passages extracted from "The Phenomenon of Man" (publisher, 1959), found in *Evolution Extended: Biological Debates on the Meaning of Life* (Ed) MIT: Boston, MA (1994):153.

Donnelly, K. (2000). *Hazards, Self-Organization, and Risk Compensation*. Perseus Books.

Eldredge, N. (1995). *Reinventing Darwin: The Great Debate at the High Table of Evolutionary Theory*. John Wiley & Sons.

Gould, S. J. (1977). *Ever Since Darwin*. W.W. Norton.

Hubbard, B. M. (1997). *Conscious Evolution*. New World Library

Huxley, J. (1957). Evolution and Religion, passages extracted from "Religion Without Revelation" (Harper & Row, 1957), found in *Evolution Extended: Biological Debates on the Meaning of Life* (Ed) MIT: Boston (1994): 234.

Jacob, F. (1982). Governors, Tinkerers, and the Role of Synergy, passages extracted from "The Possible and the Actual" (Pantheon, 1982), found in *Evolution Extended: Biological Debates on the Meaning of Life* (Ed) MIT: Boston, MA (1994): 99.

Keyes, K. (1984). *The Hundredth Monkey.* (Rev. Ed.) Vision Books.

László, E. (2000). Keynote address for Foundation For the Future - *Humanity 3000 Symposia*, August 12-16, 2000.

McMenamin, M. & Margulis, L. (1990). Governors, Tinkerers, and the Role of Synergy, passages extracted from "Marriage of Convenience", The 1990 volume of Sciences; found in *Evolution Extended: Biological Debates on the Meaning of Life* (Ed) MIT: Boston, MA (1994): 102.

Swimme, B. (1992). Science into Myth, passages extracted from "The Universe Story" (HarperCollins, 1992), found in *Evolution Extended: Biological Debates on the Meaning of Life* (Ed) MIT: Boston, MA (1994): 297-301.

Wilson, E.O. (1978). *On Human Nature.* Harvard University Press.

Global Consciousness, Global Mind, Global Brain

Introduction

Two parallel streams of enquiry pertaining to Global Consciousness/Mind/Brain are converging. One stream of enquiry is establishing the emergence of this phenomenon as a logical outcome of cultural evolution, the penultimate stage in evolution that started with the big bang and along the arrow of time passed through the particulate, galactic, stellar, planetary, chemical and biological stages. The final upcoming stage being "ethical evolution". All along adhering to and complying with the basic rules of selection for fitness and survival, in the narrow conventional sense. The stage of cultural evolution is of competition among memes, and selection for fitness of a set of them and the concurrent emergence of a metaphoric or figurative concept of global consciousness/mind/brain that is synthetic in nature, enabled by technological connectivity of the billions of humans in cyberspace, causing increasing collaboration and coordination on a variety of issues that have a bearing on the future of the species.

The second stream of enquiry, not scientifically proven, and may never be, is premised on an integration of ancient philosophical speculations. This second stream seeks to establish an implicit and *a priori* universal consciousness/mind/brain, best described by Prof. Lazlo as "the presence of a field that is strictly "information" with non-local communication between minds, and an evolutionary process that has always manifested the phenomena of sociality, connection and group altruism", but now, more evident than ever, because of the exponential increases in human connectivity on the planet.

This chapter will explore and assess these two propositions as fact or fiction and in doing so, put it in the context of the survival of the human species going forward.

Major Transitions Afoot

The dawn of the 21st century represents a unique watershed in human evolution, especially taking human evolution into account in evolutionary time frames, with particular emphasis on human cultural evolution.

A strong case can be made for the fact that as a species, we are on the pivot of major transitions. These may be described as follows.

- Belief/faith systems challenged by knowledge, specifically the exponential growth in knowledge about the human genome, and the accompanying challenges to faith and belief systems worldwide.

- The power and influence of the collective over the individual steadily eroding in favor of the power of the individual, as is evident from the global trends toward liberal democracies and free markets in their many variations and the steady decline and fall of authoritarian regimes of all varieties.

- Local, regional, national human identity giving way and forcing the need for a global and planetary identity, once again evident from the increasing interaction of humans across the planet in all realms of human activity.

Economic, political, social, cultural, and the issues confronting the human species, all of which have approached magnitudes and levels that are no longer solvable based on our earlier orientations and identities:

[A]re transforming everything from geopolitics to the structure of families. And they pose problems on a scale that humans have little experience with. As Harvard University biologist, E.O.Wilson puts it, we are about to pass through "the bottleneck", a period of maximum stress on natural resources and human ingenuity. (Musser, 2005, p.44)

Coinciding with the onset of these transitions however is the timely emergence of what might be described as the phenomenon of global brain, global mind, global consciousness, providing an opportunity for humans as a species to manage these transitions.

Global Consciousness, Global Mind, Global Brain: A Consequence?

In the words of Teilhard de Chardin (1959, pp. 245-246):

> In the eyes of the prophets of the eighteenth century, the world appeared really as no more than a jumble of confused and loose relationships; and the divination of a believer was required to feel the heart of that sort of embryo. Now, less than two hundred years later, here we are penetrating (though hardly conscious of the fact) into the reality, at any rate the material reality, of what our fathers expected. In the course of a few generations all sorts of economic and cultural links have been forged around us and they are multiplying in geometric progression. Nowadays, over and above the bread which to simple Neolithic man symbolized food, each man demands his daily ration of iron, copper and cotton, of electricity, of oil and radium, of discoveries, of the cinema and of international news. It is no longer a simple field, however big, but the whole earth which is required to nourish each one of us. If words have any meaning, is this not like some great body which is being born —with its limbs, its nervous system, its perceptive organs, its memory—the body in fact of that great Thing which had to come to fulfill the ambitions aroused in the reflective being by the newly acquired consciousness that he was one with and responsible to an evolutionary all?

Let us first look at the current situation. In simple terms, a human being can call upon the full range of human mental and emotional experiences on a global scale. In so doing we can remain solitary or collectivize on any scale. We can access, use, transmit, communicate in person or indirectly, data, information, thought, ideas, concepts, knowledge. We can initiate, organize, plan, schedule, act as individuals or collectively on any scale. It is as if we, seven plus billion individuals, replicate the exquisite beauty and complexity of individual brains. Marvin Minsky, in *Society of Mind* describes the workings of the individual human mind:

> I will call "society of mind" this scheme in which each mind is made of many smaller processes. These we will call agents. Each mental agent, by itself can only do one simple thing that needs no mind or thought at all. Yet when we join these agents in societies-in certain very special ways—this leads to true intelligence. (Minsky, 1985, p. 17)

Here, the reference is to the compartments of the human mind related to language, memory, analysis and more basic elements such as synapses, nodes, dendrites, the chemical and electrical processes that accompany the workings of the human brain. If we were to simply consider each human brain as such a component, agent or agency in the 6 billion strong brains, we arrive at the same conclusion of a provisional creation of global mind. A result of the networking of humans on the planet via the technologies of the internet, the world wide web, powerful search engines, and the stored memory of our entire history on the planet in virtual cyberspace to call upon at will. All put in service to coordinate, plan, execute at any level of organization, hierarchy, structure.

To elaborate the workings of such a society of minds, it will be useful to employ an example that illustrates the functioning of the individual mind.

"To start to see how minds are like societies, try this:

1. Pick up a cup of tea.

2. Your grasping agents want to keep hold of the cup,

3. Your balancing agents want to keep the tea from spilling out.

4. Your thirst agents want you to drink the tea.

5. Your moving agents want to get the cup to your lips.

6. Yet none of these consume your mind as you roam about the room talking to your friend. You scarcely think at all about balance, which has no concern with grasp. Grasp has no interest in thirst, and thirst is not involved in your social problems. Why not? Because they can depend on one another. If each does its own little job, the really big job will get done by all of them drinking tea. (Minsky, 1985, p. 20).

It shouldn't be too difficult to draw a parallel functioning of global mind with individuals as the elements of such coordination for the "big job". It is in this sense that one could establish the fact that "global mind" is indeed in the making for the first time in human history. This also points to the fact that "one dissects a body but finds no life inside. What is mind? One dissects a brain but finds no mind therein" (Minsky, 1985, p. 41).

There is then the problem of consciousness. If we allow for the possibility that global mind is a moving, provisional construction and not a thing in itself, what about the notion of global consciousness? Once again, reverting to the current findings on individual human consciousness can help. Understanding consciousness requires the consideration of the "movie in the brain" that we create on an ongoing basis and the "self" that is participating, observing and owns the movie in the brain.

Current research points to the fact that:

> [T]he idea of spectator is constructed within the movie, and no ghostly homunculus haunts the theater. Objective brain processes knit the subjectivity of the conscious mind out of the cloth of sensory mapping. And because the most fundamental sensory mapping pertains to body states and is imaged as feelings, the sense of self in the act of knowing emerges as a special kind of feeling-the feeling of what happens in an organism caught in the act of interacting with an object. (Damasio, 1999, p. 117)

In other words, there is no specific thing identifiable as "self", the conscious observer; as such the act of being conscious is also a provisional construction. It should be obvious that this can be extended to incorporate and accept the notion of "global consciousness" operating with individual brains acting as collaborating creators of the movie. Otherwise, if we were to insist on :

> [T]his notion of a homunculus—a little person inside each self—leads only to a paradox, then, that inner self requires yet another movie screen inside itself, on which to project what it has seen, and then to watch that play within a play—we would need another self-inside-a-self. (Minsky, 1985, p. 50)

The insistence, therefore, on the separateness of the brain, mind, and consciousness as entities that can be objectified and understood is proving to be wrong. "I think therefore I am" is an erroneous proposition that served us in good stead within the paradigm of a mechanistic world view in laying bare a lot of smaller truths, but no longer valid.

> Nearly all our scientific colleagues still seek "mechanisms" to "explain living matter", and they expect laws to emerge amenable to mathematical analysis. We demur; we should shed Descartes' legacy that surrounds us still and replace it with a deeper understanding of life's sentience. (Margulis & Sagan, 1997, p.182)

Vernadsky and Teilhard De Chardin stipulated that:

> [We] have detected one and the same fundamental processes, always recognizable. We saw geogenesis promoted to biogenesis, which, turned out in the end to be nothing else than psychogenesis. With and within the crisis of reflection, the next term in the series manifests itself. Psychogenesis has led to man. Now it effaces itself, relieved or absorbed by another and a higher function-the engendering and subsequent development of the mind. In one word, noogenesis. (Margulis & Sagan, 1997, p.182)

We have thus far explored the notion of global mind and global consciousness as a synthetic outcome of the evolutionary paradigm since the big bang, culminating in the final stages of human collaboration and coordination on a global scale, signaling the final phase of cultural evolution.

Global Consciousness, Global Mind, Global Brain: The First Cause?

At the outset it should be stated without equivocation that the alternate postulate of *a priori* global consciousness, mind, brain that we are about to explore are not proven scientific facts and may never be proven. Even so let us not ignore Kuhn's warning and stay imprisoned in a paradigm that does not currently show or allow for the possibility of an "*a priori*" existence of consciousness, mind and brain either.

There are alternative postulates regarding global consciousness/mind/brain that need to be examined; postulates that illuminate and point to a more integrated coherent, and certainly appealing conceptual framework perhaps. This framework is in contrast to the notion of "emergence" of global mind and global consciousness described above in a narrow sense, as a logical extension of evolutionary processes in the cultural realm in the conventional sense. An end point described as "Omega Point" by Teilhard De Chardin (1959). Professor Ervin László in his book *Science and the Akashic Principle* states that the postulates are premised on the philosophical and scientific speculations pertaining to the presence of *a priori* universal consciousness/mind, of the now Scientifically defensible concept of Gaia within an enlarged and expanded comprehension of evolutionary processes inclusive of Synergism and sociality, the indications from physics of the possible presence of an "Akashic field" of information that allows for non-local communication, collaboration and coordination.

The fundamental starting point for this alternative paradigm has to be speculations about Universal consciousness as laid out in the Vedanta of Indian Philosophy.

> The identity between the world and Brahman is explained. On this ground that all is known when the "one" is known is accounted for. Since all entities are real only as the effects of Brahman and as ensouled by Brahman, it has been said, "That is True". In no other way are they real. Just as, in the illustration of clay and its products, the products are real only as of the nature of clay, even so the world is only as sustained by the indwelling Brahman. (Raghavachar, 1956, p. vi)

The universal, omniscient backdrop of Brahman as the primary stage for all further acts and scenes of the evolutionary drama, Maya, as described in Vedanta, explains the onset of the multiple layers of differentiated consciousness, mind, brain, Matter, actually in the reverse, as manifestations, that are distinct and yet one and the same as the original consciousness. A logical fallacy it would seem but defended as follows:

> The signification of an identical entity by several terms which are applied to that entity on different grounds is coordinated predication. In the illustration of (say) a purple robe, the basic substance is one and the same, though purpleness and robeness are different from it as well as from each other. That is how the unity of a Purple Robe is established. The central principle is that whatever exists as an attribute of a substance, that being inseparable from the substance is one with that substance. (Satprem, 1968, p.63)

In that all is undifferentiated Brahman (Nirguna Brahman) giving rise to differentiated Brahman (Saguna Brahman):

> [W]e shall realize that there is but one force in the world, a single unique current which passes through us and through all things and which puts on one substance or another according to the level of its action. It is this force which links up everything, animates everything; this, the fundamental substance of the universe: consciousness force, Chit Agni (consciousness heat). (Satprem, 1968, p. 53)

Which then leads to the realization that:

> [T]here is a consciousness also in the plant, in the metal, in the atom, in electricity, in everything that belongs to physical nature; we shall find even that it is not really in all respects a lower or more limited mode than the mental. (László, 2004, p.155.

As Professor Ervin László puts it:

> The Indian Vedic tradition regards consciousness not as an emergent property that comes into existence through material structures such as the brain and the nervous system, but as a vast field that constitutes the primary reality of the universe. In itself, this field is unbounded and undivided by objects and individual experiences. Underlying the diversified and localized gross layers of ordinary consciousness there is a unified, non-localized and subtle layer: pure consciousness. (László, 2004, p. 19)

The paradigm of "evolution" has also come a long way from its original moorings in Darwinian Selection for fitness and survival of the individual. New comprehensions in Biology, especially the decoding of the DNA molecule caused subsequent reframing of the survival argument in terms of the selfishness of the gene but still confined to the notion of individual fitness, selection and survival. But a lot has happened since then. A large body of work now supports a much more comprehensive view of evolution itself. The most important of these new findings are that the mind body separation is an aberration. An expanded and extended version of evolution, Gaia and self-organizing criticality are important new additions to our repertoire for considering human futures. It is not in the scope of this paper to delve into great detail about these concepts but to state the essence of these ideas briefly. Extended versions of evolutionary theory are inclusive of the notions of group altruism, synergy, non-linearity, symbiosis and the like. Gaia is the idea of the Earth as a single organism, depicted as Mother Goddess and we as humans but a connected part with everything else and self-organizing criticality applied to humans, as a process that allows for individual(s) participation but not the determinants of the final outcome.

And modern physics is on the verge of leading us toward an affirmation of some wondrous old postulations.

> As long as a particle is not observed, measured or interacted with in any way, it is in a curious state that is the superposition of all its possible states. When, however, the particle is observed, measured or subjected to an interaction, this state of superposition becomes resolved; the particle is then in a single state only, like any ordinary thing. Because the state of superposition is described in a complex wave function associated with the name of Erwin Schroedinger, when the superposed state resolves is said that the wave function collapses. (László, 2004, p. 31)

Professor Lazlo then goes on to say:

> At the quantum level, reality is strange, and it is nonlocal; the whole universe is a network of time and space transcending interconnection. Could the non-locality of the most basic elements of the universe be due to a fundamental field? (2004, p. 35).

Could it be that the Akashic field is active in not only the cosmological scale, but also the ultra-small scale of physical reality? (Lazlo, 2004, pg.34).

> Is this why we wake up in the middle of the night with a brilliant idea because others have been thinking about the same thing giving us the benefit? Or is this

why a dog knows that his master has arrived long before he walks through the door? If one accepts the fundamental continuity between body and mind, thought is essentially like all other physiology and behavior. Thinking, like excreting and ingesting, results from lively interactions of a being's chemistry. If what is called "thought" results from such cell interactions, then perhaps communicating organisms, each themselves thinking, can lead to a process greater than individual thought. (Teilhard de Chardin, 1959, p. 181)

Conclusion

Two different perspectives on the nature and content of global brain, global mind and global consciousness have been presented thus far. The first as an emergence at the end point and the second as an *a priori* starting point. Both are of course provisional hypotheses. What cannot be contested however is that something is afoot at a level higher than the brains, minds and consciousness of humans at the individual level. It can be described as brains, minds and consciousness operating as an entity at the planetary level. An operating unit above and beyond that of the sum of the awareness of the billions of individuals. It will be safe to conclude that at this point, that the idea of global brain, global mind and global consciousness is neither fact nor fiction.

It is, for all intents and purposes, a unique time for humans on the planet. We are at a crossroads as a species. Our survival as a species will depend on how we conduct ourselves. In this context, the idea of global brain, mind and consciousness may be fiction or figments of our imaginations. Even so, it may be necessary for us to invent one or pretend that this exists to energize and motivate us to act in our collective interest to survive. Nothing less will do and we are running out of time.

At the planetary level a "perfect storm" is brewing. A storm comprising multiple elements that portend disastrous outcomes if we don't pay heed and attempt to resolve them at that level incorporating the notion of global brain, mind and consciousness. Elements such as:

- the failure of governance at the level of the nation state based on narrow, provincial identities for humans;

- anthropogenic climate change (which, as many scientists have concluded, may already have reached a stage of "irreversibility");

- global poverty and inequality for a majority of the planet's inhabitants, pointing to a failure of existing sanctities in economics;

- nuclear proliferation;

- global demographic transitions pointing to political, economic, social and cultural turmoil; and

- the centrifugality of "individualism" overpowering the "centripetality" of the collective, leading to a multitude of pathologies, and so on.

It is not an accident that a manifestation of the idea of global brain, mind and consciousness is what is now current in the terminology of future studies, viz. conscious evolution. A term that allows for the notion of human involvement as "Active Walkers" (Lui Lam) in an evolutionary process, where we have the opportunity to guide ourselves into a safe haven. Failure to do so may very well result in our going the way of the dinosaur.

Reprinted with permission from the conference organizers of

ISIS Summit Vienna - The Information Society at the Crossroads [Conference]. July 2015.

References

Damasio, A. (December 1999). How the Brain Creates the Mind. *Scientific American*. https://www.scientificamerican.com/article/how-the-brain-creates-the-mind/

Teilhard de Chardin, P. (1959). *The Phenomenon of Man*. Harper and Row.

László, E. (2004). *Science and the Akashic Field*. Inner Traditions.

Margulis, L. and Sagan, D. (1997). *Slanted Truths*. Springer-Verlag.

Minksy, M. 1985. *The Society of Mind*. Simon and Schuster

Musser, G. (September 2005). The Climax of Humanity. *Scientific American*. https://www.scientificamerican.com/article/the-climax-of-humanity/

Raghavachar, S.S. (1956). *Vedarthasamgraha of Sri Ramanujacarya*. Sharada Press, p.V.

Satprem (1968). *Sri Aurobindo, or the Adventure of Consciousness*. Sri Aurobindo Ashram Press.

Teilhard de Chardin,. 1959. The Phenomenon of Man. New York: Harper and Row, pp. 245-246.

Humans and The Planet: Evolution, Transitions and Trajectories.

Introduction

Science has established the fact that the evolutionary process started 13 plus billion years ago with the Big Bang. Professor Eric Chaisson of Harvard, in his widely used textbook *Epic of Evolution* (2007) illustrates the same as the "Arrow of Time" (see Figure 2, overleaf), and describes the seven stages of it as follows: "The Big Bang followed by the *Particulate*, the *Galactic*, the *Stellar*, the *Planetary*, the *Chemical*, the *Biological* and the *Cultural*, with an exhortation for "ethical evolution" if we are to survive as a species."

Descriptions and scientific explanations of the stages up to and including the biological are abundant and need no further elaborations. The cultural and ethical aspects of evolution, however, do need to be addressed, in that they pertain to how our civilization has evolved over the last 160 to 200 thousand years with the advent of Homo sapiens, their migrations out of Africa, where we are as a species and what we can look forward to by way of the future. Mesoudi (2011) notes that:

> Cultural evolution is the idea that human cultural change—that is changes in socially transmitted beliefs, knowledge, customs, skills, attitudes, languages and so on—can be described as a Darwinian evolutionary process that is similar in key respects to biological/genetic evolution.

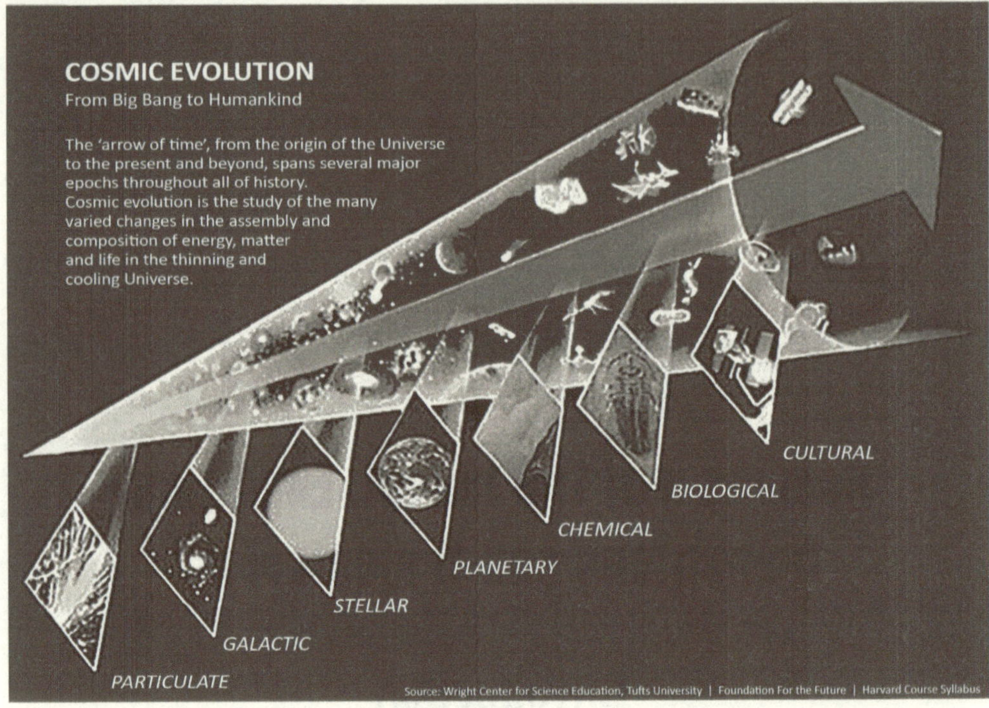

Figure 2: 'The Arrow of Time" and its seven stages (Eric Chaisson)

Cultural evolution has more recently also been described as "memetic evolution". Richard Dawkins is widely credited with the invention of the term *meme* defined as "a noun that conveys the idea of a unit of cultural transmission or a unit of imitation." (Dawkins, 1989). He likewise has stated:

> Proponents theorize that memes are a viral phenomenon that may evolve in a manner analogous to that of biological evolution. Memes do this through the process of variation, mutation, competition and inheritance, each of which influences a meme's reproductive process. (Dawkins, 1989; Wikipedia, 2021).

It can then be shown that all aspects of human society, all the way from the past to the present, are outcomes of memetic evolution. Religions, cultures, political systems, economic systems, varieties of social organization and on and on. The competition and struggle to survive is ongoing. For example, at least 200 some varieties of belief systems still exist, even though in terms of competition between them, it can be stated that only a few are dominant and hold sway over most of humanity. Similarly, in the present, there exist a variety of political, economic, and cultural systems where some are dominant, and others are on the decline.

These systems are rooted, in a foundational sense, on ideas, or a paradigm that describes the relationships between humans and humans, humans and nature, and belief in how things came to be, either as divine creations or outcomes of evolution described above.

Therefore, looking at the present, a set of memes that have survived and can be described as dominant and pervasive are the three major faith/belief systems of the Abrahamic religions, based on their books—the *Bible*, the *Torah* and the *Koran*—and deriving from them, through iterations over time, democracy, with many variations emphasizing the supremacy of the individual; capitalism as a system to organize economic activity; and scientific humanism. Scientific humanism puts the human at the center of all considerations and is best defined as:

A form of humanist theory and practice that is based on the principles and methods of science, specifically the doctrine that human beings should employ scientific methods in studying human life and behavior, in order to direct the welfare and future of mankind in a rational and beneficial manner (*Lexico*, n.d.).

Given the foreground, it is now possible to assess the outcomes of the paradigm that, in terms of measurable criteria, has been dominant for a couple of millennia. Such assessments can lead to conclusions as to the implications for humans and the planet and illuminate lessons to be learned by way of continuing with the same. It can also variously assess the need to change course (if it appears that imminent threats that plead for a modification lurk around the corner), or to effect a complete reversal of the foundational ideas of the dominant paradigm.

Transitions

Cultural evolution, starting with the migrations of modern humans or *Homo sapiens* out of Africa over the past 160 to 200 thousand years, and accelerating over the last 10 to 12 thousand years with the transition of humans from constantly moving hunter-gatherers to stationary agricultural communities. In this time frame, several major transitions can be identified. It should be noted, however, that these transitions cannot be identified or understood in terms of time frames of years, decades or even generations, because over these time frames these transitions will show cyclicality above and below the trend line that prevails over the long term. It is extremely important that we understand these transitions if we are to project where things are headed into the future and accordingly take measures by way of preparing for and preserving human survival.

Transition from faith and belief systems

Transition from faith and belief systems vis-à-vis *knowledge and its accumulation over time. See Figure 3 (below).*

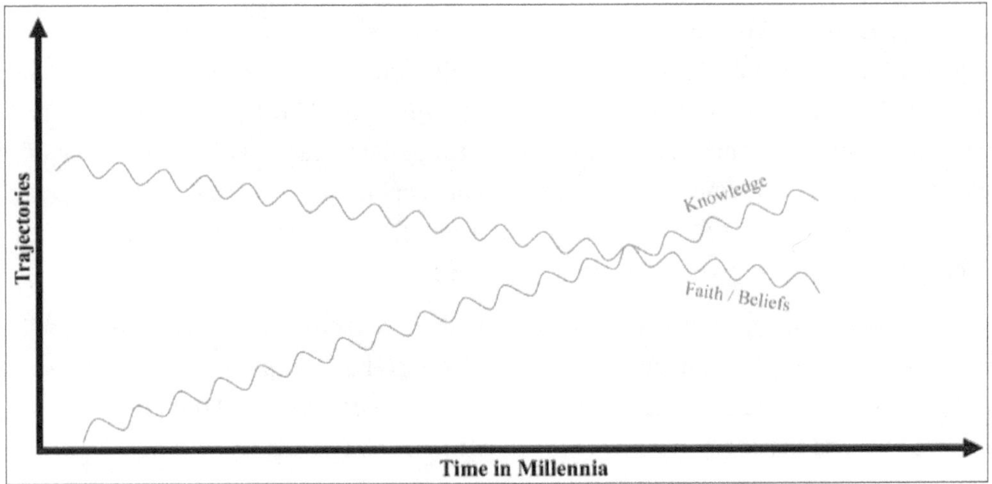

Figure 3. Belief to knowledge transition (Illustrations are only intended to be approximations of trajectories)

Humans have traditionally explained their own existence and the world around them as creations of the divine. However, even as the earlier explanations continue to exist and influence human life, it cannot be argued that new knowledge being produced by the hour is steadily subtracting from that influence. The long-term trend is unmistakable. Knowledge of ourselves and the world around us is likely, over the long-term future, to eliminate our need for and dependence on the old explanations. Globally, trends to this effect are already observable. However, vested interests will spare no effort to stall the transition, as is evident in the resurgence of religious fundamentalism in all the major faith/belief systems. This, however, is a temporary phase, and the long-term dominance of knowledge is inevitable.

Transition from "collectivism" to "individualism"

See Figure 4 (below).

What is implied in this transition is the notion that the organization of human societies, in terms of governance, authority and hierarchies, has evolved over time from pyramidical structures of feudalism, theocracies, autocracies, monarchies, dictatorships and the like, to varieties of democracies. The underlying idea is that the influence, power, and control over the individual was with the group; the collective. It is apparent that, even as such pyramids persist in parts of the world, the predominant form of governance, politically and economically, is now democracy, with its attendant extensions such as capitalism etc., based on social contracts between the institutions of the collective and the individual. The "individual" is the focus. Individuals choose their leaders. All power, influence and control are what individuals in a bottom-up fashion grant to those whom they choose to be led by.

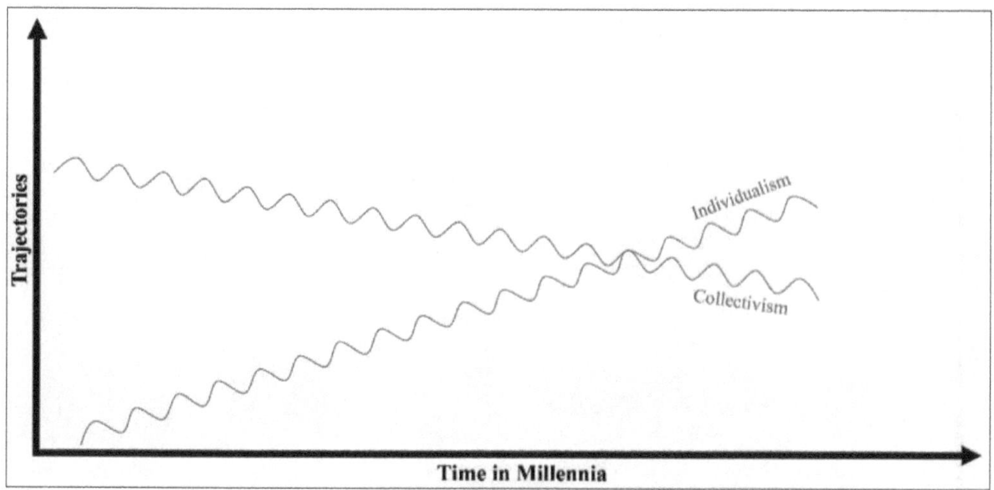

Figure 4. Collectivism to individualism transition (Illustrations are only intended to be approximations of trajectories)

Additional observations with regard to this transition is warranted. Social organizations based on the "collective" can be described as essentially "centripetal" by nature, meaning, drawn toward the center, whereas organizations with the "individual" as the focus are "centrifugal" by nature, meaning pulling away from the center. If, in such set ups, equilibrium between the centripetality and the centrifugality is not maintained, then adverse consequences accrue. In fact, considering the current state of affairs, it can be justifiably concluded "dysfunction" is the norm worldwide. The symptoms are too numerous and readily observable and is laid out in detail in what follows.

Transition from nation state to planetary governance

See Figure 5 (below).

As it pertains to humans, and their sense for who they are by way of "identity" starting with "self" to "family", to neighborhood, to city and so on extended, there has now been a change from earlier identities of tribes, kingdoms, etc. to being a member of a "nation state". However, a transition that started with humans emerging out of Africa, and populating the entire planet, spawned another phenomenon also underway; namely "globalization". What is important is that the relatively recent phenomenon of the exponential pace of globalization has caused a profound fracture in the notion of human identity and the ability of the nation state to solve any of the major crises confronting us, circumscribed within its borders. Poverty, war, pandemics, climate change, terrorism, energy, economics and trade, water, migrations are all issues that have spilled over into the global arena.

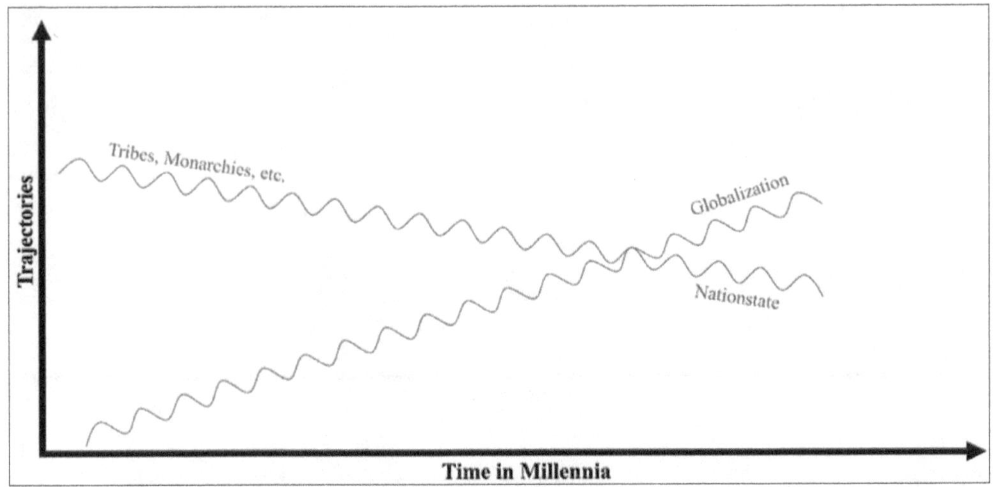

Figure 5. Nation state to planetary governance transition (Illustrations are only intended to be imprecise representations of trajectories)

In fact, the evolution and emergence of entities to address these crises have arisen over the last century with little or no success: The League of Nations, the UN with its multiple arms (political, social, economic etc.), the Security Council, NATO, SEATO, CENTO, ASEAN, MERCOSUR, NAFTA, THE EU, UNESCO, The G7, the G20, the OAS, OPEC, World Economic Forum, and on and on and on, is proof enough.

Even as the obvious transition is there for all to see, recent reactionary tendencies of vested interests to preserve the status quo also abound. The rise of fascist tendencies, nativism and nationalism across the globe are but a few examples. However, in terms of long-term time frames, they are but temporary distortions and will not stop the rising tide of globalization.

34

Transition of external world knowledge

vis-à-vis *knowledge of the human code. See Figure 6, below.*

A profound revolution took place in 1954: the discovery of the DNA molecule by Crick and Watson. While pursuit of knowledge of the external world continues in terms of physics of matter, the cosmos, chemistry, geology, astrophysics and so on, the discovery of the DNA molecule has caused an irreversible rupture in our sense of who we are and our relationship to the biosphere, the zoosphere, and even the stars, clearly pointing out that based on evolutionarily caused mutations in the distant past, our nearest relatives are the chimpanzees, and too distantly mice, and pigs and horses(!), or even a grain of rice: all arrangements of the same A T C and G, resulting in genes and genomes.

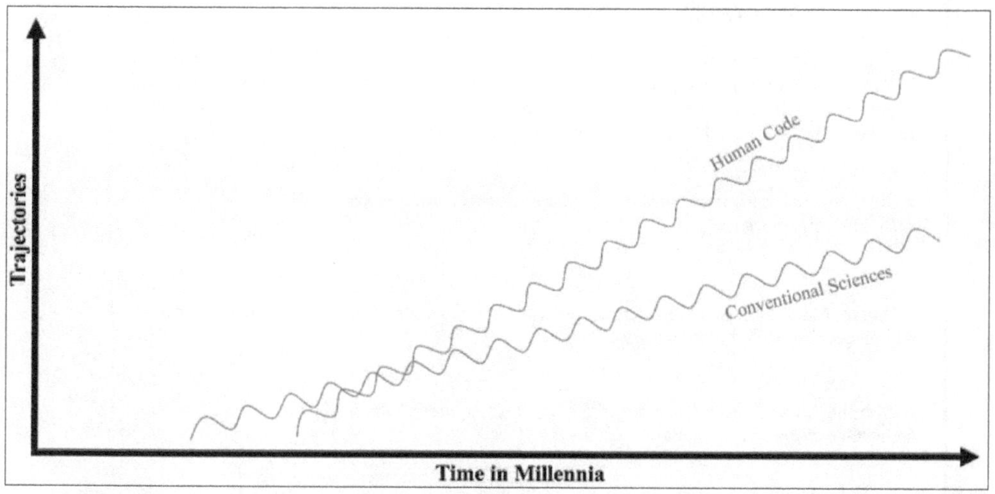

Figure 6. Rise of knowledge of the human code and sciences (Illustrations are only intended to be approximations of trajectories)

No longer can we escape the fact that we are the stuff of stars and require no divine creator to explain our presence. In fact perhaps, as we have suspected all along, we have created the divine in our own image and not the other way around. Our connections to all that is around us is a fact; a fact, the understanding of which, can awaken us—or maybe already has—to better manage our futures.

Trajectories

The consequences, better described as trajectories of "symptoms", caused by the dominant paradigm in use and the transitions that are taking place are outlined as follows. See Figures 7-10 on population, consumption, atmospheric CO^2 and extinction of species, below (Ayres, 2000).

THE POPULATION SPIKE

Millions of People (6,000 million = 6 billion)

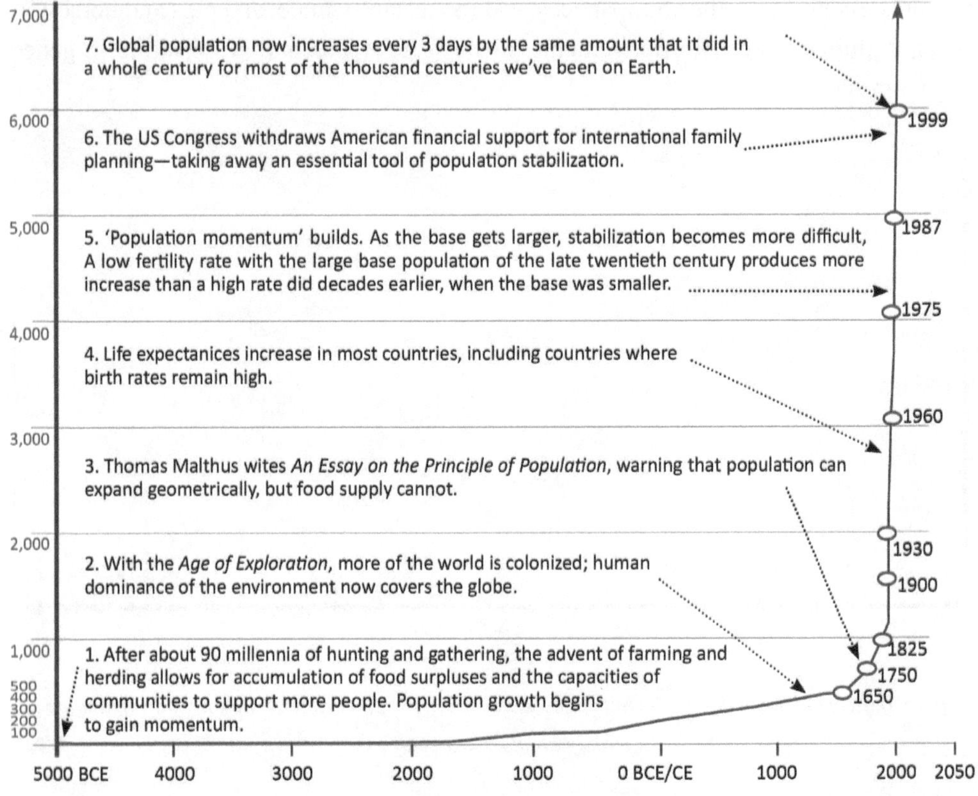

Figure 7. Population spike.

Population and Consumption

"The population problem has no technical solution. It requires a fundamental extension in morality". (Hardin, 1968)

Human populations on the planet have burgeoned from an estimated 300 million in 0 AD to 1 billion in the 1900's, nearly 8.5 billion in 2000 and is projected to

THE CONSUMPTION SPIKE

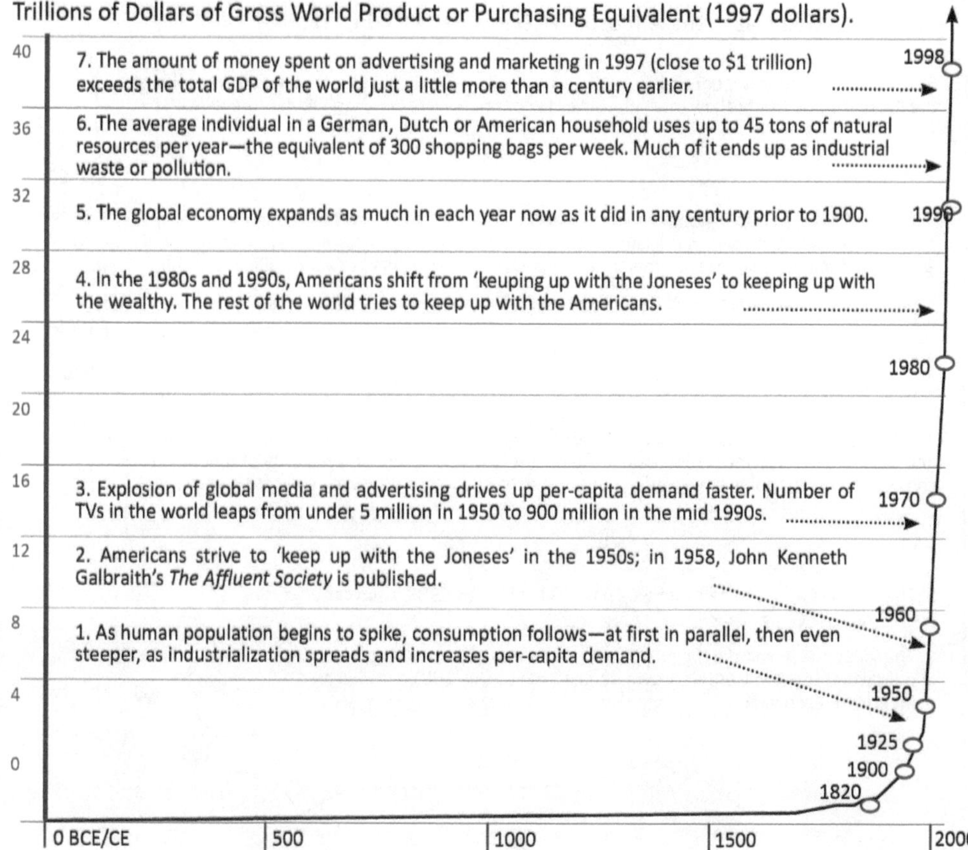

Figure 8. Consumption spike

level off at between 9 and 12 billion in the next few decades (see Figures 7 and 8). A number by itself is of little importance, unless you consider that these 12 billion have expectations of living standards by way of consumption that are equal to the so-called developed societies. What this translates to, according to experts, is exceeding the carrying capacity of the planet by at least a multiple of three. As Gandhi famously stated: "The world has enough for everyone's need but not enough for everyone's greed".

Atmospheric CO_2

CO_2 in parts per million is an indicator of the potential for drastic, irreversible climate change (see Figure 9, overleaf). It has risen from 290 parts per million in the atmosphere in the 1900's to nearly 400 parts per million now and on a path to

THE CARBON DIOXIDE SPIKE
Concentration of CO2 Gas in the Atmosphere (Parts Per Million, Volume)

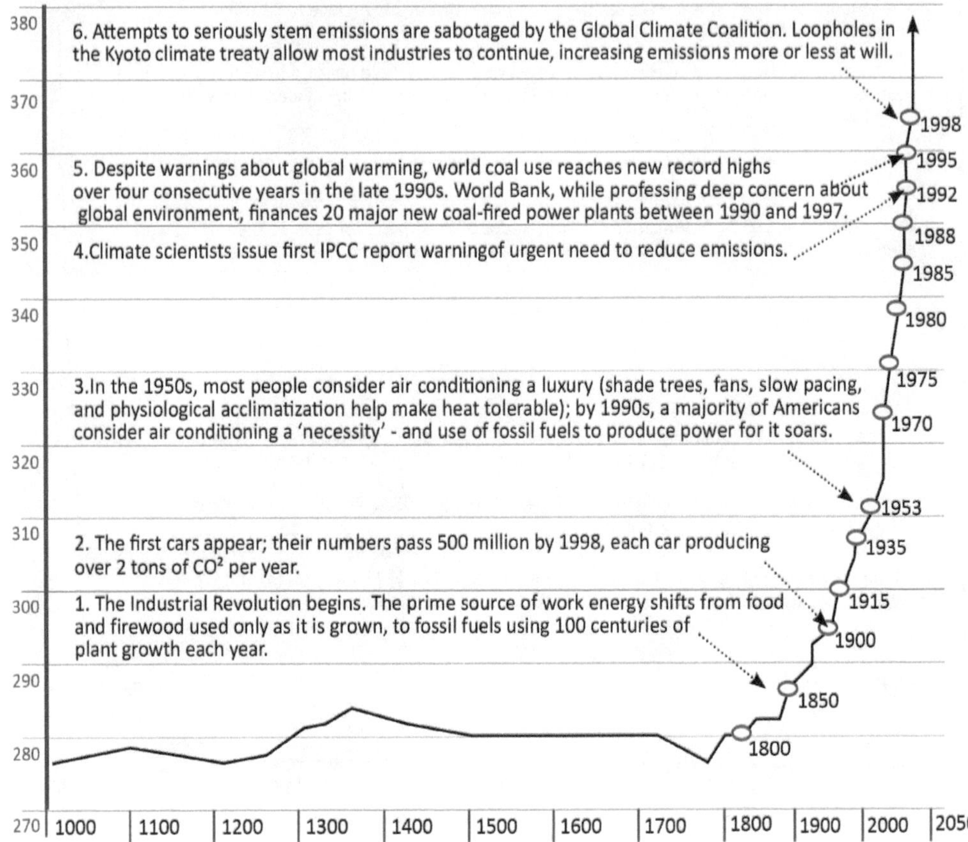

Figure 9. Carbon dioxide spike

reach 500 parts per million in the next several decades. The obfuscation of "deniers" notwithstanding, human-caused climate change is a fact, according to an overwhelming majority of scientists. The Intergovernmental Panel on Climate Change has begun to sound alarm bells that, unless efforts are undertaken to mitigate or reverse the accumulation of CO^2 in the atmosphere, we will reach the point of no return on climate change with drastic adverse consequences for the survival of several hundred million of us. Another important fact that is being understated in IPCC reports, which note that the half-life of CO^2 in the atmosphere is 14 years, is that new evidence states that the half-life is nearly 200 years (Archer et al., 2009). Scientists now go so far as to say that climate change is currently in a positive feedback loop state, meaning the change is already irreversible and accelerating (Wasdell, 2010).

THE EXTINCTION SPIKE

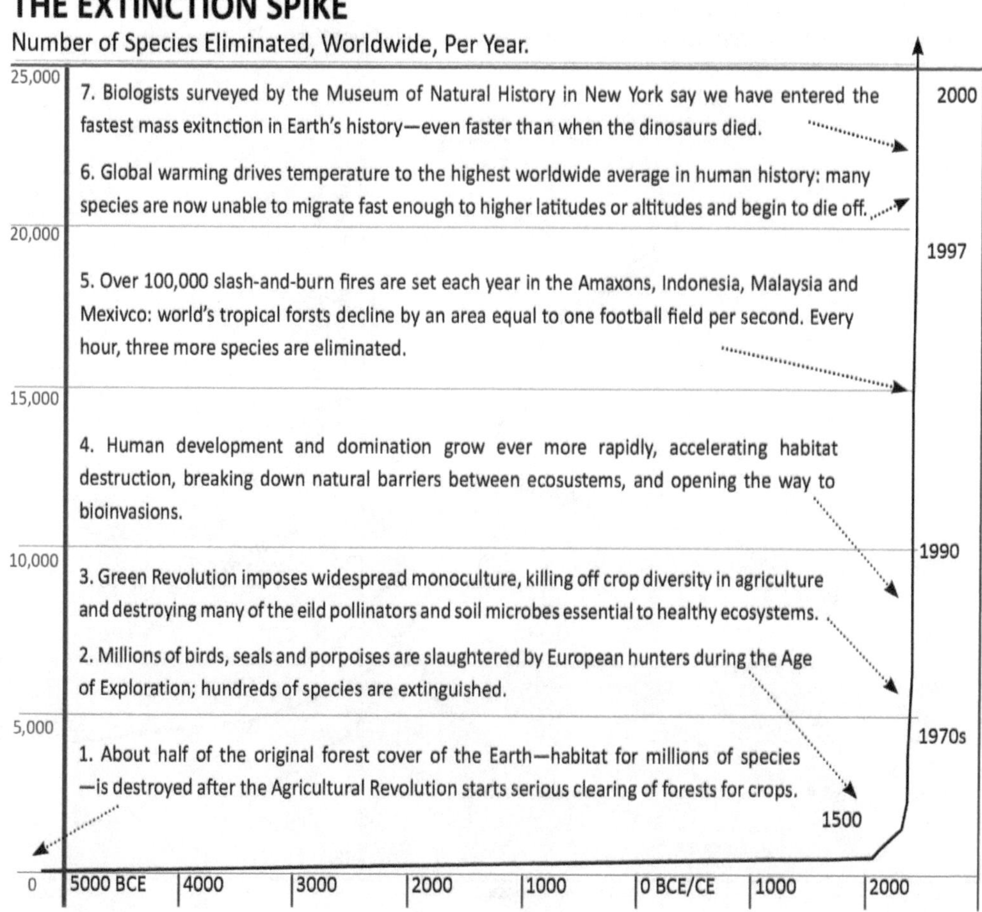

Figure 10. Extinction spike

Species Extinction

And finally, perhaps the most important is the extinctions of species numbering in the millions that has already occurred and is continuing into the present (see Figure 10). Harvard Professor E.O. Wilson, in an interview as recently as Oct. 2021, made an impassioned plea that a mandate to preserve at least 50% of the current green cover on the planet must be issued and implemented to stem the downward slope of our civilization (Kimbrough, 2021).

In the 1970s, Donella Meadows et. al. published a seminal work titled *Limits to Growth* (Meadows, Meadows, Randers & Behrens, 1972). In that work they noted that, given current economic and other policies, the prevailing idea of unlimited economic

LIMITS TO GROWTH: A REVIEW
Historical and Predicted Trends overlaid by Observed Outcomes from the 1972 Study,
The Limits to Growth (Meadows et.al.).

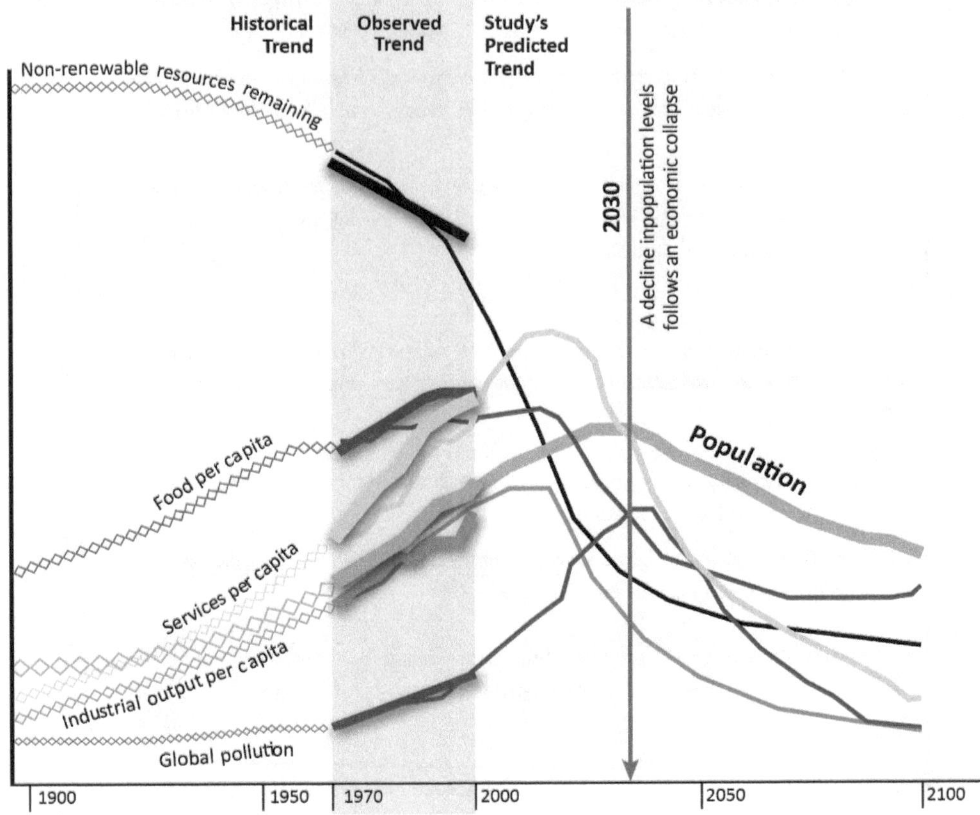

Source: *Smithsonian Magazine*: Looking Back on the Limits of Growth. Mark Strauss, April 2012.

Figure 11. Limits to Growth

growth is unsustainable. To verify if their projections were true or not, a recent review of their study was undertaken. Figure 11 (above) clearly shows that they were essentially correct in their prognostications. As it pertains to the most critical raw materials that fuel economic growth, the lifespan of most of them, including most importantly fossil fuels, is reaching exhaustion or will occur within the next several decades (see Figure 12, opposite).

For further evidence as to the state of the planet, see Figures 13-19 that follow, featuring images of different parts of the planet taken by NASA over a 20 to 25-year period. They are self-explanatory. They show green cover depletion to make room for urban sprawl, devastation of areas as a result of mining, and disappearance of large bodies of water.

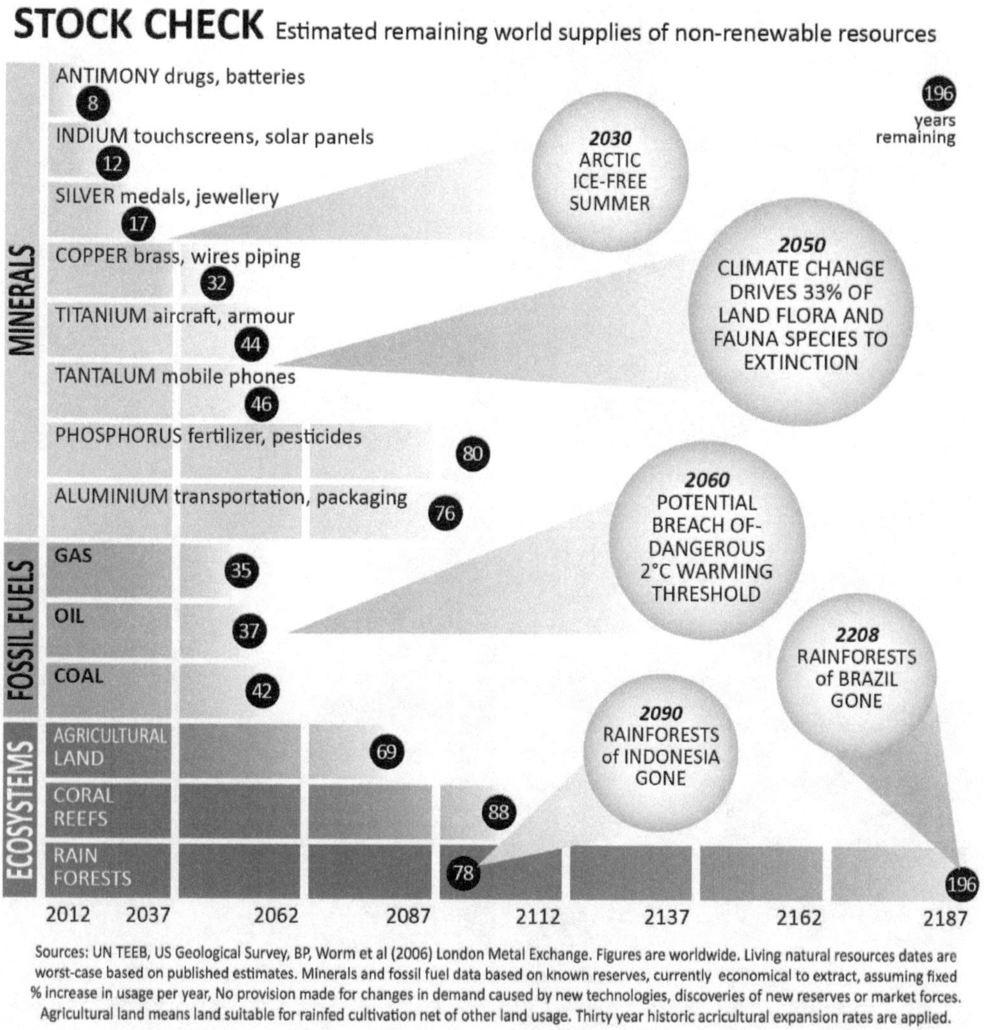
STOCK CHECK Estimated remaining world supplies of non-renewable resources
MINERALS
ANTIMONY drugs, batteries
8
INDIUM touchscreens, solar panels
12
SILVER medals, jewellery
17
COPPER brass, wires piping
32
TITANIUM aircraft, armour
44
TANTALUM mobile phones
46
PHOSPHORUS fertilizer, pesticides
80
ALUMINIUM transportation, packaging
76
FOSSIL FUELS
GAS
35
OIL
37
COAL
42
ECOSYSTEMS
AGRICULTURAL LAND
69
CORAL REEFS
88
RAIN FORESTS
78
196
196
years remaining
2030 ARCTIC ICE-FREE SUMMER
2050 CLIMATE CHANGE DRIVES 33% OF LAND FLORA AND FAUNA SPECIES TO EXTINCTION
2060 POTENTIAL BREACH OF- DANGEROUS 2°C WARMING THRESHOLD
2090 RAINFORESTS of INDONESIA GONE
2208 RAINFORESTS of BRAZIL GONE
2012
2037
2062
2087
2112
2137
2162
2187
Sources: UN TEEB, US Geological Survey, BP, Worm et al (2006) London Metal Exchange. Figures are worldwide. Living natural resources dates are worst-case based on published estimates. Minerals and fossil fuel data based on known reserves, currently economical to extract, assuming fixed % increase in usage per year, No provision made for changes in demand caused by new technologies, discoveries of new reserves or market forces. Agricultural land means land suitable for rainfed cultivation net of other land usage. Thirty year historic acricultural expansion rates are applied.

Figure 12. Stock check

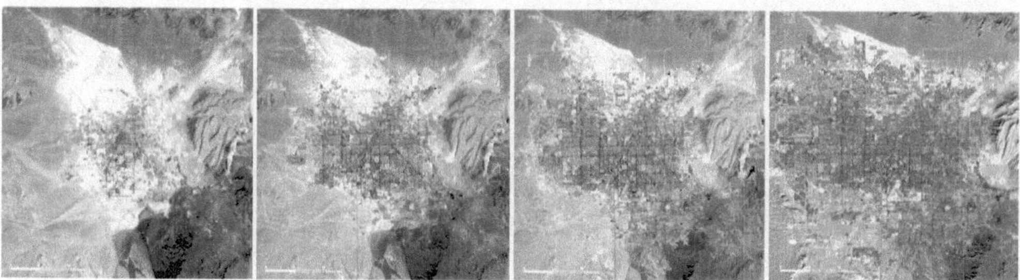

Figure 13. Growth of Las Vegas

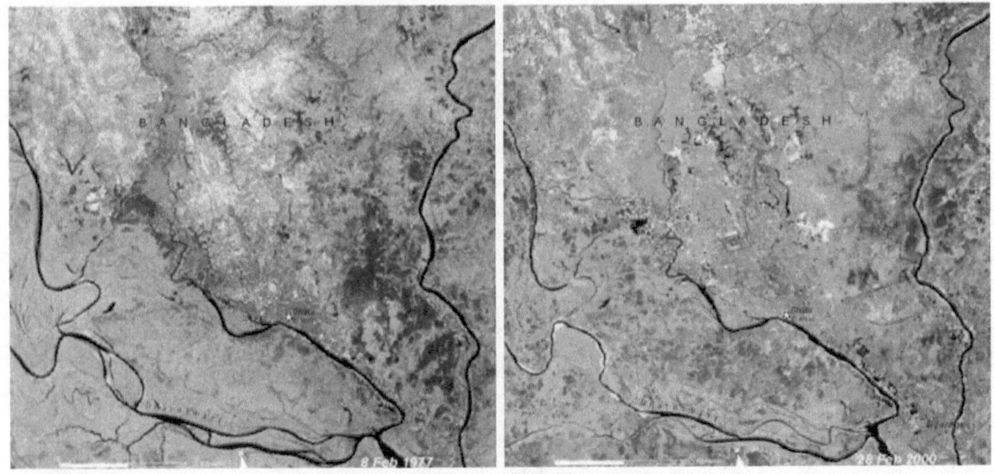

Figure 14. Population growth in Dhaka

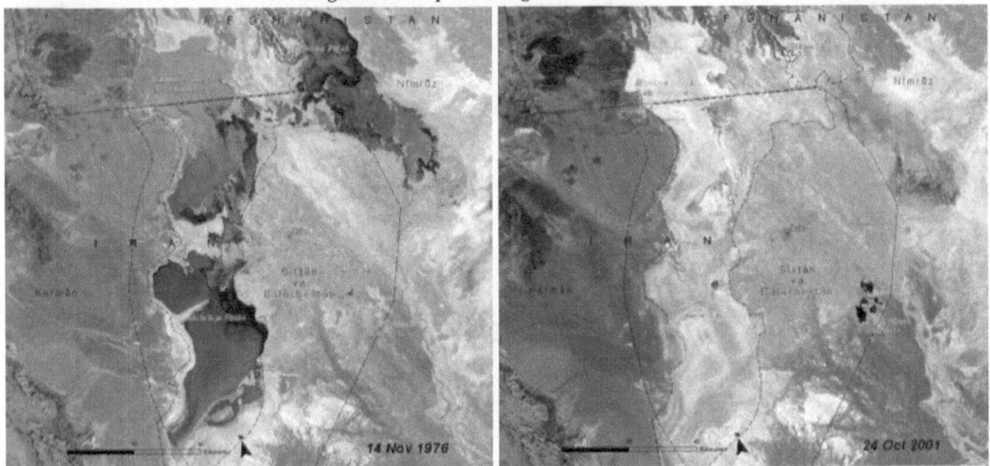

Figure 15. Disappearance of Lake Hamun

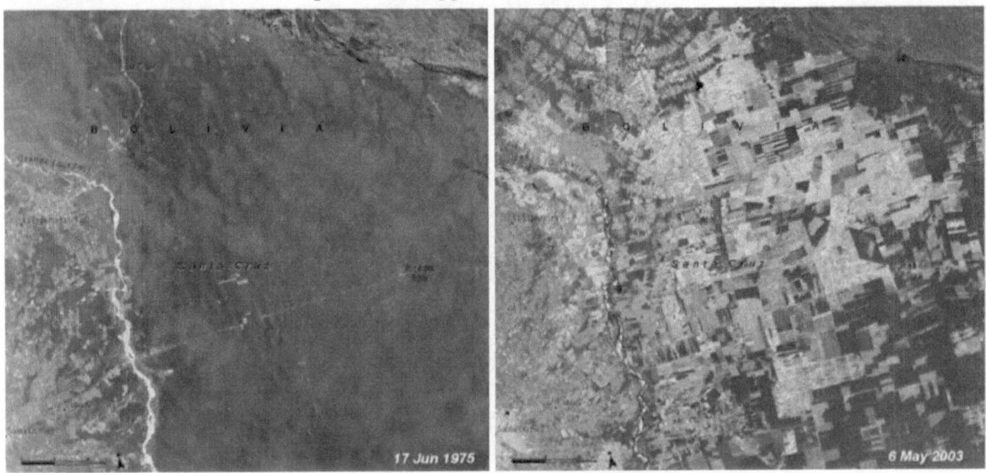

Figure 16. Deforestation in Bolivia

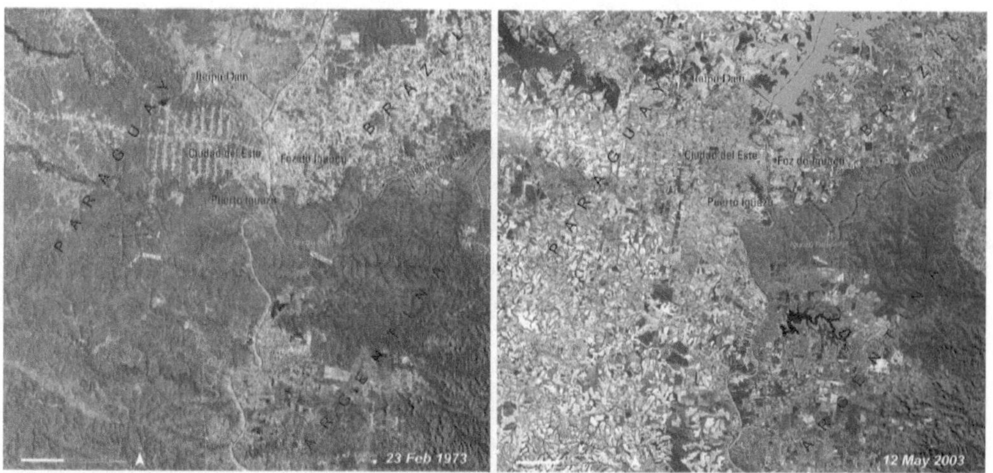

Figure 17. Deforestation in Argentina

Figure 18. Urban growth of Santiago, Chile

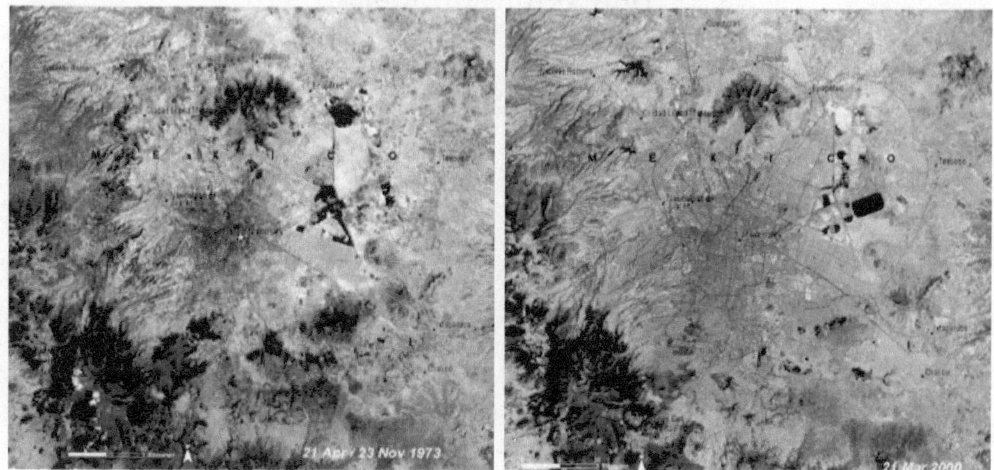

Figure 19. Urban growth of Mexico City

Ethical Evolution: The Future

We are at a crossroad as it pertains to the current state of the planet and the survival of humans as a species. As evolution has already established, 99% of all that ever existed is extinct and it should be clear that we are not exempt. Several world-renowned experts warn that we have perhaps 30 years or so to change course if we are to survive. No half measures that offer solutions without altering the dominant paradigm will do. The dominant paradigm of conquest, conflict and consumption (see Interview with Ervin László, page 99) must give way to cooperation, connection and conservation.

The approach to the future, described by Professor Chaisson of Harvard must be within the framework of ethical evolution. Ethical evolution requires enlightened human participation in evolution with future generations in mind. It is ethical in the sense of positioning ourselves as active participants, in a complex interdependent and interactive system that, as shown, evolves with the interests of all the stake holders—animate and inanimate—taken into account.

The most important idea to keep in mind is that this approach is for our survival as, opposed to the foolish idea we often hear being promulgated of "saving the planet". The planet has been around for four-plus billion years and is going to be around for several more billions of years. It is we who are at risk of disappearing!

IT MUST ALL START WITH A COMPLETE AND TOTAL ERASURE
OF ALL THAT WE KNOW AND HOLD TO BE TRUE AND THE
RE-EDUCATION OF OURSELVES IN THE ELEMENTS
OF A NEW PARADIGM.

References

Archer, D., Eby, M., Brovkin, V., Ridgwell, A., Cao, L., Mikolajewicz, U., Caldeira, K., Matsumoto, K., Munhoven, G., Montenegro, A., & Tokos, K. (2009). Atmospheric Lifetime of Fossil Fuel Carbon Dioxide. *Annual Review of Earth and Planetary Sciences*, 37(1), 117–134. https://doi.org/10.1146/annurev.earth.031208.100206

Ayres, E. (2000). *God's Last Offer: Negotiating for a Sustainable Future*. Basic Books.

Chaisson, E. (2007). *The Epic of Evolution*. Columbia University Press.

Dawkins, R. (1989). *The Selfish Gene*. (2nd ed.). Oxford University Press.

Hardin, G. (1968). The tragedy of the commons. *Science*, 162, 1243-1248. https://www.jstor.org/stable/1724745

Kimbrough, L. K. (2021, October 20). *Half-Earth, conservation, and hope: An interview with E.O. Wilson, Paula Ehrlich and Sir Tim Smit*. Mongabay. Retrieved November 23, 2021, from https://news.mongabay.com/2021/10/half-earth-conservation-and-hope-an-interview-with-e-o-wilson-paula-ehrlich-and-sir-tim-smit/

Meadows, D., Meadows D., Randers, J., and Behrens, W. (1972). *The Limits to Growth*. Universe Books.

Mesoudi, A. (2011). *Cultural Evolution: How Darwinian Theory Can Explain Human Culture and Synthesize the Social Sciences*. University of Chicago Press.

Scientific Humanism. (n.d.). Lexico. Retrieved November 23, 2021, from https://www.lexico.com/en/definition/scientific_humanism

Wasdell, D. (2010, November). Critical Issues in the Domain of Climate Dynamics. *Dept. of Land Economy*. University of Cambridge.

Wikipedia. 2021. "Meme" Last modified November 17th, 2021. https://en.wikipedia.org/wiki/Meme.

Worst-Case Climate Change and Foresight

What follows is the transcript of a talk titled Imagining the Worst: Foresight, Ethics and Extreme Climate Scenarios, *which I presented on March 6, 2011 in Ljubljana, Slovenia. The conference, "Anthropogenic Climate De-stabilization: A Worst-Case Scenario", was convened by UNESCO for the purposes of exploring climate destabilization impacts resulting from anthropogenic activity on the planet.*

Listening to all the talks yesterday, as I was thinking of what I am going to say, it seemed to me that all that needs to be said, has already been said. And so, the only thing that I am going to attempt to do is to put the same things differently.

I'd like to start with the usual disclaimer. Even though I am attached to Foundation For the Future, I am not representing the views of the Foundation. One of the things about the Foundation For the Future is the fact that its Mission is to simply "Increase and diffuse knowledge concerning the long-term future of humanity" without taking positions on what needs to get done, or who will do them, or why. What I have to say is strictly my personal views, however, much of what I have to say is based on conclusions that I have drawn over the last decade or so organizing and moderating think tanks on a variety of topics relating to the long-term future of humanity in a multi-disciplinary setting, especially one on the "worst case scenario of anthropogenic climate destabilization." I should also point out that I am not a climate scientist, nor would I describe myself as being in the forefront of the community of people involved in Foresight either. Even so, I would want to state that whilst establishing and directing programs at the Foundation For the Future, I have evolved formats and approaches that point to Foresight as the need to present the unvarnished complexity in major issues of concern, including pros and cons, advocates and dissenters, agreements and disagreements, in their entirety at the level of the common person—creating the possibilities for informed choices and decision-making—basically premised on the future as an "emergence" out of a complex, competitive interplay of memes across the universe of stakeholders. And that is what I hope to elaborate a little bit on here.

The challenge lies in presenting the array of memes in an unvarnished fashion and literally letting the public decide, one individual at a time. It is necessarily slow and messy but, in my view, the only way forward. It could very well turn out that such an approach could well amount to "too little too late", especially given the fact that we are hamstrung by political correctness, scientific caution, and fear of causing panic. This is especially so with a subject like climate change, not to mention the community of reputable scientists and important, ideologically-driven government leaders who have cast doubt in the minds of the general public as to whether the problem even exists, let alone the urgency and magnitude of it. It is important to point out that there are numerous sources for understanding the field of foresight, but three come to mind and deserve mention. The first is the work of Dr. Sohail Inayatullah; a friend and a brilliant scholar whose body of work on methods, tools, content and nature of futures thinking, in my view, is by far the standard in the field. Secondly, the Foundation itself funded a study carried out by Richard Slaughter to elaborate on the state of the field of futures studies, and thirdly, of course, the Millennium Project has done a study on the entire gamut of all that is available, and of who is doing what in futures studies. You may want to avail yourself of these resources.

An elaboration on these methodologies, given the limitation of time I have, is not possible. But suffice to say, the field is generally biased towards "preferred futures" and provides prescriptions for desired outcomes with little or no chance of ever materializing; the improbability of such desired outcomes increasing proportionately with the size of the issue being considered, such as global climate destabilization.

I state my point of view in the abstract as follows:

In numerating, analyzing and understanding all aspects of the worst case of climate change, evaluating the consequences in every dimension of human affairs and then outlining coherent strategies via foresight is a bewildering complexity and possibly, a nearly impossible proposition.

Climate change is a complex phenomenon in the making. Science and technology associated with comprehending it is far from complete. The civilizational norms and values within which all this is occurring are in a necessary state of flux. The variety present within politics, economics and culture across our societies precludes generalizations or consensus of any kind and the current state of the art and methodologies of foresight as they relate to capacity for addressing the issue of climate change is lacking, if not absent.

The case can be made to the effect, therefore, that addressing climate change boils down to "bottom-up" strategies of logical incrementalism in a reactive mode, primarily at the local level. Such strategies are premised on individual humans persuaded as active walkers, as opposed to random, passive walkers in the statistical sense, and essentially approach a transformation while, perhaps, holding a passage through ruin as a distinct possibility in the foreseeable future. I might add that, with respect to providing a clean slate for future generations, ruin is not an altogether-undesirable outcome in the near-term—especially as it pertains to the question of ethics. I should point out here that in evolutionary terms, 99% of all that ever existed is extinct, and we are not exempt. Also, the fact that on an evolutionary timescale, human beings represent a split second before midnight on a 24-hour scale and possibly may not go beyond one second past midnight in the future.

To begin with, what do we mean by "worst case climate change"? Yesterday, the scientist who pointed out the different elements of climate change did a wonderful job and I don't think there is much to add to it, except to point out a few things. One of them has to do with the fact that replicable climate models indicate that the concentration of carbon dioxide in the earth's atmosphere will reach approximately 1000 parts per million by the end of the present century and remain above this level for thousands of years. At present, 400 to 600 parts per million is considered the red zone and current levels are already approaching this level, unlike the popular literature that suggests that CO_2 in the atmosphere is a century time scale issue: this is the important thing to keep in mind.

Scientists, especially David Archer of the University of Chicago who has done extensive research on this aspect of CO_2 in the atmosphere, point out that the time to recover from the presence of excessive CO_2 in the atmosphere is in the order of 100,000 plus years (Archer et. al, 2009). It is doubtful that the projection of 1000 parts per million should be dismissed as unlikely or lacking credence. This projection is two or more times above the tipping point. The direct consequence of the increase of CO_2 concentration in the atmosphere is rising temperatures around the globe. By the end of the century, global average temperatures will rise by more than 5 degrees Celsius and will continue to rise for centuries. Consequences of such rises in temperatures include the direct effects of heat waves and stronger hurricanes. A recent study found that the maximum speed of the strongest hurricane of the last 25 years would increase by 5 meters per second for each degree of ocean warming. Since the power and destructive potential of hurricanes are proportionate to the velocity, a 50% increase in speed would imply a tripling increase of destructive potential. Sea levels could rise by two meters during the present century; a one-meter rise will affect over 150 million people in Asia. A sea level rise of 10 meters will affect 500 million people. A recently published study on what might happen to Bangladesh under said circumstances revealed that almost all of Bangladesh is in tremendous jeopardy.

Climate impacts on the Atlantic Thermohaline Circulation is a dangerous component of the climate system, because it is capable of rapid reorganization, resulting in abrupt climate change with temperature shifts of up to 10 degrees Celsius in a matter of decades. This has been shown through work carried out by scientists in our own backyard, Professor Calvin of the University of Washington, Seattle, USA. His article in the publication *The Atlantic Monthly* focuses on the conveyor belt system of the Atlantic current and what would happen if that current was stopped, which is a distinct possibility (Calvin, 1998).

More importantly, a scientist at the Meridian Institute in the UK, Dr. David Wasdell, using a "systems dynamics-approach" based not on modeling, but on tracking complex feedback dynamics, states that addressing climate destabilization is not about stopping catastrophic impacts but about stopping run-away behavior in a dynamic system. He believes that the earliest stages of run-away climate changes have already commenced with no naturally occurring negative feedback processes able to contain the effect (Wasdell, 2010). Most of the systems are already in net-amplifying feedback, so the hotter the earth gets the faster it gets hotter. In order to deal with it, we will have to generate a negative feedback intervention of sufficient power. Another way to state this is that the global heating that is underway—a gap between the energy received by the earth from the sun and the energy radiated back out—is running at approximately 2 watts per square meter of surface area and the amount is increasing by 25% per decade under a "business as usual" model. Three tipping points have already been identified. For example, with respect to the pine bark beetles in Northern US and Canada: the winters are not cold enough to kill the larvae of the beetle which is killing vast areas of pine trees, adding yet more carbon to the atmosphere. Secondly, the acidification of the oceans due to increasing temperatures, leading to massive changes in the lower part of the ocean food chain, is causing the disappearance of coral reefs in the Caribbean Sea. Thirdly, climate change has begun to affect human health worldwide with the extent of the impact expected to increase along with increasing climate change, leading to worldwide concerns for malnutrition, diarrheal disease and malaria. Other health impacts are death due to heat waves, flooding, air pollution and a wide range of food and water diseases.

Coming back to the issue of foresight and ideas for addressing the worst case, I will outline my view of how the future emerges, and the means and methods that may apply to addressing the worst case of climate change. Let me first point out that when it comes to foresight strategies etc., I am not disputing the relevance of traditional methods as applicable to micro issues at any level. However, it is my view that these methods are essentially inapplicable to a wide range of macro issues that we face at a planetary level, as in climate change or alternative energy, or the impending crisis of water, or sustainability, or species extinction, or wild cards and pandemics. A lot of that complexity was brought up yesterday in this conference, which demonstrated the dynamics and the tensions in the conversation, especially when talking about rights, duties, different methods for foresight, all of the model and practical issues that are involved and the situational context that must be considered. All basically point to the fact that it is indeed a very complex thing to approach, let alone to address successfully.

For issues at the macro level however, there are two important elements. On one hand there are the bottom-up choices and decisions that individuals make within their social, political, cultural, economic, and religious context, while on the other hand, there is the opportunity to obtain the full picture of a given issue with all the complexity laid bare as well as it can be. Given this, the analogy I would use by which the future emerges is akin to the sand pile that is articulated by Per Bak in his seminal work *How Nature Works* (1996). Even though his work is limited to natural phenomena, I do think that the same approach works quite satisfactorily in human affairs.

The analogy goes somewhat like this: Imagine a flat surface and grains of sand being added across the surface from all different points above it. As the process continues, individual piles form at various places on the surface, and further down the line, adjacent piles merge, creating a new pile, and so on, *ad infinitum*. Over time, all these piles collapse into forming a single pile. This essentially points to the fact that we are all inputs to the system, however, the outcome is not under our control. We are contributors, we are participants, but processes such as self-organization, complexity, tipping points or non-linearity all operate across the surface of the same pile as it relates to these inputs, creating an outcome that we really have no control over, nor can we predetermine or act towards. As such, in a system, what can be affected is the quality, relevance, timeliness and value of the input of each individual, to eventually effect an emergence that constitutes the future.

Let me return to the subject at hand. In terms of the worst case of climate change and what it is that can be determined by way of foresight would essentially amount to intervening and helping manage the inputs that would enhance the probabilities of a desired outcome. As a starting point, this outcome to shoot for can (at best) and should be, minimalist; minimalist in the sense of survival rather than some pie-in-the-sky desirable future. Survival of the self and the species is a starting point, the "greatest good of the greatest number" articulated in the utilitarian philosophy put forward by Bentham and Hooker as the driving value. This value, simply put as "happiness" or "wellbeing", is being increasingly articulated and implemented in many policies in the UK, Canada and even the Kingdom of Bhutan, which has implemented the idea of "gross national happiness", based on measurable metrics. This is because conventional metrics of GDP and per-capita income etc. have, in effect, caused the problem in the first place.

Climate change, or any other issue currently being approached, is based on an untouchable, primary preferred assumption to simply to stay entrenched in the prevailing operant paradigm, and merely offers care and caution as the remedies. I might add that, over the last decade, almost universally, I have talked to audiences at the level of the individual and I can report that, when these crises and their implications—and more importantly, the fact that we are simply, severely, diminishing the possibilities for future generations—are put forward to them, along with ideas on what we can and must do, their reactions, without exception, are best described as the desire and the willingness to participate and actually do something about it!

Given this approach, what then to do about climate change and how to do it? In a nutshell, it is my view that addressing the worst case of climate change involves overcoming what is described as the *normalcy bias*. This bias, as described in the literature, occurs as follows: The *normalcy bias* refers to a mental state people enter when facing a disaster. It causes people to underestimate both the possibility of a disaster occurring as well as its possible effects. This often results in situations where people fail to adequately prepare for a disaster and on a larger scale, the failure of the government to include the populace in its disaster preparations. The assumption that is made in the case of the normalcy bias is that since a disaster never has occurred, that it will never occur in the future. It also results in the inability of people to cope with the disaster once it occurs. People with a normalcy bias have difficulties reacting to something they have not experienced before. People also tend to interpret warnings in the most optimistic way possible, seizing on any ambiguities to infer a less serious situation. I cannot think of a more appropriate description of the issue of climate change and our current states of mind. There are two aspects to the normalcy bias. The first has to do with the fact that the current civilizational paradigm is premised on the universal applicability of the limitless possibilities of progress, growth and development, even though we know that these are the very same values that have caused the issue of climate change, or any of the other crises, in the first place! Specific to climate change, or for that matter, the impending depletion of fossil fuels and water, or burgeoning human populations directly implying limits to the carrying capacity of the planet, the normalcy bias seems to be at work in full force.

Thus, with respect to addressing the issue of climate change and overcoming the normalcy bias, what should we do and how should it be done? This is one area where some of the routine techniques of foresight would come in handy. Once again, I'll revert to citing from the findings of our conference at the Foundation For the Future, and specifically Professor William Calvin, who gave one example of how we might go about this. Basically, his approach would be to approach the public with a plausible worst-case threat that will quickly require addressing on a war footing. More than just awakening a long-term sense of responsibility or empathy for people impacted by an event, the depiction must elicit an emotional response that includes dread or fear. Because there is so little time for effective response, his suggestions were to focus attention on something big that could happen in only a year or two, for example, a two year El Niño that dries out much of South America and Southeast Asia, resulting in a cascade of problems worldwide. The presentation of this would be the next challenge.

Such a scenario should be presented in a way that, as a first requirement, would ensure comprehension by ordinary citizens. Several means were described. Examples: A graphical presentation of great global populations as affected over time, depicting the actual impact of past events as well as anticipated future climate-related events; a simulation game that connects the present with future conditions through interactive causes and effect linkages; computer games, films and similar media created for the purpose of communicating the climate destabilization story; a *disaster yardstick* to graphically depict the response to the question of how bad it could really get, with respect to breakdown of the social order, failed states, anarchy and ultimately, extinction; narratives, stories and books to illustrate health issues and regional impacts, extended droughts in Sub-Saharan Africa and the consequences or water issues depicting different areas with too little or too much in the wrong places at the wrong time; graphic illustrations of disappearing ice on the planet and what it would mean to different places on the planet. I already mentioned the thermohaline circulation and how a sudden reorganization of it might result in climate changes and consequences thereof, for instance, for most of Europe.

This all boils down to a good specification of scenarios, timelines and stories identifying the worst case, taking one small thing at a time but depicted and represented in an appropriate manner for the general public to understand. Another recommendation to come out of our conference was the need for the establishment of a global climate alliance that would be an aggregation of the global activist agencies across the planet, to provide an organized, coherent, bottom-up force to address the issue. Additionally, we need entities organized at neighboring levels, like FEMA, minus the incompetence that it demonstrated with regard to Hurricane Katrina in New Orleans.

In the largest sense, there are two overarching issues. One is the ethical implications of the worst case of climate destabilization, and encircling this, the larger issue of the untenability of the dominant paradigm as it relates to the relationship between humans and the biosphere, the zoosphere, the geosphere, the atmosphere, or to state it more generally, the planet. As one of the philosophers in our conference correctly pointed out: Mankind is now in the grip of the "perfect storm" on both counts. On the one hand, those who have contributed the least to climate change will suffer the most. This is specifically true to perhaps 90% of the human population on the planet today, and of course, generations to come who will inherit the planet. Secondly, we carry the responsibility for committing acts easily described as "criminal" that inflict great harm on current and future people and the animals of the world and nature generally. It is an issue that again is perhaps less amenable for consideration and conclusion with respect to solutions and approaches in a top-down fashion, but one that is more easily impressed onto the present generation as it pertains to everyone's own children, grandchildren and great-grandchildren.

I will conclude by pointing out, the issue of climate change is best addressed at the level of every person. Every person must take the time to examine his or her own "normalcy bias", educate themselves with regard to these two overarching issues and act accordingly with enlightened self-interest as the guiding principle. Thank you.

References

Archer, D., Eby, M., Brovkin, V., Ridgwell, A., Cao, L., Mikolajewicz, U., Caldeira, K., Matsumoto, K., Munhoven, G., Montenegro, A., & Tokos, K. (2009). Atmospheric Lifetime of Fossil Fuel Carbon Dioxide. *Annual Review of Earth and Planetary Sciences*, 37(1), 117–134. https://doi.org/10.1146/annurev.earth.031208.100206

Bak, P. (1996). *How Nature Works: The Science of Self-Organized Criticality*. Springer-Verlag.

Calvin, W. (1998, January). The Great Climate Flip Flop. *The Atlantic Monthly*. https://www.theatlantic.com/magazine/archive/1998/01/the-great-climate-flip-flop/308313/

Velamoor, S. (2011, March 6). *Anthropogenic Climate De-stabilization: A Worst-Case Scenario* [Conference presentation]. UNESCO Conference, Imagining The Worst: Foresight, Ethics and Extreme Climate Scenarios, Ljubljana, Slovenia.

Wasdell, D. (2010, November). Critical Issues in the Domain of Climate Dynamics. *Dept. of Land Economy*. University of Cambridge

International Affairs in the New Millennium: A Futures Perspective

*"The planet has enough to meet every human's needs
but not for every human's greed".*

- M. K. Gandhi.

Introduction

Mistaken and foolish notions about "saving" the planet have become the central focus of global efforts, whereas what is urgently needed is a focus on humans "saving" themselves from extinction. The planet has been around for nearly 4.5 billion years and according to estimates is likely to be around for another 6 billion. It is important to note and heed the fact that 99.9% of all that ever existed is now "extinct" and humans as a species are not exempt.

The following is an attempt to outline the nature of the megacrisis, the attendant symptoms and causes in temporal scales that are "long term", and an appeal to pause, rethink and help participate in and create a new paradigm to ensure survival going forward, provided it is not already too late.

The Megacrisis

The "megacrisis", simply put, can be described as the impending collapse of the planetary system inclusive of humans, due to the ideas, values and assumptions that have formed the basis for human endeavors as it relates to progress, development, the limitless power and value of human agency on the one hand, and the resultant devastation of the planet on the other. It should be pointed out that a basic fact has been overlooked, that with the exception of one external input, the Sun, the planet is a closed system with everything that is on it being a "fixed" amount, even as humans have multiplied into the billions and continuing to grow in numbers thereby pointing to the inevitability of "exhaustion" of every resource, known and as yet unknown, due to the notion of progress and development measured in economic terms of material consumption without limits.

Symptoms of the Megacrisis

The list is long. Symptoms abound at all levels of human society and organization, from the local neighborhood, to the community, the city, the state, the nation and yes, much more obviously and profoundly at the global level. To name a few: climate change; economic collapse; the recent implosion of the free market system; the impending end of the fossil fuel age; the threat of a nuclear holocaust; and extreme poverty for more than three quarters of humanity, accompanied by paralysis on multiple fronts—a paralysis that is rooted in the conduct of international affairs via strategies that imply continued enslavement to a set of ideas, but with caution and with the hope and prayer that this will somehow produce a different outcome, a strategy Einstein described as "insanity". Examples of the paralysis are numerous.

The debates about a sustainable future for humans mired in "nationalism", the failure to adopt global climate change protocols, or the lack of seriousness in getting to the abolition of nuclear weapons, economic models/paradigms of progress, growth, development based on gross summing of the value of the monetary exchange of each transaction without consideration of whether each of these transactions is a positive and negative in terms of the well-being of society as a whole. For example, the monetary value of building hospitals for dealing with diseases is "progress", as well as jails for holding criminals, are added instead of being subtracted? Or for that matter these computations do not consider the cost of repairing resulting tragedies of the commons in the future, or the cost of robbing future generations of their share?

Perhaps the most intractable symptom is the fact that all of the symptoms described above are being dealt with and being treated as "problems" or "root causes" in and of themselves, thus masking the need to look deeper to determine the real "root cause". An approach that will do nothing more than ensuring the consummation of the collapse. An utter and complete absence of "critical thinking", because arriving at the "root cause" would undermine the very foundations of the dominant paradigm. And the reluctance to look deeper is reinforced, because it would mean the beginning of the end of the "vested interests" who control the political, cultural, and economic realms.

The Operant Paradigm

The operant paradigm is rooted in a set of civilizational driving forces that can be described in terms of the nature of the relationship between a) humans and humans, b) humans and the planet, and c) humans and higher powers. These driving forces have evolved over time and emerged through thousands of years but have gathered momentum and dominated human affairs only over the last two millennia. The Royal Geological Society described it best as the onset of the "Anthropocene", meaning the dawning of an "epoch" where humans dominate the planet and have altered it irreversibly and therefore, have caused an impact similar to geological events of the past that had profound effects on the Planet including extinctions. All previous epochs had their origins in geological or other factors.

The fundamental ideas of this operant paradigm are as follows. It should be pointed out at the very outset that the origins of the fundamental ideas are not an outcome of reasoning or knowledge, but articles of faith and belief handed down presumably by agents and agencies of the supreme!

- Humans are the apex of creation, divinely ordained to be in charge;

- humans and nature are apart and separate from each other;

- nature has been given to humans to subjugate, exploit and use over the last couple of millennia and more recently;

- reinforced with notions of the power of human agency, human infallibility, autonomy and ability to design and create futures at will; and most importantly,

- The divinely ordained "obligation" to do so.

Along came the "scientific method", and a newer set of ideas that progress can be linear and unlimited, and that we as humans are duty bound to pursue such progress, defined as "scientific humanism". The "supreme" is in the process of being dispensed with and replaced by the crowning of "humans". Translated into modern economic terms as "Per Capita Income", "GDP", "Free Markets" and so on without comprehension or concern about the attendant tragedies of the commons. Additionally, at the social, cultural and economic levels, intellectual dishonesty that reinforced the above, with ideas of "free will", and "individualism", equality, accompanied by contempt for the "collective", and so on. A devastating combination of ideas that are squarely responsible for the current state of affairs and what is worse, an unquestioned continuation of faith and belief in them with absolutely no inclination to examine or revise any of them.

Let us not forget the human propensity to create and rely on wrong ideas is nothing new. Our history is replete with examples. It was not long ago that humans thought the Earth was at the center of a single universe only to find out that is not so. That we are at the center of the Solar System and that the Sun revolved around the Earth, that the Earth was flat, that we were divinely created, apart from and above all other forms of life, only to find out that all we see around us has existed for billions of years before we arrived and that we are descendants of the Bonobo, sharing 98.4% of their genetic make-up, that a grain of rice has more genes than we do.

Course Correction

So, what is best descriptive of the present moment is that we stand at the threshold of a plethora of planetary issues of our own making but faced with the need to recognize and acknowledge our own insignificance and unimportance as a species and our godlike sense of "self" shattered and in ruins, calling for a thorough rethinking.

The overriding question is whether we are prepared to think in terms of a major course correction with regard to our sense of who we are and our relationships with all that is around us, or continue to operate within the current paradigm, unable to extricate ourselves from it. The prospects are not encouraging.

It seems we are evolutionarily speaking hardwired to look no farther than the current generation or at best the next, as to the implications of what we are doing, and only the capacity to "react" and change course. What may be the case however is, that this time around, we may not have the time or capacity to react, given the magnitude of the megacrisis about to unfold. For sure what is evident is that there is a vague unease about it all, that there is something seriously wrong. The vocabulary and the narratives being used in our discourses are no doubt shifting. "Sustainability", "Earth as Mother Goddess (Gaia)", "voluntary simplicity", "Gross National Happiness" as opposed to

"GDP," our "obligations to future generations" etc. are bandied about, but essentially strategies, that do not dare question the central themes and ideas of the operant paradigm. Strategies best described as "more of the same" with lip service to the need for course correction.

Future as Emergence

An important exercise that needs to be undertaken is to understand how the future actually comes about. It is not in the scope of this essay to present a detailed picture. Suffice it to point out that the Future, contrary to our belief that we create it, is actually born of emergence. An emergence that is best understood in evolutionary terms. Cultural evolution to be exact. A process in which competing memes are selected for fitness over long periods of time. Memes inclusive of all of our ideas as inputs to a system, and the outcome as an emergence that we have no control over.

It will be important to note that, in this sense, what might seem like a spectacularly successful paradigm for nearly ten thousand years based on our ideas is what has created the outcomes that we are currently grappling with. And so the indications are clear. Our ideas over the last ten thousand years are actually wrong and on the verge of obsolescence, and actually the reasons for the disappointing and destructive results seen until now. Another way to look at this is that we are doomed to continue functioning within the operant paradigm if we do not stretch and extend the time frames of consideration of such phenomena.

Three Axes of Emergence

A thorough overhaul is in order. As an aside, it is important to point out that for any course correction to take place, education of the billions of humans is what is now needed. Education that does not reinforce the ideas and the values of the dominant paradigm, rather, education that presents the truth as reverse of the ideas of the dominant paradigm, so as to permit informed choices and decisions.

It is important to briefly explain the concept of emergence. Simply put, emergence is the result of a complex interplay of variable on three axes.

The first Axis is the individual, at once functioning with multiple identities at various levels (individual, family, community), the second Axis is the varieties of social, cultural, religious, economic and political systems within which we are located, and the third axis is the biological, zoological, geological and atmospheric domains.

The process is one in which individuals are not random walkers but are actually active walkers by virtue of their participation, conditioned by and operating within a set of ideas and values, but the outcomes are entirely outside of their control, simply by virtue of the fact that the complexity of the interactions is too great for any approach that would result in a desired outcome. Complicated further by the fact that such inputs and participations are provided within a framework of individuals with the autonomy to optimize self-interest. The emergence has elements of: criticalities, tipping points, self-organization, chaos and stasis.

The process is best illustrated by the oft-repeated example of a butterfly flapping its wings in one location causing a tornado in another distant location.

Students and theoreticians and practitioners of international affairs would do well to familiarize themselves with these ideas, if they are to be more effective in their pursuits. And to reiterate, enable a bottom up revision of ideas and norms that facilitate reasoned and informed participation by individuals within the framework of a substantially altered "Paradigm" of ideas and values is what may avert the crisis.

It is entirely likely that even such a course correction may be too little too late.

International Affairs:
Specific Planetary Transitions

Specific to International Affairs, given the preceding as it relates to the importance of comprehending things in terms of evolutionary processes and timeframes, it will be useful to outline the major transitions that are occurring on the planet. Five key transitions that would not otherwise be readily apparent because of the extremely short time frames in which students of international affairs operate.

Firstly, the beginning of the end of the nation state.

It should be fairly apparent that the nation state as a unit of consideration will never disappear but that its relevance for solving the major issues of our time is diminishing on an hourly basis. This conclusion will be self-evident by asking a simple question: Name a single issue that is being currently debated internationally that is amenable to be solved by and within nation states? The answer is NONE. It is also fairly apparent, aggregations of supra national entities in every realm of human affairs, are being put together also on a daily basis. Entities and entreaties for global governance is the overarching need. It will come about sooner or later, in more and more formal ways. This is not to say that the Nation State will disappear, but what will occur is that the

Nation State will decline in its dominance as the unit of identity for humans.

Secondly, knowledge vs. faith and belief systems.

The intersection of the accumulation of knowledge on the one hand and ideas of faith and belief systems that have been around ever since humans have existed on the planet is now approaching a criticality or a tipping out. It was pointed out earlier as to the Shattering of the myths that humans accepted and believed and now proven to be false. This process is now accelerating as a result of human mobility across the globe and globalization and will soon create an untenable situation for the basic tenets of faith and belief systems. In this sense, this author will dare to suggest that the so called "Clash of Civilizations" or regression of societies to religious and cultural fundamentalism is actually the last phase in their respective fights for survival and will soon give way to reformations across the spectrum. This is of course not to say that "God is dead". It is unlikely that God will be given last anytime soon, because ultimately humans will have a difficult time getting used to the idea of the absence of meaning and purpose in their lives and will therefore need God and the idea of a life hereafter. This recourse however is likely to be contained and constrained within their personal domains.

Thirdly, the individual vs. the collective.

For centuries the power, influence and autonomy of the individual has steadily increased, even if at different rates in different societies and thus in a "Zero Sum" sense has eroded and in instances eliminated the power of the collective in many ways in formal structures relating to human affairs. But we are at a threshold of reconsideration of this drive to individualism. Many of the pathologies of human society, the excesses of the economics of *laissez faire*, the multiple tragedies of the commons are pulling humans back to an appreciation and importance of the "collective"—a balance somewhere in the middle is what is likely to emerge.

Fourthly, bottom up vs. top down.

Even as the need for global governance is emerging in all matters of significance, the intractable and inflexible structures below, middle and bottom are beginning to be on shaky grounds. New knowledge and technologies are making it abundantly clear that humans can communicate and organize for common goals across and outside of all levels of formal governance. A powerful new force on the planet that is likely to cause upheavals in many of the areas of human affairs with utterly unpredictable outcomes. Wikileaks, the Arab Uprisings are only the beginnings of this transition and is likely to gain in its momentum toward change. It should be pointed that the danger of such runaway revolutions is limited. Limited because of group selection, altruism and sacrifice of self for the collective are also phenomena that are present in the evolutionary process of emergence of the future described above.

Finally, globalization.

This theme has been explored to exhaustion. But it will be worthwhile revisiting it. Globalization is prevalent in the current discourse as if it is something new. This author would like to submit that globalization started when modern humans emerged out of Africa nearly 60-80 thousand years ago, and the process has continued. What is new of course is that globalization is reaching a tipping point.

What needs to be understood is that this is a process that cannot be designed toward desirable outcomes or that there is a moral or ethical or other value of "good" or "bad" that is assignable to it. What we are witnessing is globalization at warp speed whereas it used to be at snail's pace in earlier times. It will have implications in every aspect of human affairs. What might emerge, much to our chagrin, is a homogenization of all of the variables- culture, politics, religion, genetics, and over evolutionary time a "planetary imprint" but of course passing the test of "selection for fitness" and survive. There is no point or use in lamenting this outcome. It is not a question of "if" but "when" and the evidence in favor is already fairly apparent.

Conclusion

As it pertains to "international affairs" and the "planetary issues" that we as humans are facing, solutions exist, and the future will emerge with or without our intervention. We would be well advised however to undertake a serious re-examination of our most passionately held ideas about ourselves and our place on this planet. "The Pale Blue Dot." The only home we know and have. It must start with each individual making an attempt to ask and answer the simple question: WHO AM I?

It requires us to understand that all our identities at multiple levels and the complex interactions that we are part and parcel of described in this essay must be circumscribed within a supremely critical identity for ourselves. That we are, first and foremost, Citizens of the Planet and all other identities must take second place and not the other way around. Anything less will doom us to extinction and time is running out. That we are part and parcel of the "System" and not over and above and independent of it.

We would do well to know and understand that 99% of all that ever existed is extinct and that we are not and will not be exempted.

John Donne's immortal verse comes to mind:

> No Man is an Island. Entire of itself. Every man is a piece of the continent, a part of the main. If a Clod were to be washed away by the Sea, Europe is the less, as well as if a promontory were, as well as if a manor of thine own or of thy friends...Every man's death diminishes me because I am a part of mankind. So, do not send to know for whom the bell tolls: It tolls for thee. (1624)

Reprinted with permission from the Journal of Futures Studies.

Journal of Futures Studies, March 2012, 16(3): 99-106.

References

Donne, J. (1624). *Devotions Upon Emergent Occasions, and several steps in my Sickness.* Church of England.

CHAPTER 7

Asia Past, Present and Future: A Civilizational Perspective

Paradigms and Civilizations

Human civilizations can be studied as transformations of culture, beliefs, traditions, and political systems. In order to understand the evolution of a people or culture over time, it is first necessary to identify the dominant paradigm which drives that society. In some cases, the same paradigm has remained intact within a culture for centuries. In other civilizations, dynamic change has resulted in the adoption of new paradigms over time. It is in this last group that we find Asian civilization today. Between paradigms.

Asia, in its drive to modernity over the last century, has superimposed a set of new driving forces upon a millennia-old system, willingly and unwillingly. These new contradictory driving forces are rooted in the Judeo-Christian traditions and within extensions of this tradition. These extensions have been universalized and secularized into an irresistible package of liberal democracy and egalitarianism, a package which is comprised of three main components. These three components are clearly laid out by Professor S.P. Udayukumar as "the triumvirate of Nation-statist-democracy, scientism, and developmentalism which have very broad implications". Udayukumar's discourse on the "axiomatic Western three-in-one" speaks to religion generally as an underlying force (Sardar, 1999). In the case of the west, this underlying force is the Judeo-Christian tradition. The primary precepts of the Judeo-Christian tradition are these (Elredge & Gould, 1995):

- God and man are wholly separate.

- Man is unique and at the top of creation.

- Man has dominion over nature.

- The fall from Eden has to be regained by good works.

- All that are not of this tradition must be brought into the flock (conversion).

- The Anti-Christ must be defeated (prepare for righteous battles).

The important eras, stages, and episodes of western civilization with respect to itself and the "other" can be satisfactorily explained as an outcome of the implementation of these tenets (Nobel, 1999). Understanding this backdrop is crucial in order to understand the state of contemporary Asian society. Each of these tenets is centrifugal in nature. This centrifugality is apparent in the denuding of the earth's resources, in the creation of bigger and bigger "tragedies of the commons" now assuming global proportions, in the alienation and anomie of individuals in the ongoing proliferation of the number of disenfranchised groups seeking equity, worth, identity and rights (Hardin, 1968). This powerful force of centrifugality has gradually taken western civilization to near exhaustion, whereupon certain patterns have begun to emerge. These are patterns of discontinuities which could be qualified as "punctuations", according to the model set forth by Stephen Jay Gould (Elredge & Gould, 1995).

Deceptions

The superimposition of forces of centrifugality has fundamentally altered, in some ways surreptitiously, contemporary Asian civilization in two ways. Foremost, the adoption and integration of the concepts of "individualism", "rights", "autonomy" and "atomization" in their western denotation have catalyzed a storm pitting the individual against the collective good. This storm is grounded in the relegation of duties, obligations, and responsibilities accompanied by a removal and enforcement of the same to the "commons". These institutionalized system of rules, laws, and codes had ensured centripetality in Asian societies for centuries. The rapid move to the western paradigm resulted in the undermining, corrupting, and the almost overnight replacement of these social, cultural, political, and economic structures. Though, these structures were formerly hierarchical, traditional, patriarchal, they did contain some unique pluralistic and democratic features. In Asian history, these structures had coerced the cohesion and integrity of the whole and the collective, by placing primary emphasis upon duties, roles, obligations, and responsibilities.

There has been a second major deception implicit in this attempted transformation by and of Asian societies. This deception, or error, was the belief that the transformation towards a more western system would be relatively painless, swift, and manageable. Asia, thus, entered the proverbial Faustian bargain.

The bargain, of course, required that in exchange for democracy, developmentalism, and scientism, which together held the promise of individual rights, sustenance, and survival, Asia had to first give up its inherent paradigm of centripetality. To the majority of these populations, entrenched in tradition, hierarchy, and patriarchy, this proposition seemed a good bargain. These populations were lured into agreeing to the proposition by the radical literate and liberated intellectuals of these societies. Unfortunately, these radical intellectuals were had and allowed themselves to be misled by the promises of idealism implicit in this bargain. In all fairness, who wouldn't?

Civilizations in Transition

What is happening today in Asia is a transition between these paradigms, where the Asian paradigm has been submerged by the western model. The Asian paradigm is diametrically opposed to the Judeo-Christian model in every respect, the implications of this transition are enormous. The basic precepts of the Asian paradigm are these:

- Humanity and God are one and the same.

- Humanity is of nature and part of it.

- Righteous behavior and responsibility serve the larger interest of the community first and the individual second.

- Humanity's search for meaning and God is a process internal to oneself.

- Divinity is omniscient.

The irony here is, tragically, two-fold. First, many societies anchored on the Judeo-Christian traditions have become increasingly aware of the impending exhaustion of their paradigm as the logical outcome of the inherent centrifugality. However, these societies continue to energetically promote the same panaceas, only now with some measure of sobriety. This sobriety can be seen as attempts to moderate the heretofore evolutionarily unstable strategies in newer but ultimately anthropocentric prescriptions and imperatives.

In many academic, holistic, and long-term forward-thinking communities in the west, "sustainability", concern for "future generations", "global ethics", "cosmic evolution", "Gaia", and "systems" approaches have all become cardinal concerns. All are pale imitations of profound intuitions and understandings which have been addressed for millennia in Asian philosophies and cultures. This intuition is something that cultures such as the Tasadai of the Philippines, certainly, understood from day one.

Second, most Asian societies that have embarked on the path towards things western have found that the road is arduous, long, and painful. Furthermore, it has become clear that this transformation will take centuries for these societies to become equals of the so called "advanced economies" of today, in contrast to the presumption that only mere years of decades were needed to attain that objective.

Today there are more illiterate, undernourished, impoverished people in Asia than at any time in Asian history. Similarly, there exists more social discord, ethnic conflict, and racial and caste hatred today than the Asian culture at large has ever known before. Groups, which may have been historically disenfranchised due to their tradition, hierarchy, or patriarchy, have become even more marginalized. By enshrining centrifugality and discarding old "evil" structures of centripetality, vacuums have been created and are now filled by caricatures of democracy, scientism, and developmentalism. All of these democratic movements are practiced in the main. However, they are built on rampant ignorance and illiteracy that now elects godmen, kings, dictators! Notwithstanding these "formalities", very little else has been changed. For Asian civilization, the Faustian bargain has been a bad one. It is time to look at the very real possibility that Asian cultures have been had. The signs are everywhere and can be readily identified on many levels, yet many remain unwilling to face the truth. This manifests itself in the vociferous demonizing of the west for the presumed demonization of the non-west.

The current situation of Asian societies can be likened to a high wire act, on which they have gone a quarter of the way across, are losing balance, yet have no possibility of returning to the starting point. The picture painted here is a somber one. It is the only means, however, of coming to terms with this crisis which exists in Asia.

Leadership into the Future

The strategy for moving Asia forward, therefore, is to manage the problem within the evolutionary context. If Asia were to take a managerial view of things (which incidentally is a western invention premised firmly in positive convictions about human agency, control over one's destiny, and the possibility of realizing desired futures) at a minimum, the requirements are:

1. Extend the time frame under consideration to centuries instead of the delusional approaches often taken in terms of decades.

Given the nature of the representative democracies or the business sector, the planning horizons adopted for definition of national objectives or commercial strategies rarely ever exceed five years. This is true even with the understanding that the consequences of almost any policy or decision, in either realm, will not be known in the same time frames chosen. Decisions for the building of a highway, dam, chemical factory, or the policy of one man-one vote, are attractive "industrializing" and "egalitarian" propositions. However, the consequences of these propositions spread not across one, but many generations and are often invariably negative. These environmental fluctuations and the political corruption in Asia have, not surprisingly, been considerable. What is needed is an expansion of time horizons in terms of envisioning local, regional, and national destinies.

2. The units of consideration should be top down from the largest and the most general to the smallest and the particular. Example: start with the earth as the unit of measure and view smaller aggregations in order down to the individual. In other words, optimize the larger first and the smaller next.

It is now becoming increasingly clear that mankind's understanding about its "position" or location" has to be changed. The boundaries that man circumscribed himself within, be they economic, social, or political, have become obsolete. It has become irrevocably clear that the denuding of rain forests in the Amazon, the burning of forests in Indonesia, the eruption of Mt. St. Helen's in the United States, affect not one civilization but all. Legislation issues by the U.S. Congress to fight terrorism- touches religious, social, and cultural nerves around the globe. The Aids virus is not the localized, African, phenomenon that it once was. This is now a pandemic. Individuals such as the Dalai Lama, Mother Teresa, and even Michael Jordan, are no longer nationally or regionally bound icons.

The point which can be made from these observations is that when examining either one Asian country or Asia entirely, in an outward sense, it is irresponsible to limit the perspective to thinking in terms of a "part" of the whole. In days past, this may have been a reasonable approach. Today, however, demands that there must be a wariness of man's inherent nature to look at the whole as a reflection of his own image. What one man, or even a collective, sees, feels, and desires, from a singular vantage may not be that which is objectively true. This being the case, a plea must be issued that considerations be made in terms of local and regional issues within the framework of larger, more relevant boundaries. Every man is a part of the whole. The whole circumscribes and defines the part, not the reverse. Asia, thinking about its future, must begin by thinking about what it is a part of. Likewise, any Asian country must think about itself first as a part of Asian and then, of itself as an entity within it.

3. Focus on the paradigms that will guide Asia into the future, even as we are respectful of what evolution teaches us, however distasteful those lessons might be.

In the rush to modernize, most countries in Asia welcomed the western paradigm eagerly. Now they struggle with the reconciliation between who they really are, and the implications of the western paradigm upon their lives. The Chinese advising the US to mind its own business regarding human rights is a classic example. The reversion of Pakistan to a theocratic dictatorship is another. The current situations of Singapore and Saudi Arabia, still more. In other words, these countries have learned that the importation of paradigms in total is unworkable. What is needed instead is a paradigm that takes Asia's own deep codes and structures into account. Visions that honor and retain the deep civilizational codes, as well as incorporating new ones with caution, are the ones that will meet with success. If not, Asia will most certainly perpetuate the conditions that prevail today- suffering from the onslaught of ramifications of employing the inappropriate western paradigm. Many point at the new paradigm as yet another western "agent of colonization". In all of these protestations, what is often ignored is the simple fact that Asia has willingly and enthusiastically embraced the western paradigm. The old dog of blaming everything on colonialism, capitalism, imperialism will not hunt anymore. That dog is dead.

4. Consider things in a framework of hierarchic, interacting multi-system complexity and focus on boundary areas, the areas where systems interact rather than internal to any system.

It is commonly known that when two tectonic plates rub against each other, earthquakes and mountains are caused. It is easy to conclude that the focus of any examination of this should be upon the areas of interaction of the tectonic plates and not simply the plates in isolation. One example of this is Kashmir, the area of intersection of India and Pakistan. East Timor, though internal to Indonesia, is another. To understand and solve problems therefore, focus is needed on such intersections as a primary effort, rather than as a secondary concern. It is the areas of intersection that often have the most to reveal.

As another example, the various government bureaucracies must begin to manage the areas where the results of their autonomous partitioned decision-making show. A dam constructed by a department of public works must be coordinated with the department of agriculture, social welfare, forestry, flood relief, and so on, and not as an isolated edict arising out of a five-year plan.

5. Concentrate on the processes that will carry us to our objectives rather than the events that we desire.

Many are familiar with Deming's great contribution to the quality improvement miracle of Japan. The underlying premise is simple. It can be explained through analogy. In a harvest of apples, rotten apples can be sorted out from healthy apples in the process of harvesting. Depending on the size of the crop, and the portion of the crop lost to rotten apples, once can then investigate the magnitude of cause after the fact. This is what I call "management of the event". Deming would argue that if one can identify all of the reasons that some of the apples have become rotten, and also what causes other apples to remain healthy, one would find that good apples happen because all the various inputs to getting good apples must be within an acceptable range (Deming, 1996). These various inputs within a range and sequence can be defined as the process for producing apples. The imperative then, is to preemptively manage the process of producing healthy apples, rather than managing the event of harvesting bad apples.

This same rationale can be applied to a myriad of other phenomena. One could just as easily approach crime, the population explosion, or disease in the same manner.

6. Insist on discipline in the problem-solving process. Identify the true, deep, underlying causes rather than the ones too near the effect.

This dictum is a continuation of the ideas described above. Most problem solving usually takes the form of attacking the symptoms rather than the cause. For example, take potholes of a given street. Generally, if the pothole is the problem, the quick solution is usually to fill it. However, one must first determine whether this is truly a solution or simply a treatment of the symptom, which will most likely reoccur? Effective problem-solving procedures first identify the true cause. In this scenario, it could be defects in the asphalt mix, inappropriate design for the traffic that utilizes that road, or poor drainage. One tactic is to ask the question "why" five times. Usually by the fifth "why", the cause is identified, and a solution is readily apparent.

7. Keep in mind evolutionary lessons as they pertain to human capacity and limitations when it comes to size of organization, clarification of roles and responsibilities alongside of rights and privileges.

Asia has, as have other regions of the world, succumbed to the charms of developmentalism, scientism, nation-statism. In country after country, bureaucracies have attempted problem solving on a national scale. The result has been the creation of unmanageable behemoths, whether they be in the industries of steel, public works, banks, or airlines, while simultaneously proclaiming rights, votes, and privileges for all. However, two glaring omissions remained clear. First, reasonable interpretations of what constitutes the appropriate size for a given organization is absent. The second is the absence of duties, responsibilities, or obligations, or more generally, the absence of accountability on the part of its citizens.

At a minimum, Asian civilization must walk away from the "one-minute manager" concept that has captivated and enthralled so many. This enthrallment has resulted in the use of perspectives based on short time frames used by everyone in their respective pursuits, despite the best of intentions in every case. This is exacerbated by the gross neglect of "complexity" and "evolution" in decision-making and consideration.

Conclusion

The interactions of multiple solutions, multiple inputs, and multiple entries into the solution space often results in some self-organized outcome. This implies that diversity, difference, and uniqueness must be maintained as inputs because they are the grist of the evolutionary mill. It must also be acknowledged that the evolutionary mill is a slow-moving mill. If it took the West two thousand years to get to where it is, then Asian civilizations must understand and accept that the process it has now undertaken will take just as long if not longer, simply because of the circumstances and conditions that prevail. It would require the idealists and the radicals amongst us to moderate rhetoric into a slower and less strident mode. Otherwise, they must be prepared to accept responsibility for turbulence and turmoil unleashed by revolutions driven by impatience, arrogance, and servitude to any single belief system or alternative and, more importantly, disregard for the evolutionary juggernaut. History is replete with single utopian ideologies and designs as alternatives that have failed. The only overriding requirement of these alternatives should be that they are rooted in our own paradigm.

Contemporary Asian civilization must muster the courage, the appetite, and the strength of will to take a more radical approach. It requires Asia to stop the train of transformation and for its passengers to get off and in a sense, redirect themselves. Asian peoples must redirect themselves not only in terms of their own paradigm, but also in the evolutionary context. The benefits of implementing these alternative strategies are clear. Asia would do well to set up enclaves that experiment with a hundred visions that provide fresh inputs to the evolutionary process in terms of the socializing of the individual and varieties of social economic, political organization. It will likely be the interplay of these varieties within its own all-encompassing paradigm that will yield the results we need. There can be no more lost, and simultaneously everything to gain.

All human civilizations evolve. The evolution of these civilizations occurs within a variety of dominant paradigms which compete with one another for dominance. In the case of Asian civilizations, what history is witnessing is a paradigmatic shift to the western paradigm, even as the current dominant western paradigm with its one dimensionality is nearing its end. The re-emergence of Asian paradigms is timely and relevant. Over the course of the next two centuries, Asia should and will most certainly return home, to its own paradigm, which emerges from within. Dr. Sohail Inayatullah (1999) once described such a paradigm as one which cultivates "communities that are ecologically conscious, spiritually aware, socially progressive, and embedded in the culture of the area".

Reprinted with permission from the Journal of Futures Studies.

Journal of Futures Studies, August 2000, 5(1): 61-71

References

Deming, E. (1996). *The New Economics*. MIT Press.

Elredge, N. (1995). *Reinventing Darwin: The Great Debate at the High Table of Evolution*. Wiley Publishers.

Galtung, J. & Inayatullah, S. (1987). *Macrohistory and Macrohistorians*. Praeger.

Hardin, G. (1968). The tragedy of the commons. *Science*, 162, 1243-1248. https://www.jstor.org/stable/1724745

Inayatullah, S. (1999). *Situating Sarkar*. Gurukul Publications.

Nobel, D.F. (1999). *The Religion of Technology: The Divinity of Man and the Spirit of Invention*. Penguin Books.

Sardar, Z. (1999). *Rescuing All Our Futures*. Adamatine Press.

Managing the Future

"No man is an Island, intire of it selfe, everyman is a peece of the Continent, a part of the maine; if a Clod bee washed away by the Sea, Europe is the less, as well as if a Promontorie were, as well as if a Mannor of thy friends or of thine own were; any mans death diminishes me, because I am involved in Mankinde; And therefore never send to know for whom the bell tolls; It tolls for thee..."

- John Donne: *For Whom the Bell Tolls* (1624)

*T*he *Harvard Business Review* has a daily radio spot on management problems and solutions reminiscent of the "one-minute manager". There has yet to be a single reference to management's responsibility for our future.

An MBA program at an American university took students on visits to prisons to talk to executives behind bars for white collar crime, but they were not taken to the executive suites of Fortune 500 companies to discuss global warming, or the hole in the ozone layer, or pollution in metropolis after metropolis, even though these corporations are directly or indirectly responsible. These multiple `tragedies of the commons" escape their notice. The scope of management thinking and management practice has been confined to the four walls of a business, dealing with people as `human resources" as opposed to "human beings", with the business enterprise being the focal point vis à vis competition, but not as a component or aspect of human society. There is no need to reiterate the fact that humankind is at a crossroads. We are now faced with problems that are larger in scope than any business or nation state can cope with. At best, we react at various levels ranging from municipalities emphasizing recycling to the "Rio Summit". We read daily about sustainability, climate change, genetic engineering, population, depletion of fossil fuels and the like. Yet it is an exception, rather than a rule, when a university includes curricula on management of the future, or a government has cabinet level positions or ministries committed to a study of the future. Managing the future requires an overhauling of existing paradigms of management thinking, given the new context of human affairs. This new context is characterized by the following important shifts as it relates to humans, their institutions, and worldviews:

- Globalization in the cultural, economic, social and political domains that are blurring our views about identities, about ethics, about nation states. We are now being forced to contend with the idea of humanity in a planetary sense.

- Revolutionary advances in the fields of information technology and genetics are causing us to re-think our notions about what it will mean to be human.

- The increasing power and influence of humans on other humans, on the environment and on other systems (ecosystems, biosystems etc.) that now have empowered us, in some part, to govern evolution.

And yet, other than reactions and ideas articulated by interest groups, academics and NGOs, there is an absence of any organized mobilization to rethink the now obsolete ideas and concepts of management. We continue to operate at the limits of an antiquated paradigm that is essentially a view of things in this particulate, functionalized, compartmentalized view of human affairs: extensions of existing business management models that are on the verge of exhaustion. We are confronting major "discontinuities", to quote Drucker, of which managers are blissfully unaware, and we still mouth clichés like "value proposition", "customer satisfaction", and "total quality", without really understanding the true meanings of the words even as these managers, with their daily decision making, impact the lives of generations to come. The following is an outline of some ideas that we must consider in the articulation of this new paradigm:

The unit of consideration has to be the planet and humanity first, and then on down to the consideration of our multiple identities, not the other way around. Multiple identities as citizens of nation states, employees of corporations, members of neighborhoods, members of families and then of ourselves as individuals, must be secondary to the global community. It is this systems-view, which structures us in our various roles, in our institutions and in our support systems (eco-, biosphere, etc.), that puts the proper perspective on the nature of interactions and relationships in a more enlightened, yet real, way.

A serious attempt must be made, on a global scale, to articulate the deep human civilizational code that will govern our thoughts, words, and deeds. This code need not be any more onerous than a set of ethical principles held inviolate and above our narrower value sets. These principles need only articulate behavior norms in service to a consensus set of values, such as:

- the earth must be preserved;

- species extinction must be averted;

- weapons of mass destruction will not be deployed; and

- other behavior standards of benefit to all humanity...

...a time horizon for deliberations that takes a really long-term view, well beyond the 5–20-year spans that we currently limit ourselves to. This cannot be overemphasized simply because human actions and their consequences are almost never visible in these shorter time frames, eg. global warming or sustainability. Even more importantly, shorter time frames legitimize existing paradigms and extend their life cycles because the perspective and objectivity to see its obsolescence is simply absent or excluded. For example, the idea of a flat earth survived for thousands of years, dictating an erroneous world view. Problems usually occur when interactions take place, and these areas of interactions are usually identifiable at the boundaries of subsystems. So, the focus of management must be on the boundary areas and interfaces rather than the ideation contained completely within the domains. For example, population growth is a problem that, in order to be managed, must be looked at in the framework of interactions between men and women, women and education, and society and its religion, as opposed to dealing with the symptom of overpopulation by distributing millions of condoms as an overlay on the deep structural interactions that are the cause of the problem. The above discussion leads to another important principle relevant to the management of the future. It can be stated as a commitment to managing a "process" rather than "events" as a measurement of progress. Thus, management is the implementation of a set of principles that monitor and maintain the variables that interact to produce a result rather than the measurement of the result itself. To revert to the example of "population", it would therefore be more appropriate to manage and monitor women's education, women's empowerment and women's financial self-sustainability as the variables in the process to control population. A more detailed elaboration of these ideas is outside the scope of this essay. An attempt has merely been made to show that:

- management studies must include "human futures" in their purview because these futures have to be managed;

- the underlying principles of current management practices need to be overhauled for relevance and applicability to the new paradigm described; and

- the paradigms we have used thus far for understanding and managing human affairs are outmoded and obsolete.

Reprinted with permission from Foresight.

Foresight, June, 2000, 2(3)

References

Donne, J. (1624). *Devotions Upon Emergent Occasions, and several steps in my Sickness*. Church of England.

Management Studies and a Changing World

Introduction

Students of management study finance, operations research, marketing, entrepreneurship, organization theories, strategic planning, etc., with the primary focus being the safeguarding of the future of businesses and shareholders. Concern with the effects of implementation of such knowledge on the commons and the management of them is left to institutions that fall outside the purview of the business being managed. Such an allocation of responsibility would be appropriate if the institutions that fall outside the purview of businesses had primacy, influence, and control over the business world. It is fairly apparent that this is not the case. Economics (businesses, management, industry) has become the predominant force and the institutions that are supposed to provide the checks and balances have in fact become the aiders and abettors of such dominance.

Economics has been the preeminent force, and the rationales and justifications for it have been provided by a larger set of values, assumptions, and imperatives that have now become universal: the profit motive, the laissez-faire system, economic development, growth measured by GDP and per-capita income, and so on. These universal imperatives are based on an even deeper set of values and assumptions, including the concepts that humans are a species separate from and superior to all other life; the planet was placed at our disposal by "the almighty" to be explored and exploited for our own good; and material progress is the necessary and sufficient condition of progress. These concepts compose the larger paradigm within which human affairs have been conducted for the last several centuries... and then something happened along the way in this rush to bliss.

The vocabulary has changed. We now hear of sustainability, voluntary simplicity, climate change, the end of oil, extinction of species, the consumption spike, water wars, concern for future generations: terms that denote impending disaster but, again, without particular attention to the institutional arrangements, frameworks, and structures within which these issues are to be resolved or an examination of the deeper values and assumptions that have been in force in a civilizational sense. I should say, more appropriately, in a Western civilizational sense, because it is the West that has been at the forefront of outlining the dominant paradigms for centuries if not millennia and thus the direct cause of these unfolding scenarios. It should be noted that all other societies that subscribed to different and even opposite notions have abandoned them in favor of wholesale adoption of the Western paradigm. The modus operandi is still to conduct human affairs without challenging and altering the larger paradigms and as such it is "business as usual" for students of management and management studies, with no profound changes to the curricula that students of management need to undertake.

The assumption is that these issues are externalities that do not fall within the purview of management studies or the world of business and industry, and that the multiple tragedies of the commons that have emerged are to be addressed outside the framework of management and business. Governments, NGOs, and international bodies are expected to address these issues while the business world and its managers proceed with continued emphasis on profits and shareholder gain as their primary and only focus, with (in exceptional cases) a course or two thrown in to include "corporate social responsibility." This would be an accurate assessment if managers and industry were viewed as secondary to the larger frameworks of governments, NGOs, and international bodies, but as has been pointed out, it is actually the other way around. Unless and until economic entities of business, industry, and management take the lead in changing the modus operandi and the paradigms within which they operate, the chances (already low) for preemption of the larger crises may well disappear, forcing us to REACT to continuous and ongoing catastrophes.

This paper will attempt to show that there has to be a radical change in the approach to economics and, more important, management curricula to be mandatorily inclusive of a new set of comprehensions and responsibilities to serve as a basis for implementation of their roles. Basically, this implies a complete redesign of education in the fields of economics and management, a re-education that builds on what is already studied but with curricular additions that cause a much-needed sensitization to and awareness of the issues of the commons that are fast approaching criticalities.

Redesign in Management Studies Curricula

This chapter will attempt to outline the basic content of such a re-education, with an itemization of the aspects that should be included in management studies. Though a detailed review of the nature and content of these aspects is not included in the scope of this paper, a brief elaboration follows:

1. Critical Thinking

2. A Primer in Biological and Cultural Evolution

3. The Planet as System

4. Chaos Theory and Tipping Points

5. Globalization and Emerging Transitions

6. Economics and Finance

7. The Question of Human Identity

1. Critical thinking:

Briefly, what is prevalent in education generally and certainly in management education is emphasis on "what" is to be learned, with either a complete absence of or at best a passing reference to "how" to learn. The "how to learn" method is what results in critical thinking. A basic and nonnegotiable prerequisite in management studies should be critical thinking, inclusive of the scientific method. Students would be exposed to basic concepts of "inductive" and "deductive" reasoning; the rigorous process of collecting, organizing, analyzing, testing, evaluating, and synthesizing data; and the subsequent formulation of correct conclusions, beliefs, or action. In addition, emphasis needs to be put on scientific literacy, which would be inclusive of aspects such as the meaning of scientific facts, scientific truths, the role of theory and conceptual schemes in science, and the basics of experimentation. What typically happens is that the sciences are studied without describing the scientific method; causes are extracted from correlations despite the well-known fact that correlations do not necessarily imply causation; symptoms are confused with problems and dealt with as ultimate causes; and decisions are made with partial or compartmentalized knowledge, providing partial and short-term relief with serious detriments to accrue later. A good case can be made that the tragedies of the commons we are facing as a species have much to do with the absence of critical thinking. Reliance on "belief," whether as "given from up above" or acquired through education, is the chief culprit in the multiple tragedies of the commons that we confront.

Another aspect of critical thinking that is typically missing is the appropriate emphasis on the totality of a given inquiry, in terms of inclusion of the inherently multidisciplinary and complex interdependent nature of it. This is true not only internally, in the narrow sense of businesses and managers charged with functional responsibilities with incentives tailored to the execution of them (thereby completely missing the notion of problems and solutions existing in the spaces where functions interact in the boundary areas), but also neglect in consideration of the fact that the business itself is interacting with the entire outside world and not just its competitors. For instance, the ethical, moral, and legal implications of decision-making, in terms of, say, "downstream" consequences to the commons, are usually absent. Another example is a business arena in which multiple players optimize their individual positive outcomes while creating a devastatingly negative effect on a specific area of the commons itself. An example might be the impending exhaustion of fossil fuels.

2. A primer in biological and cultural evolution

A comprehension of the processes by which we have arrived at where we are as a species is of paramount importance. These ideas include a) selection for fitness, both in the genetic and memetic sense; b) a deeper understanding and appreciation for how our sense of time and change differs radically from what evolutionary processes indicate; and c) humans acting as participants in a complex interactive process—involved, as opposed to being sole agents. This comprehension will provide an understanding of how things actually come about *vis-à-vis* human agency, time, and change. It would be hard to continue to argue the persistent belief in the paradigm of "humans as sole agents," with the implicit assumptions and expectations about change and time (instantaneous and immediate), when compared to evolutionary processes with respect to change, time, and complex interactions. Though the evidence suggests that these comprehensions may in the short term hold true, in the longer term, it is evolutionary processes that dictate the outcomes, which are usually exactly the opposite of what we intend. The record of large experiments based strictly on these three errors is rather sketchy. Utopias have come and gone, and the human condition has remained essentially the same with respect to classes, castes, and conflicts between humans on the planet. No doubt material progress based on scientific and technological advancement would indicate that we have come a long way, but by the same token we would be hard-pressed to deny that the magnitude of the problems we have created as a result are far greater than the solutions we have obtained thus far. The question to address is whether we are indeed active walkers completely in control, or are we merely passive participants, actors on a stage, with roles to play but without control over what emerges as outcomes. An interesting thought experiment would be to examine whether humans and the planet would be better off if we were still in the hunter-gatherer stage without any of the paradigms—better off in the sense of sustainability, climate change, and depletion of planetary resources. Would the content of our emotions and our experiences with respect to each other be any different? At least we would not be in peril and at the threshold of complete and utter destruction through nuclear weapons or a devastated planet. The point of including such study in our curricula is to allow for asking such profound questions, and to proceed with forethought and caution as opposed to proceeding headlong into the future with delusions of grandeur based on erroneous and ill-conceived convictions about our predominance as a species.

3. The planet as system

It is absolutely correct that systems thinking has been very much a part of the curriculum of management studies, but it has been systems thinking that promotes the idea that the business is a system with interacting and interconnected parts, both hierarchic and lateral, and that "holistic" approaches to problem solving should be chosen. Well and good, but what has been missing in these studies is the idea that the world around the business, the planet Earth, is also, in fact, a system. One may or may not choose to subscribe to higher and higher levels of this abstraction all the way up to thinking about the Earth as Mother Goddess Gaia (Lovelock, 2006), but we certainly cannot discard this larger idea in its entirety or be ignorant of it. The fact that the planet Earth is a system at any level need not be proved here. It is important for students of management to understand that the system that they are guiding into the future is a part of a larger economic system that, in turn, is part of an even larger system, and that the economic system in its entirety is in itself a part of the planetary system, inclusive of the biosphere, the zoosphere, the atmosphere, the geosphere, and so on. Any action or reaction in any of these systems in the final analysis will have an effect in every one of the other systems, usually within the framework of a negative "zero-sum" game unless consciously managed to create a synergy in the positive sense throughout the system. Once again, it should be evident that what has thus far resulted is the former and that there is now an urgent priority to think in terms of creating conditions for the latter. The point here is that management studies curricula must incorporate an introduction to this idea of the larger planetary system. This suggestion accompanies the notion of including emphasis on "critical thinking" as it relates to the emphasis on the multidisciplinary, interdependence, and boundary area implications already discussed above.

4. *Chaos theory and tipping points*

In the past couple of decades, new approaches to understanding phenomena have emerged. These can be lumped together within the terminology of "chaos theory" and "tipping points," inclusive of terms such as "complexity" and "criticality." Once again, the scope of this paper does not include a detailed elaboration of these new approaches but merely an introduction to the basics of these ideas and to implore that they be included in curricula to facilitate a basic understanding of the theory, leading to a better understanding of the phenomena and the context in which management of business occurs. Two ideas lie at the base of the study of chaos theory and tipping points.

1. Chaos theory starts with the supposition that systems that we function within and seek to manage are complex systems and that chaos, not order, is what is ubiquitous, as in weather or the stock market or for that matter the status, internally or externally, in a system of any size. This is precisely the opposite of what is usually assumed as conditions that prevail with methods, processes, policies, and decisions that follow. Secondly, the theory posits that the slightest change in initial conditions of a complex system has a profound impact resulting in completely different patterns and outcomes.

2. Tipping points essentially refer to levels in complex systems at which momentum for change becomes unstoppable. This idea is commonly illustrated with the example of a butterfly flapping its wings and eventually resulting in a tornado! Why are these studies important? They are important because such studies would require us to understand and accept that a reorientation as to the basic assumptions under which we have operated thus far is an important imperative. They would also drive home the realization that the absence of such an approach is what has caused us to be oblivious to the possibility of several unforeseen and adverse "tipping points" that have already occurred, are occurring, or will occur.

5. *Globalization and emerging transitions*

Management studies already include consideration of globalization, but, again, in a narrow sense. Such consideration considers things that have occurred or are occurring and the connections and implications to the business at hand. Examples are the onset of the worldwide web and the internet as used in web-based sales and marketing; the instantaneous movement of financial capital across national boundaries; trade agreements and protocols; the unfettered movement of labor across national boundaries, and the like. But the real phenomenon that is occurring is the entire idea of globalization as being at a "tipping point," not just in aspects described above, but in many other far more critical areas. The reference to the "tipping point" is to emphasize that globalization is not anything new. It started with the movement of humans out of Africa in the distant past. It included the movements of individuals, economies, and empires since time immemorial. What is important is to study, acknowledge, and understand that globalization is reaching a tipping point. It is a tipping point that poses an entire set of new possibilities. Are humans on the verge of a global culture? Are we beginning to witness the end of the nation-state? Are religious and belief systems in a competitive struggle for the hearts and minds of populations across the globe? Are knowledge and the accumulation of it on the verge of rendering religious and belief systems less and less effective and even obsolete? Is a global bottom-up revolution dismantling existing top-down structures of governance?

These questions do not fall just in the realm of academic debate and discussion. It should be obvious that the outcomes of these processes will affect every man, woman, and child on the planet. Therefore, a study of these is important to put in proper perspective the role of human agency amidst a complex interactive system and therefore render more realistic and feasible the faith in human agency to manage these processes successfully.

6. Economics and finance

These two subject areas are in need of perhaps the most significant revisions to realign with current realities. Major questions now loom on the horizon. Are the traditional contents of economics and finance relevant in today's globalized economy? What is the true cost of a gallon of gasoline—or, for that matter, what are the true labor and material costs of inputs in businesses? Are gross domestic product and per capita income valid measurements to indicate the economic health of individuals and a national economy? For example, should the economic value of the criminal justice system and the medical industry or the costs for environmental remediation or the storage of nuclear waste be added to or subtracted from the GDP? Do markets and the stock exchanges correctly reflect the value and use of current and future use of natural resources of the planet? Is human capital existing in a business properly represented on its balance sheets? Are adverse downstream consequences caused by an upstream business properly measured and charged to the business? Are taxes levied and paid commensurate with the function and maintenance of the commons for current and future use? How are the diminishing futures of generations to come considered in current economic models? These are the questions that now loom on the horizon.

The idea of human capacity for rational individual decision-making, resulting in optimal outcomes for the collective at all levels, has been at the heart of economic and financial theories and decision-making since the time of Adam Smith. While it can be argued that this has created the great wealth of nations, it can also be conclusively shown that this approach is what has resulted in the great tragedies of the commons that we witness today. The enormous future cost of rectifying many of these tragedies, allowing for the fact that they even can be rectified, is not accounted for in the wealth of nations and certainly not shown in any profit and loss statement or balance sheets of businesses or the budgets of nations. This willful negligence can be traced to another belief: that human ingenuity and science and technology will always come forth with solutions. Whether this is justifiable or not, what is apparent is that there needs to be a serious rethink about concepts of economics, finance, and profit and loss, at all levels of human activity. Minor tinkering within these disciplines to make incremental changes will only postpone the inevitable. At a minimum, students of management need to be made aware that important concepts and understandings are missing in their academic pursuits—if nothing else, to create awareness and perhaps the incentives to cause them to think outside the mainstream and build on ideas that are currently being generated by thinkers outside the mainstream of academia.

7. The question of human identity

Through millennia human identity has evolved, or has it? As a species, we started out as members of nomadic tribes and today we find ourselves as members of nation states but retaining at the same time all our prior identities, moving back and forth between them as required. It appears that we function within these identities, starting with the tribal and expanding it as needed to the larger ones. Racism or warfare or economic sanctions or holocausts or religious intolerance all manifest regressions to identities that reinforce separateness of one's group and, more important, demonization of the "other." This would not be an issue if functioning within compartments at the smallest group level were the dominant condition, as it used to be, because wars and other interactions had only localized consequences. This is no longer the case. Multiple interactions within the group and simultaneous complex interactions at multiple vertical and horizontal levels are now the norm and not the exception as they used to be. It has been shown that any human on the planet has only six degrees of separation from any other human, and we know now that a volcano erupting in Iceland has consequences for billions of people on the planet! We now approach a condition that precludes going forward with business as usual, especially as it pertains to our identity. Every major issue that we face has now surpassed the capacity of nation-states to address and solve.

And yet, operating from our national identities, we extend out toward supra-national structures, organizations, and agencies on an "as needed" basis, in fits and starts, with little or nothing accomplished. National identities seek to subdue the issues to soluble elements within the scope of the state, again with the primary motivation being optimization of outcomes for one's own state. The only alternative toward a hopeful and potentially successful resolution of the issues is, as a mandatory starting point, to recognize the need for an "identity" for ourselves that goes beyond the nation-state, an identity that causes us to think in planetary terms as citizens of the Earth. Anything else would be insufficient, inadequate, and incomplete. There is no more important question to ask, study, and find answers to than the question of "Who am I?" This question must be asked in education from the earliest age all the way to the highest levels in academia. The poet John Donne had it right a long time ago:

> No Man is an island unto himself. Every man is a piece of the continent, a part of the main. If a clod were to be washed away, Europe is the less, or if a promontory were, or if a manor of thy friends were, or a manor of thine own. Every man's death diminishes me because I am part of mankind. Therefore, do not send to know for whom the bell tolls, it tolls for thee.

Conclusion

An attempt has been made in this paper to show that curricula in management studies need to be structured around a core of knowledge that will facilitate a correct locating by students of themselves *vis-à-vis* all that is external to them and a better understanding of the world around them as to what is happening, how it is happening, and why it is happening. This is an urgent need that must be addressed because our survival as a species and the safeguarding of the planet, our only home, depends on the stewardship of enlightened managers.

Reprinted with permission from the Journal of Futures Studies.

Journal of Futures Studies, September 2010, 15(1): 91 – 100

References

Ayres, E. (1999). *God's last offer: Negotiating for a sustainable future*. Four Walls Eight Windows.

Brand, S. (1999). *The clock of the long now: Time and responsibility*. Basic.

Diamond, J. (2005). *Collapse: How societies choose to fail or succeed*. Viking.

Elgin, D. (2010). *Voluntary simplicity: Toward a way of life that is outwardly simple,*

inwardly rich (2nd Revised Edition). Harper.

Gladwell, M. (2000). *Tipping points: How little things can make a big difference*. Little, Brown and Company.

Gleick, J. (1987). *Chaos: Making a new science*. Penguin.

Hardin, G. (1968). The tragedy of the commons. *Science*, 162, 1243-1248. https://www.jstor.org/stable/1724745

Hawken, P., Amory L., & Hunter L. (1999). *Natural capitalism: Creating the*

Hawken, P. (2007). *Blessed unrest: How the largest movement in the world came into*

being and why no one saw it coming. Penguin.

next industrial revolution. Little, Brown and Company.

Inayatullah, S. (2004). *The causal layered analysis reader: Theory and case studies of*

an integrative and transformative methodology. Tamkang University Press.

Lovelock, J. (2006). *The revenge of Gaia: Earth's climate crisis and the fate of humanity*. Basic.

Shamos, M. H. (1995). *The myth of scientific literacy*. Rutgers University Press.

Smil, V. (2008). *Global catastrophes and trends: The next fifty years*. The MIT Press.

Taleb, N.N. (2007). *The black swan: The impact of the highly improbable*. Random House.

Ward, P. (2010). *The flooded earth: Our future in a world without ice caps*. Basic.

Wells, S. (2010). *Pandora's seed: The unforeseen cost of civilization*. Random House.

Wilson, E. O. (1998). *Consilience: The unity of knowledge*. Alfred A.

Knopf.

Wright, R. (2000). *Non-zero: The logic of human destiny*. Vintage.

Ethics in Business:
A 21ˢᵗ Century Perspective

Introduction

To begin with, the word "ethics"—itself being one of those words that everyone has an idea as to the meaning but would be hard pressed to define—brings to mind a case before the supreme Court of the United States, dealing with pornography, which is also another word that defies definition or description. As a result of its consternation over the word, the court decided that "pornography" is indeed one of those words that cannot be defined, but anyone will know it when they see it. It seems that the same would be true of the word "ethics".

In order to clarify what the word means, let us begin by asking ourselves a set of questions. At the most basic level, none of the questions have anything to do with ethics in business: we will get to the subject of ethics in business shortly. The idea behind these questions, however, is to establish an understanding of what "ethics" refers to at the most fundamental levels of our day-to-day activities.

How many of us have driven the wrong way on a two-way street because a legal U-turn to go the right way is too far away? How many of us use the horn in our cars to get someone's attention in a neighborhood at 3 in the morning? How many of us have bribed a policeman to get out of a traffic violation or bribed an official in a bureaucracy to get something done? How many of us have failed to buy a platform ticket at a railway station? How many of us have thrown out garbage or a cigarette butt out of our car windows onto the street? How many of us have gone in the wrong way into a parking lot to get to an empty spot before someone else did? How many of us have jumped a queue?

And now a few questions at a slightly higher level: How many of us leave a light switch on when we are not in the room? How many of us shave with the water running in the faucet? How many of us indulge in the modern fashion of buying and using water in plastic bottles? How many of us use a car or a two-wheeler even when the distance is short enough to walk? How many of us clear all the trees from our building sites to optimize the built-up area and/or a view?

One could go on and on with questions like these for the rest of the day. The point being made is that at the level of the individual, all of them have to do with behavior and actions that have a consequence to others and the commons, and eventually to oneself, indirectly in the short, medium or the long term. All of them have to do with right and wrong and good and bad behavior and encompass the range of behaviors that are uncivil, immoral and in a legal sense, ambiguous or outright illegal. If it is not already obvious, it should be that if our answers to any or some or all of the questions is in the affirmative; simply put, we have been unethical.

Definitions of Ethics

Let us also now get the definition of ethics in general and ethics in business in particular out of the way: A simple search on Google will show that there are literally thousands of entries on the subject. A couple of definitions that make the most sense are as follows:

In the most generic sense, a study of the subject of ethics has to do with "the art and science of good and bad, right and wrong moral behavior that has consequences to whom we know and those we don't know." (Miller, 2016). Attached to this definition would be the notion of ethical behavior defined as "enlightened self-interest" where enlightened has thus far implied the utilitarian notion of the greatest good of the greatest number of HUMANS only!

Specific to a definition of ethics in business, Anil Chopra, a consultant on corporate ethics and an ex-Tata employee, states that "best practices in corporate governance can only emerge when informed by an established set of business principles and a defined approach towards organizational behavior." And further: "that the sooner companies begin discussing and enacting business processes for managing integrity standards within their organizations the better" …. Who can argue with this?

And further, another elaboration about ethics in business by the same consultant is that "every functional area of business must have a set of these principles that guide and dictate ethical behavior". For example, as it relates to accounting, prohibiting misrepresentation of revenues, or prohibiting capitalization of things that should really be expenses or getting vendors and suppliers and to collude in the avoidance, or, as it relates to employment practices, avoiding use of child labor or forced labor or production in sweat shops or violation of rights of workers or ignoring health and safety and environmental standards. Behavior of employees that is clearly dishonest, disrespectful, irresponsible, unfair or uncompassionate. It should be noted that the above definition strictly pertains to the notion of ethics as it applies to the internal functioning of a business and in a minimal sense to certain aspects what might be described as "inter-business" and in the larger social context as well.

Given the above definitions it would be inarguable that if this was all there is to it, we would have had ethical systems long ago. What we instead have in the most general sense is everybody's favorite oxymoron, not only at the level of the individual but certainly in business viz; business and ethics as a perfect example of a contradiction in terms.

At every level of activity, as individuals in intra-business, in inter-business and for that matter at a local, regional, national, global level and in the political, cultural, religious, economic domains, unethical behavior is the rule rather than the exception. Why this is the case is what we need to explore and understand. That is what will be attempted at this point with a view to reframing the context in which the idea of ethics must be incorporated from the outside in and from the top down.

The first thing to comprehend is that there is no such thing as ethics in business. Peter Drucker has pointed out that ethics in business has to start with the understanding that there is only ethics.

The Existing Context and Framework
for Ethics

An important aspect is the existing framework or the context in which humans have placed themselves at the apex of creation and subordinated and subjugated all the other important interacting spheres on the planet.

Enlightened self-interest thus far has been construed to mean self-interest contained within the utilitarian notion of "the greatest good of the greatest number", the greatest good of the greatest number being understood to mean "humans", but we are now beginning to understand that the greatest good of the greatest number needs to be revised to mean the greatest good of the planetary system. More about this later.

Given the existing context and framework, the question of ethics can be examined at three different levels. The planetary level, at the level of the nation state and finally at the level of the business. What will be apparent is that our current understanding and pursuit of ethics has serious shortcomings. And the single most important cause for these shortcomings has been the use of GDP as the metric for measuring human progress.

It is inarguable that progress as measure by GDP internationally and nationally has been the driving force for economies, and businesses in turn, have perfectly legally used profit and enhancing share-holder values as the overarching goal and sole reason for existing. Norms for ethical behavior have been defined and used in subservience to this overarching goal. GDP, it should be pointed out, is the sum total of all transactions that involve a monetary exchange.

What is only beginning to be understood is that this paradigm has caused and is causing multiple tragedies for the commons that can be best described as patently unethical.

Multiple Tragedies of the Commons

Ethics and the planet: The following are some examples at the level of human civilization and the planet:

- According to statistics produced by the UN, human populations are expected to rise to between 9 and 12 billion in the next thirty years. Our models of economic growth have been built in the expectation that humans can have per capita consumption at the level of the American of today. What is not understood is that this simply cannot happen. Stated another way, it has been determined that human populations have already exceeded the carrying capacity of the planet by a multiple of 3.

- According to Professor Ed Wilson of Harvard, world renowned socio-biologist,

25,000 species are going extinct every year and we do not know as to when the next extinction will cause the entire complex interlinked system of life on the planet to collapse.

- Study after study of CO_2 levels in the atmosphere (too numerous to cite) show that the levels of CO_2 have gone up from 290 parts per million to nearly 400 in the last several decades, heading to 500 parts per million shortly, leading to climate change that some scientists now say is irreversible and that it will cause or has already started causing devastation for hundreds of millions of humans.

- That we will be at the end of the fossil fuel era in about 30 years. (Roberts, 1994)

- That time frames by which planetary processes work is not a quarter as in business or a 4- or 5-year election cycle or even a human generation that is of 25 years, rather it is in terms of multiple generations or centuries and even millennia.

Ethics and the Nation State

Following are a few further illustrations that should suffice to prove the point of how incomplete, inadequate and misguided our ethical norms have been at every level of national economic and business activity based on GDP, profit and shareholder value as indicators of progress.

Consider the fact that any major city in India employs policemen, courts, prisons and security systems to combat crime of all varieties. An important question that needs to be asked is: is this investment a social positive or negative? Any child will say that it is a reaction and that it is a negative one, because it does not at all do anything about the causes and is nothing more than an attack on the symptoms. Yet the monetary value of all the transactions involved in crime prevention are added to the GDP.

Similarly, specific to India, all monetary transactions involved in addressing diseases directly assignable to "progress" such as the rising epidemic of heart disease, pulmonary diseases, cancers, obesity, diabetes and the associated investments in hospitals, doctors and clinics, are all added to GDP.

The question to ask is: Should not the value of all these transactions be actually subtracted from the GDP?

Ethics and Business

Let us now consider the subject of ethics in business from a different perspective. Here are examples of perfect oxymorons in terms of businesses that may be completely ethical internally, but with respect to the common good, looking from the outside in, would be considered overwhelmingly unethical.

- Coal-fired power plants (the main source of power in India and China) that spew CO^2 into the atmosphere by the hundreds of millions of tons every day exacerbating the problem of global climate change.

- Automobile factories exhorting us to buy cars that are being put on the road in the cities of India at the rate of tens of thousands every month, worsening the situation of pollution and accelerating the exhaustion of fossil fuels.

- Extraordinary compliance with ethical practices inside cigarette manufacturing companies even as they are causing pulmonary diseases and multiple tragedies for the commons, not to mention skyrocketing costs down the road for cures and medical support systems.

And finally, it has to be recognized that all of our concerns about ethics have been with this generation of humans and at the most the next. What is completely absent from out discourse is the "ethics" or rather the absence of it with respect to what we are bequeathing to future generations. An inheritance that is best described as a horribly disfigured and denuded planet.

A New Context and Framework for Ethics

Unless we define and institute a new paradigm to mean survival and prosperity of the planetary system of which we are an integral part, including rights of future generations as the first and foremost priority, all bets are off and best estimates indicate that we have about a thirty-year time frame to make course corrections or we humans as a species are at serious risk of extinction. It should be pointed out that 99.9 percent of all that ever lived is extinct and we should take heed of the fact that we are not exempt from such a possibility.

Simply put, the paradigm, the context, the framework, the context within which we must make sense of ethics has to radically change. Given this, what is an individual to do? What does enlightened self-interest in this new, emerging context mean?

Even as it seems reasonable to assume that we as humans are not capable of preemption and that a collapse at the civilizational level is clearly possible, because of too many vested interests that have much to lose by changing, one needs to retain the hope that there is still time and that something can be done to delay the inevitable, if not avoid it.

It is this writer's view that the survival and well-being of our planetary system, with humans as an integral part, must be the driving ethic in a top-down, outside-in the fashion. Nothing else will do. It is within this context that humans must practice the art and science of enlightened self-interest. Again, to emphasize, enlightened here means the greatest good of the planetary system with us as the dominant force but inclusive of the biosphere, the geosphere, the zoosphere and the atmosphere not only for ourselves in the present but for future generations. The planetary system is best explained by the concept of "Gaia" referring to the fact that the planet with its contents is a finely tuned self-regulating organism inclusive of humans interacting with the biosphere, the zoosphere, the geosphere and the atmosphere.

To this end, as individuals in our multiple parallel roles including as employees, we must take a stand and refuse to compromise, even if it means making other choices like opting out or being a whistleblower or an activist demanding change or an entrepreneur in relation to these new opportunities, and at a simpler level, change oneself and seek to change another person. As Gandhiji put it, you become the change you wish to see and secondly, sustainability here is defined as meeting our needs in the present but keeping in mind the needs of future generations.

Sustainability as it relates to strategies for radical improvement in resource efficiencies, providing service as opposed to products, investing in regeneration of natural systems and emulation naturally occurring bio systems and processes, such as biomimicry (Benyus, 2009) to create new industrial processes. Much work has been and is being done in these areas to create new businesses.

Businesses and their employees must at the highest strategic levels realign their mission to visualize and incorporate an ethic that mirrors the survival and well-being of the planetary system and every thought word and deed must reflect a commitment to the same. Nothing less will do.

It should be pointed out that businesses need to reinvent themselves, even if it means creative destruction. They will need to align their missions, strategies, goals and objectives to be truly ethical. It is entirely likely that by doing so, they will gain huge competitive advantages. Profitability, enhanced shareholder value and acclaimed social standing are sure to follow.

Reprinted with permission from the Journal of Management and Entrepreneurship

Journal of Management and Entrepreneurship, March 2012, 18-26.

References

Benyus, J, (2009, August). *Biomimicry in Action*. [Video]. TED Conferences. https://www.youtube.com/watch?v=k_GFq12w5WU&ab_channel=TED

Miller, J. R. [J. R. M. (2016, September 20). *What is ethics?* [Video]. Youtube. https://www.youtube.com/watch?v=8XFZdU9JZBU&ab_channel=J.R.Millerhttps://www.youtube.com/watch?v=8XFZdU9JZBU&ab_channel=J.R.Miller

Roberts, P. (1994). *The End of Oil: On the Edge of a Perilous New World*. Houghton Mifflin.

11
CHAPTER

The following are transcripts of interviews of world renowned scholars conducted by the author on a range of subjects specific to the Future: Evolution, Science, Education, Human Genome, Medicine, Culture and Society.

An Interview with Michio Kaku and Ervin László (2000)

Michio Kaku

Dr. Michio Kaku is one of the world's most widely recognized figures in science today. He is a professor of theoretical physics, NY Times best-selling author, TV and radio personality. As co-founder of String Field Theory, Dr. Kaku carries on Einstein's quest to unite the four fundamental forces of nature into a single grand unified theory of everything.

Ervin László

Dr. László is a Hungarian philosopher of science, systems, as well as a proponent of the theory of quantum consciousness articulated in his book, *The Akashic Principle*. He is also the founder and president of the "Club of Budapest" which sees itself as a space for addressing current and future issues that affect humanity as a whole. It aims to raise awareness of global responsibility and build bridges between cultures and generations. His work related to mind and consciousness and morphogenetics also addresses the idea of a "grand unified theory."

An Interview with
Michio Kaku and Ervin László

(2000)

Dr. László and Dr. Kaku were interviewed together in 2000.
The transcript of this conversation can be found on the following pages.

Seshadri Velamoor: Good evening Dr. Kaku, good evening, Professor László, thank you very much for agreeing to join me in this conversation. I'd like to start as I normally do these conversations, since we've been doing them for some time, if you had to choose one person that you could conjure up from History and have a conversation with, who would it be and what would it be about?

Dr. Michio Kaku: I would probably choose Sir Isaac Newton to have a conversation with because if you look at the world before Newton, it was the world of Magic, a world of superstition, a world where spirits and ghosts rule the solar system, where there were no rules, there was no Mathematics for the cosmos. After Isaac Newton, suddenly, we had Mathematics, we had the Calculus, we had the Laws of Motion, and we had a framework of Space and Time and the universal law of Gravitation. So, from darkness we went to light and enlightenment. His rules of course, lasted 300 years. Even Einstein, when he made his tremendous contributions, did not create a new Mathematics. He borrowed the old Mathematics of advanced Calculus. He did not invent new the scientific marvel of Space and Time, he simply bent the Space and Time of Isaac Newton. So, I think a mind like that would be fascinating to interact with.

Velamoor: What would you be interacting about if you had the opportunity? What might you ask or talk about?

Dr. Kaku: In hindsight, Isaac Newton gave us a paradigm for unification. Heavenly physics and Earth-like physics were supposed to be totally different. On Earth, there were supposed to be sin. Evil, sin and different kinds of sin, like mortal sin. The Heavens were supposed to be perfect. He unified the earth-like physics and heavenly physics to give us unified physics of the cosmos. Today, we physicists are trying to unite Curved Newtonian physics and the Quantum Theory, the Theory of the Atom. To unify them in a Cosmic theory, that will give us a theory of everything.

Velamoor: Within the new context, do you suppose Isaac Newton would have come up with just as brilliant ideas as he did for the time?

Dr. Kaku: It's hard to say. I think Newton in the later years of his life, began to dabble in Alchemy and stuff. But then again, Alchemy was the science in the 16th century. If you were a Chemist in the 1600s, you would dabble in Alchemy because that's all there was in terms of the laws of science. I think today if he were alive, he would be fascinated by the greatest unification of all. The unification of atomic physics, the quantum theory with the Big Bang and the universe. That is the theory of everything.

Velamoor: And Professor László: yourself?

Dr. Ervin László: I wouldn't mind having conversations with Sir Isaac either, but I think my choice would be Albert Einstein the philosopher and perhaps even more specifically, Alfred North Whitehead. Whitehead took his cue from Einstein. He undertook a project which needs to be done today because it needs to be done over and over again. And that is to take the latest theories of the sciences and build a conceptual framework that will unite them, so that we can have not only a physics of everything, but a metaphysics. A metaphysics includes the physical universe, which includes the living world, and it includes the human being. I think that's a project that needs to be done at all times because if you have truly a theory of everything it has to be a theory of human consciousness as well as of biological organism as well as of the quantum as well as of the cosmos.

Velamoor: And how would the physicist react to that?

Dr. Kaku: I think it's very difficult. Someone once asked Einstein about taxes, and he said that it was much too hard. It would take a philosopher to understand taxes. So, Einstein realized that in some sense, the fundamental laws of the universe are fundamental. They are simple, elegant, and pure. The laws of humans are messy. We're talking about passions that are irrational, but this doesn't mean that we can eventually have a tapestry by which we can see unifying themes within human behavior. It just means it's very hard.

Velamoor: Do you foresee a science of humans that would be as precise as the physics of particles eventually?

Dr. Kaku: Maybe, maybe not. Isaac Asimov in his Foundation Series books (1991), wrote about a secret second foundation. Maybe a foundation similar to the Foundation for the Future. But a second foundation that wrote the laws of meta history, so that you could predict the history of a Galactic Empire. Now, when we physicists today look at Asimov's theory of a second foundation, we try to be much more modest, and we try to say that the best we could do is look at civilizations on the basis of energy consumption. That's very easy to measure. We have three types of energy sources in the universe. We have planetary energy, stellar energy, and galactic energy like in the second foundation. Therefore, in civilizations far beyond ours, we expect to have different types of civilizations: type 1, type 2, and type 3.

We are type 0. We are a civilization run by nations and wars and fundamentalist passions, however, in the next hundred years or so, we expect to see the birth of a type 1 civilization. A truly planetary civilization that harnesses planetary energies, that can control the weather for example, and I'm proud to be alive in an era where you can see the birth of this type 1 civilization. A type 1 telephone system. The European Union is the beginning of a type 1 economy. English is going to be the type 1 language of the future. Nation states are withering away giving birth to perhaps a type 1 planetary political system and we're beginning to see the birth of a type 1 culture. Blue jeans, rock and roll and rap music… my god! Who would have predicted that would be the culture of a type 1 civilization?

Velamoor: Professor László, how would you fit conception of the future over 100-year time frame as an expert, as a theorist, as somebody who knows evolution inside and out?

Dr. László: I agree that we can have a highly encompassing kind of idea of all things that go on because the key there is development, or as I prefer to call it, evolution. That is progressive, irreversible change. Not indeterminate as to everything that is happening but on the whole, irreversible and moving in some different directions. As we look at the cosmos, as we look at life on Earth, as we look at civilization, it's moving in some determinable direction and these are then general laws of evolution which are statistical laws, and they give us a handle for understanding how the human arose out of the non-human biological matrix. How the biological matrix arose out of a physical matrix, how all of these arose out of the Big Bang and how possibly the Big Bang arose out of a metaverse, which could have been a multi cyclic universe as well.

I believe that the evolution in a systemic and holistic but rigorous perspective, gives us a handle not for telling everything, not for foretelling or predicting, but for understanding the general thrust of where things are going. Now, I find this idea of the type 1 type 2 type 3 civilization based on energy fascinating but I'm not using it as the basic concept because it uses one parameter (energy parameter) as the key concept and I think when you deal with this life and these humans, a number of complex parameters are coming into play as well. When I think of civilization, I think of many things that are there in addition to the consumption of energy

Velamoor: And what would your perspective on evolution be, as a physicist and in the context just described, Dr. Kaku?

Dr. Kaku: I think evolution must have a driving force, an engine, behind it. In Darwinian evolution the driving force there is simply survival, and species mutate in response to changes. Here on the planet earth, we have the fact that the gross national product of nations grows at about three percent per year on average and that's because people want a better life. They want a better distribution of wealth, and they want middle-class comforts. So, given the fact that we have an engine driving the economy at roughly three percent a year, if you would extend that therefore to hundreds or thousands of years into the future, you begin to realize that within a hundred years, you would then attain planetary energies. Within a few thousand years, you would begin to attain stellar energies capable of manipulating stars. Then on a scale of hundreds of thousands or even millions of years, growing at three percent a year, you would begin to have galactic energy similar to the second foundation and Isaac Asimov series.

I think that this evolution is not inevitable because I think the most dangerous transition is between type 0 to type 1. By the time you have a type 1 status, you have a planetary culture, a planetary ethic, a planetary spirit, a planetary way of looking at crises around the earth like global warming. In type 0, you're talking about a fragmented civilization based on nation states, based on greed, plunder, the strong make the rules. So, the transition between type 0 to type 1 is the most stupendous and we're seeing it all around us. Every day when I open the newspaper I say, "Ah, the foundation for a type 1 civilization is being laid". But it's also the most dangerous. Global warming - we have no planetary government that is capable of dealing with global warming for example, or even pollution or nuclear proliferation. The United Nations is simply not powerful enough to stop India and Pakistan from going at it with nuclear weapons and so I think that this is very dangerous, and I think we're seeing this happen. Not only do we see the Internet forging a planetary culture of our language and a planetary economy, but we also see fragmentation in the world. Which trend will win? I don't know.

Velamoor: I see a similarity in terms of that line between zero and one that Dr. Kaku draws with the concept that you articulate, Dr. László, as it relates to the three C's that need to transition to a new set of three C's. You describe the current situation or the immediate past as the three C's—conquest, colonization and consumption—having to be transitioned into the three C's of connection, communication and comprehension, which seems to me to have a very close parallel to the notion of a movement from a type 0 to a type 1. Could you make a comment on that?

Dr. László: I see a lot of similarities. I think, how we package this, how we prove what kind of framework we put on it, can differ. I think the outcome of the analysis is similar. I see a human civilization as unfolding directed by certain myth. It's ideas that people have. The biological evolution is directed by inborn genetic determined behavioral patterns and relations to the environment. As soon as you reach the level of the human, another kind of coding takes over, called cultural coding, other than just genetic coding. That means ideas now no longer have the separation between genome and phenome. Now, you have a total system that creates innovations and changes itself constantly by its innovations.

The driving forces is what you can call technology - but technology in a very broad sense. For example, we speak about fire as technology, the invention of the wheel, as well as the invention of writing which was a major technological breakthrough. And since then, we are having a series of technological innovations that constantly rock and transform society. The kind of technologies that we will be using in the Western world starting at the Levant for the past 10,000 years had a particular thrust. Elsewhere in civilizations, like in India or in the East or in the southern hemisphere, this was not the case. But starting in the Neolithic communities in the Levant and then into Europe and some parts of Asia, there has been a particular thrust. This thrust was to transform nature to serve human needs and human ends. That enabled tribes to settle, to create settled communities, enabled always an ever-larger use of energy and ever more food production, enabled population to grow, and society had to complexify. Therefore, it also changed culture as a general category, the ideas that people had, the myth that had to change.

To summarize this point, ever since this process of colonizing nature and conquering nature started it has been extended to other peoples. The aim has been to subjugate, and this has resulted in a tremendous linear development. We share not a lot of nonlinearities, but an upward development - more and more complex societies, more and more complex technologies, powerful technologies, larger and larger population size. And this has now spread over the planet. So, we have basically Western civilization with its extensive kind of evolution aimed at conquest, colonization, and the last 200 years increasingly at increasing consumption. This is now a worldwide phenomenon, and it has probably reached safe limits, or limits of safety. If we go push it any further without any further thought of the qualification of the way it should go, it could move into very dangerous territories.

Velamoor: There is an interesting proposition that is being floated right now. It goes along the lines of what might be described as memetic evolution paralleling genetic evolution. So, to that extent the notion of purpose, or foresight is absent even in memetic evolution, in the sense that the idea is seeking to perpetuate itself and that we just simply become agents of that perpetuation. Any thoughts on that?

Dr. Kaku: The process of evolution is sometimes said to be a blind Watchmaker, so we're not talking about a designer per-se, we're talking about the fact that it can create higher forms. But we must also look at the engine that drives these things, either in the area of ideas like with memes or in the in creation of species. There must be a driving force pushing it. In biological evolution, it's basically survival of the fittest that is, people must have things to survive. With memes, it's survival of the marketplace of ideas. So, there has to be a driving force.

With society, we look at a type 0 civilization based on nation states. Nation states are very new. There was no Germany in 1870, there was no Italy in 1870. The driving force of nation states was the development of capitalism, because to be a capitalist with large markets, you need to have a common language, common currency, and common borders and this of course is almost by definition the creation of a large nation state. So, the rise of capitalism also gave us the rise of nation states and that was the engine pushing forward the type 0 civilization. Now we're going to be entering type 1 where we have the forces of globalization, where nation states are simply too small as a meme, too small as a concept that motivates Joe Public in the streets. In the future, with the internet we will feel more in common with somebody in Australia and somebody in Borneo than we will with our next-door neighbor and the President of our country. So, in the future, countries will be mainly for fighting skirmishes, with wars that are sequential because big wars can never be fought. It's simply too dangerous to fight. Politicians will then start to wave the flag and start to collect taxes but as far as the public, as far as memes, as far as the idea permeating within the bulk of humanity is concerned, they will see themselves with more affinity with their bridge player in Borneo and their bridge partner in Beijing than with the leader of their country. Nations know this, and politicians know that their power is going to end and they're going to try desperately to hold on to their elite power. That's a law of history: elites will always cling, tooth and nail, to whatever power they have. But the forces of history will sweep them over.

Kings and queens tried to hold on to their power too, and yet revolutions, wars and so on swept over kings and queens. National capitalists will try to cling to the national boundaries of their culture, but now we have Germany and France burying the hatchet saying, hey we have to compete against Americans. Forget competing against the French and the Germans now. So, I think what's happening is, the forces of globalization are blind—there's no guiding force behind them—but it is an engine. It is an engine creating a type 1 economy. This of course, could create excesses, it could create maldistribution of wealth and that's why I think that this transition must be guided. We must be conscious of the fact that this transition is taking place right before our eyes. One of the greatest transitions in the history of humanity - from fragmentation and sectarianism, fundamentalism driven by the dominant members of society, to a situation where people feel more affinity being earthlings and being more affiliated with people because of hobbies and because of interests rather than because President so-and-so happens to be the governor of whatever. So, we're talking more about ideas that cut across national boundaries, which requires a global ethic to guide the transition so that we don't have a maldistribution of wealth.

Velamoor: Even though you might concede that it is really a competition between memes, you are asking for, allowing for, the requirement of human agency in terms of the transition that needs to be managed.

Dr. László: Driving forces, I think, we have to include as a moving force of ideas, what I call the "myth". They need not always be very specific and very conscious of what they're actually doing but people individual and collectively hold a set of ideas. You can call them values, beliefs or you can call them ideologies, but because they do this, they behave in a certain way. Now, not all society at all times behave the same way.

We have in the modern world, in the Western world, which is now spread worldwide, this kind of civilization and kind of value system, although not entirely everywhere, but it's just penetrating in all parts of the world. It means that this kind of behavior system is reaching a point where it's eating into the Physical, biological and Psychological limits of the earth, so I agree with Professor Kaku that we are in the greatest moment of transition, perhaps in the history of humanity, certainly one of the greatest in the last 10,000 years. A similar great thing occurred from the Paleolithic to the Neolithic. My last book is called Macroshift 2001 – 2010: Creating the Future in the early 21st Century (2000) and is precisely saying that in the next ten years, we must somehow make the beginning of this shift. I am saying that we are shifting from basically a value system that guides evolution along extensive levels of always more quantitatively, always more conquests, always more consumption, toward the kind of evolution that you can characterize as intensive and therefore, which creates more and more connections, creates deeper understanding and also creates structure. This is the kind of thing that occurs in biology all the time.

We have reached the limits of the planet. Unless we colonize other planets, and for the time being we have to make do with earth, we have to move into another kind of evolution, and this evolution has to be, as Professor Kaku also said, guided consciously. And the key factor here is ethics.

Velamoor: In a sense then, we could say that this blind watchmaker, with the capacities we have at our disposal, those eyes need to be open.

Dr. Kaku: In some sense because we've come of age. The Foundation for the Future for example, often asked the question "What's going to happen in a thousand years?" and of course then, wild speculation starts to jump out. But if you have a methodology, a framework by which to view the next thousand years, then it's not so strange to begin to talk about the year 3000 in terms of this framework that we're talking about.

In the year 3000, we'll be laying the groundwork for a type 2 civilization. Now, between type 1 to type 2 is a factor of 10 billion. That's the difference between a planet and a star—a factor of 10 billion. Which means that for the next thousand years we're going to be stuck on the planet earth. We're not going to be building starships to go to colonize Alpha Centauri and the nearby stars. We're not going to be able to terraform Mars instantly and have gigantic civilizations grow on other planets. We will have small outposts. It's not like Columbus where with a little energy expenditure you can take a sailboat and basically can go across the Atlantic Ocean. Starships are a whole other matter. Consequently, we'll have a thousand years to build this intensive infrastructure that we're talking about. We're not going to be going to the planets, to the stars, but we're going to be here on planet Earth working out planetary problems and working out a planetary system of equitable distribution of wealth, working at a planetary discussion of the economic and the politics of power, so that everyone has a fair shake when we lay the foundations for type 2. Not only this of course, but technology at that point will give us the ability to even change the human form. Evolution has more or less stopped in terms of the physical evolution of humans; there's no more bottlenecks like Australia. Anyone can have children, so the physical evolution of our form has more or less stopped. In a thousand years that could change again. We could have guided evolution. Hopefully it'll be by consensus, hopefully we will not have dictators decide to create super warriors to subjugate other humans, hopefully it'll be done by consensus, and everyone will have a wall screen to talk to the Internet and we collectively decide whether or not we should begin to alter the nature of the human being to give us a form of perhaps even immortality. A merger of carbon and silicon, so that we replace human organs with silicon—with genetically grown organs—extend the human lifespan, so that by the year 3000 will be the laying the groundwork for going into the stars.

Velamoor: Now to bring it a little closer to today. One of the things that seems to kind of standout is that the speed at which science and technology is moving out relative to essentially our human incapacity to absorb, and the institutions that we now have, and their incapacity, in that sense, to manage the pace at which science and technology is moving out. That seems to have created a lot of discontinuities or disjoints and we see ungovernability emerging already in so many of these countries where expectations of population as well as the speed at which science and technologies are moving out is a big gap. Would you care to comment on that?

Dr. László: It's a case of the Sorcerer's Apprentice. We are creating all kinds of processes that become runaway processes. We can't control them anymore. We don't think about all the fallouts basically. Technology assessment is a relatively recent phenomenon. For example, after World War Two we have created de-colonization. What it has done is, it brought almost 190 nation-states into the world with the idea of the nation state as a sovereign autonomous entity - total fiction. So, we created a fictional entity, we let them on their own, they can't cope economically, and they can't adapt their cultural patterns to the market system and to the globalized system, but suddenly, we said, you are just one of us. One United States, one Malaysia, one Madagascar etc.

Velamoor: And worse yet, in those populations creating expectations that completely throw apart whatever structures that existed in some degree of coherence and cohesion.

Dr. László: So, all of this means that we are at a point where the total human world, the organization of the human world, is in question and must be reoriented in some way. Never before did we have that need for consciously guiding this evolutionary process. Up till now, we went with the idea of the more the better. The more is better for a small minority. Today 20 percent of the world's population has 1.1 percent of the global wealth, the next 20 percent has 1.9 percent, and 550 billionaires, according to the Fortune 500 listings, are having as much income as about three billion people. I mean you can't govern a world such as this.

We must move into a new phase of evolution and here I just like to bring up one word, or one concept that we so far have not touched on. That is the word consciousness. We are a species that is conscious of itself - that looks around and that can look back and also ahead of it. We have heard not long ago, a nice saying by Winston Churchill who said something along the lines of "The farther back you can look, the farther forward you are likely to see."

We are not looking into the past. We tend to forget the past. We think the future will just make itself, but I think we have got to look at ourselves as being on a trajectory from the past into the future and this trajectory now is inflected. It cannot go on as before because if he goes on as before, we risk very serious breakdowns. Whether it's on the level of population, whether it's a level of fresh water, whether it's a level of soil fertility or a level of air pollution. We have possibilities of managing these things technologically, but we are not using the possibilities and if you just continue doing what we do, we are going to have enormous breakdowns affecting most of the human population.

Dr. Kaku: Elaborating the disparity mentioned between science and the level of society, it goes deeper than that in the sense that science is not beginning to change the nature of capitalism itself. When Adam Smith conceived of capitalism he was talking about commodities; the exchange of commodities being the source of wealth with labor added in. And then comes Henry Ford who adds the concept reduction of these commodities. Now, we're witnessing a historic shift away from "commodity capitalism" to "intellectual capitalism". Commodity prices have been collapsing for the past 70 years. You see that we have fruits and vegetables at our disposal that we eat for breakfast, that a king of England could not have. A king of England would say, this is preposterous that you have foods that are cheap that even peasants can afford a king's banquet. That's because commodity prices have been dropping. Better containerization, mass production, better growing conditions, and competition.

However, intellectual capital cannot be containerized, cannot be mass-produced, you can't simply turn out software programmers. You see that wealth is being distributed in a different way because of the shift away from commodity capital to intellectual capital. You see Singapore, since, from the ashes of World War two, becoming a major powerhouse in Asia. You see China desperately grabbing for the internet when it hates the internet. The Chinese government fears the internet to its core but if you take the internet out of China you are just poor.

Velamoor: Back in India too, the export of software in dollar terms exceeds all other exports put together by quite an order of magnitude.

Dr. Kaku: And Silicon Valley is growing in India. Nations that are very small and very poor—Israel for example—are creating their own Silicon Valley and going to the top tiers of the world economy. Southeast Asia is doing this. Other countries are not. So, we see two tendencies in the world today, one is a tendency toward fragmentation and revenge with the collapse of the Cold War. Nations now see other nations as their mortal enemy because 700 years ago they defeated them at some obscure battle on some obscure hill. That's the story of the Balkans.

Velamoor: Or is it possible that that is because what was artificially held together because of an imposition of a structure of the Soviet bloc, that the removal of it has created a situation where they are regressing to their older separate identities?

[crosstalk]

Dr. Kaku: It's like a pressure cooker. You had all these neo-colonial and colonial tensions left over from World War one and held in check by the Cold War, by the two superpowers, and then it blows up. So, you have two tendencies in the world. One tendency is toward unification like with the European Union. The European Union must compete with NAFTA, and they know this. They don't want to be poor. They're putting away their individual sectarian religious differences to create a society based more and more on intellectual capital. Southeast Asia knows this too but for other areas of the world they don't, and they unfortunately will see most of their economy being reduced to dust.

And that's why we must get the message out. That the future is a freight train, and you must get on this train or else it's going to bypass you and simply move on without you. This freight train is intellectual capitalism. Capitalism itself is making a historic shift away from commodities to intellectual capital.

[crosstalk]

Dr. László: I just like to add a note about freight trains. They used to be, after the Second World War as the railroad theory of development: that everybody goes along the same track and there's the engine that's pulling and you basically have to get on it.

I am worried about the concept that there is a preferred kind of development for all of humanity. I think we're moving into an area where diversity will be essential and there will be more than one way to develop and to grow. And the kind of capitalism whether its intellectual or commodity capitalism, I think will transform. It will work for some and will not work for others, but it need not work for everyone because basically what we have to do is, create the space, the economic, social and cultural space, so that people can choose their own value systems and choose their own ways that they are living. There is a turnaround for example in Eastern Europe. I am quite often in Eastern Europe as a native Hungarian. There was first an absolute process of being enamored of capitalism and they engaged in a kind of "cowboy capitalism", where all is competition and nothing but competition. Now, there is another turnaround. A lot of people are becoming very disenchanted with the whole notion and looking for other values and I see that many parts simply do not want to buy in to the global consumption kind of economy.

At a very basic level, you mentioned the food and marvelous fruit that everybody can have —I wonder how healthy some of that fruit is. It's getting mass-produced while the kind of local produce that was produced in a healthy and organic way for example, is being very largely replaced.

I live in Italy and in Italy, the local peasants are complaining that the produce that they get on the market no longer has the quality that they would grow themselves, but they can't grow it because they are not in the market. The large companies are basically taking over. On all levels I feel that we are in front of a watershed. From the very basic food that you have on your table to the water you are getting, we cannot go on as we were. We must shift in some kind of a direction and it's not just an economic recipe. I believe there is also a cultural recipe, an ethics, and cultural beliefs - a new mythology basically.

Dr. Kaku: I agree that nations have to choose their own way, but I think we also have to realize that if their way is not consistent with the motion of commodities, capital and intellectual capital, nations will be reduced to poverty. Even Hungary is not going to go back to communism. We're talking about variations within a theme that Hungary and the Czech Republic will have their own tune but they're not going to go back to the martial music of communism because there was an un-democratic and a very un-responsive system.

Now, what is going to happen in the future is, we're going to have more democracy. Everyone will have internet connections. The internet will be universal and basically for free as a universal type of telephone system and this means much more democratic input into the way society then produces goods and services, so that Pesticides can gradually be eliminated if people so desire. I think on one hand, we have fragmentation in the Balkans, we have ethnic conflicts in Africa going back to the colonial ages, and we unfortunately will see nations go backwards and have their economies be reduced to dust. Other nations, I think, will flourish in the future.

Velamoor: Ultimately this has to do with future generations. We are dealing with the future and it has to do with people in the future generations. To change tracks just a little bit and we're kind of running out of time. What three things would you transmit to children? As values, as ideas, as convictions.? What three things would you say to the younger generations?

Dr. Kaku: One I think, is a commitment to science. Science means the world as it is, not the world as necessarily we wish it to be. It can be used for the good. Second, is caring for others to make sure that all of us enter a new age and so that there is compassion. And third, I would say democracy. I think the democratic forces of the future are getting greater than they are now - with the internet, with the fact that everyone can set up web pages and distribute all sorts of manifestos on the internet. We can have a marketplace of ideas. So, with the commitment to science, the future, a commitment to compassion to make sure that all of us get on the train, whichever train is going in the direction of the future, and a commitment to democracy, that all of us will have a voice, I think that is laying the groundwork for the future.

Dr. László: I have one major point and then perhaps a minor point. I think we have got to come to the insight that there are many ways to live but we cannot live in a way that doesn't permit other people to live in a way they want to live. In other words, we have to have a kind of a "spaceship of ethics". We have six billion people on this earth, soon eight, nine billion according to the forecast. We must learn to live in ways that are compatible with the freedom, and with the dignity of other people. That means, many other things to go along with it. I mean first of all, examining your beliefs and not simply accepting everything blindly. It means getting information from science, from the world around you using your head, so you decide in a responsible or accountable way the way that you want to live. Not only as a private individual but as a citizen, as a corporate manager or a collaborator and as a scientist. And we have the responsibility to see that our children can choose their own lifestyles and their own beliefs. That means education. Do not educate them into what we have now as ours. Inform them, allow them the freedom to choose. The one thing we all know about the future is, it will not be the past.

Velamoor: Thank you very much. It's been a privilege to talk with two brilliant, fascinating minds.

Interview sourced from the archives of the Foundation For the Future.

References

Asimov, I. (1991). *Foundation*. Bantam.

László, E. (2000). *Macroshift 2001-2010. Creating the future in the early 21st century*. Iuniverse Inc.

Further Readings

Kaku, M. (1994). *Hyperspace: A Scientific Odyssey Through Parallel Universes, Time Warps, and the 10th Dimension*. Oxford University Press.

Kaku, M. (1997). *Visions: How Science Will Revolutionize the 21st Century*. Doubleday.

László, E. (1996) The Systems View of the World: A Holistic Vision for Our Time. Hampton Press.

László, E. (1996) *Evolution: The General Theory*. Hampton Press.

CHAPTER 12

An Interview with Richard Dawkins and Norman Levitt (2001)

Richard Dawkins

Dr. Richard Dawkins is a zoologist, Darwinist, evolutionary biologist and a Fellow of the Royal Society. The work for which Dr. Dawkins was awarded the Kistler Prize in 2001 is the ethology of the gene, work that redirected the focus of the "levels of selection" debate away from the individual animal as the unit of evolution to the genes, and what he has called their extended phenotypes. At the same time, he applied a Darwinian view to culture through the concept of "memes" as replicators of culture. Dr. Dawkins' powerful contribution to a new understanding of the relationship between the human genome and society is that both the gene and the meme are replicators that mutate and compete in parallel and interacting struggles for their own propagation.

Norman Levitt

Dr. Norman Levitt was an American Professor Emeritus of Mathematics at Rutgers University in New Jersey and a fierce critic of pseudoscience. He was best known for his 1994 co-authored book *Higher Superstition*, in which the authors expressed their criticism for the "academic left" and the abuse of science for advancing political goals.

An Interview with
Richard Dawkins and Norman Levitt

(2001)

Dr. Levitt was interviewed together with Richard Dawkins in 2001.
The transcript of this conversation can be found on the following pages.

Seshadri Velamoor: If you had to think about one individual from history that you would have a conversation with, who would that be, why and what would the conversation be about Professor Dawkins? Would you like to go first?

Dr. Richard Dawkins: I'm going to have to be boring and say Charles Darwin. Also-interesting would be Lucy the Australopithecine who lived three million years ago but I'm not sure what I would ask her. Darwin, I would be fascinated to meet. He's the father of my subject and one of the greatest men who ever lived. I would ask him what took you so long? Why did you wait so long before publishing your brilliant theory? What gave you the confidence to feel that somebody wouldn't come in and scoop you? I suppose the conversation might go on to talk about what's happened since his time and a lot has happened since his time? I imagine, since he was an immensely curious man, that he would want to know.

Velamoor: Mr. Levitt?

Dr. Norman Levitt: I think I'd have to go with Einstein, not quite in my field, officially a mathematician rather than a physicist, but the great figures in my field, Archimedes for example, have very little to offer. Newton and Gauss were sort of dry old stick. While one respects them from a distance, Einstein, among figures of that caliber, was sort of unique in his ability to see how his field and his way of thinking about his field somehow tied into the rest of human civilization. Ways that were not addressed by most other physicists or most other scientists and even on top of that, there's a legend that Einstein sort of did his great work by the time he was 35 or so and after that he was bypassed by the developments in quantum theory. The ones achieved by Heisenberg, Bohr and Dirac, but I think that standard history of physics is under revision right now and the insights that Einstein had into the foundations of physics, which were poo-poohed by physicists for about 50 years, are surfacing again. So, I think that Einstein is having his gentle revenge against all the people who dismissed him as sort of a hopeless, old fogey by 1925. I'd really like to get some of his insights of where physics should go in these days of superstring theory and brain theory and so forth.

Velamoor: Would such a conversation and his insights relative to everything that has happened since his time validate his own conclusion that God does not play dice?

Dr. Levitt: With the aid of not terribly well-known physicist named David Bohm, it would at least in part. Einstein was notorious in the physics community for insisting that there were, in fact, causal models of physics even at the micro level which were dismissed by the Copenhagen inventors of quantum mechanics. And Bohm showed about 1950 that, in fact, you could get around the prohibitions that the Heisenberg and Bohr models insisted upon, and make sense of quantum physics in classical terms. That's not the only way of approaching it and it's still very contentious, but at least Einstein's insights are back into the game. The insights that are usually expressed, some with a bit of distortion, with the famous "God does not play dice" line. What Einstein was really getting at was that it should be able to do physics without making probabilistic notions irreducible. That you could get a dynamical notion of physics, even in the quantum sphere which would eliminate the sort of randomness that's associated with most quantum mechanical models. So, Einstein was aware of these developments at the end of his life, but he was doubtful about them for certain reasons. Mostly having to do with the reintroduction of action.

It would be nice to talk to the 25-year-old Einstein again, assuming that he had had a few months to bone up on things for his sense of where and how physics should go and what our picture of the universe should evolve into. It would be nice to have his views to complement those of people like Weinberg and Ed Witten who are comparable thinkers of our day but there was something unique about Einstein's insight of the things

Velamoor: Regarding your book *Higher Superstition* (Levitt & Gross, 1994), it is a departure from mathematics in no uncertain terms. And I now want to come back and want to talk about memes.

I'm sure you would say that there is really no quality that is assignable to memes in terms of functionality or dysfunctionality at the same time. It would seem that, if you were to look at current times, there are quite a few operant memes that one could categorize as dysfunctional. If that's a reasonable question, would you care to address it, Mr. Dawkins?

Dr. Dawkins: I'm not deeply wedded to the idea that memes are a good explanatory model for human culture. For me, they are a way of emphasizing that it isn't only genes that are self-replicating in the Darwinian model. The idea of a meme as opposed to a more purposive view of human culture is that these are replicating entities. They are things which make copies of themselves through the soup of human culture and human brains. You can think of them as having a kind of autonomy in the same sort of way as one thinks of genes. In neither case do they do it with any kind of deliberation.

The question is, is it helpful to explain the way human culture works by saying that certain ideas, certain fashions have a strong intrinsic tendency to copy themselves? Another way to put that is just that they're appealing to human minds - people like them, people enjoy them and that's why they copy them and pass them on. Everybody finds it a helpful way of looking at things. I find it helpful only in certain limited spheres. It's helpful in the case of religion where we have to explain why it is that people in different parts of the world, people of different ethnic backgrounds believe different mutually contradictory things about the cosmos, about life, about what's right and wrong. It does make a lot of sense to say that children especially, tend to do what they're told by their parents or by their elders and probably for good Darwinian reasons - good genetic Darwinian reasons, that it would make sense for the human brain to be pre-programmed and to believe whatever the elders say. After all it's dangerous for a child to go out there and pick up snakes or eat berries or do these things.

In a sense, for the child brain, it is a built-in rule of thumb, believing whatever your elders or parents tell you to believe. Such a rule of thumb is automatically vulnerable. To believe that if you want it to rain, you must sacrifice a goat to the great rain god. Whatever it is that happens to be the belief of the culture, once it starts, it gets passed on to the child, to the grandchild, and the great grandchild and so on. I think, that's a constructive use of meme theory that really does explain why peoples in different parts of the world believe things that have no basis on fact or evidence and are mutually contradictory. But nevertheless, they believe them extremely passionately and strongly.

Velamoor: Absolutely. In *Higher Superstition* (1994), it reflects your concerns about what has captured academia in the US and perhaps in the rest of the world. In describing those things as memes, would you assign a quality or a value to it, saying those are dysfunctional?

Dr. Levitt: I don't want to stick too narrowly to the issues that we addressed in *Higher Superstition* because the book was concerned basically with faddism and snobbery and academic life which is not necessarily the most illuminating subject in the world when you're trying to think about the general tendencies of culture.

But in the past couple of years, I have thought about the general relation of science and scientists to our culture and our society with the work we did on *Higher Superstition* as a starting point and an example. In terms of meme theory, I think it suggests something that is both interesting and very disturbing, namely that some ideas and some chains of thought tend to provoke what one might call an immune reaction. A certain instinctive repulsion or distaste for a way of handling things intellectually.

I think one of the great dangers of our time is that science seems to have this allergenic quality to a lot of people and I've been trying to think about this and to think about why a society that is so dependent on science and on technology, and on some surface level, is so enthralled by science and technology, is at a deeper level so resistant to not only its discoveries but to the way it goes about making discoveries.

Velamoor: Is it possibly because the whole idea of purpose and meaning is something that is constantly subtracted by the efforts of science and the addition of knowledge on an ongoing basis daily?

Dr. Levitt: That, I think, is part of it. The point is that science is a sort of bargain and in some ways it's a very painful bargain, that if one accepts as a mode of intellectualism on the way science generally has at of coming at problems, of all sorts of problems, the kind of categories it uses and the kind of categories that it refuses to countenance, then you can see why people are uneasy with it, aside from particular dangers of technology or particular implications of discovery.

Most people prefer, as Professor Dawkins indicates, to form their ideas and their beliefs and their opinions in ways which run along familiar grooves in all society. When you do science, or we even think about science then you have to be prepared to reject or ignore these ways of doing business and this goes against the grain of people psychologically and the danger of this is self-evident. There are enough recent issues where we can see this flaring up. I won't go into those in detail, but I think this is one of the crucial dangers of modernity, its inability to absorb a way of thinking about things that is the most efficient and accurate that we've yet been able to devise.

Dr. Dawkins: I think that's about half of it and I think that's a very important part of it, but I wonder whether also it's that science is so effective and so good at what it does and that frightens people. It's so good at getting results with great efficiency. Also, those results are often bad results as in H-bombs and germ warfare. So, science is so exceedingly good at what it does, and it can be used for bad things and if you want to do bad things then the most efficient way to do it is to use science and similarly if you want to do good things. I think people are frightened of efficiency, frightened of what works, and also frightened of what they don't understand. I think those things are added to the points that Norman Levitt has just made.

Velamoor: Coming back to evolution. Is the evolution paradigm necessary and sufficient for thinking about the future?

Dr. Dawkins: I don't know about sufficient but it's necessary in the sense that it is the truth about how we got here in the past. It's the truth about why we exist, it's the truth about why we are the way that we are and the way that we are will surely have an enormous influence on our future, so to that extent it's certainly necessary. I don't think it's sufficient. I don't think that human sociology, the study of human society, the study of human history, although it doesn't contradict anything that we know in Darwinian evolution, it's not greatly illuminated by the application of Darwinian ideas. You do have to introduce other ideas to understand human history and the future of human society. So, it's necessary but not sufficient.

Dr. Levitt: There's always the problem of a given subject; someone trying to understand his own situation, or a collective of people trying to understand their own situations, and there are always conceptual and categorical difficulties when somebody tries to do that. Maybe this is just a highfalutin way of saying that it's hard to be objective about yourself. The question of what methodology, what approaches we should use to think about ourselves and to regard our own situation is a difficult one. They're very difficult. I think there have been some noble attempts which have come finally to very little. The various grand schemes in the 19th century for trying to encompass the important aspect of human behavior in Marx's terms and historical terms or in Freud's terms, which seemed for a time to have swept the field, but we found ultimately to have disintegrated basically into a pile of cliches. That experience gives us a warning that this is a very difficult area to try to approach and I think we can only study these examples with a view to finding out why our propensity to do this kind of speculation runs into so much trouble. I think that's a necessary precondition to developing whatever theory it is and that might actually give us some positive guidance for the situation of humankind.

Velamoor: In this context, could you please put in perspective the whole idea that there's a lot of thought being given to human agency, conscious evolution, ethical evolution, all these seemingly contradictory ways of saying that, in some respects, things will evolve but we are in charge and therefore, it requires some responsibility or is that an oxymoron?

Dr. Levitt: One of my favorite daydreams is to imagine some figure from the past or even just some man in the street from the past from Egypt or Rome or medieval Europe or Tang Dynasty China and confront that person with the world we have now. It's a remark I've made to my wife more than once as I drive down past the skyline of New York. We are living in an extraordinarily strange situation for a human being to live in. We are surrounded by an environment which is completely at variance with any of the environmental factors that we had to deal with when we as a species were evolving. So, what in the world can we make of this strangeness? How can we somehow reconcile it? It seems natural to us. Extraordinary singularities in human experience, so how do we reconcile what we can understand of our biological nature which was evolved when people essentially squatted around the fire and did what they could about finding a little meat to go with what they could dig out of the ground? How do we reconcile that with the future of a people that has to live with its origins? If we were a little dumber, we'd probably be in better shape or a little smarter. But we are smart enough to get ourselves into an enormous amount of trouble and probably not quite bright enough to get ourselves out of it, at least not easily?

Velamoor: Professor William Calvin has a nice analogy (2004). He puts it in the context of the headlights of a car, basically saying, can we see past what the headlights cover in so far as what you're able to see in front of you because you're moving so fast that you won't have the opportunity to really analyze the situation in front of you? To react would you care to comment on fire and digging stuff from the ground and maybe humans having left themselves behind their own creations?

Dr. Dawkins: I think considering that we are Stone Age creatures in modern times, we're doing remarkably well. I'm amazed we're not completely driven out of our minds by the environment in which we find ourselves. It says a lot for something that we can cope at all and of course some of us can't and get driven mad by it.

Your original question was about the problem of human agency, and I think that's more of a philosophical problem. But it is true, I suspect in the future it is one we're going to face increasingly because we come historically from a time when we regarded individual humans as responsible agents who were responsible for their actions and could be blamed for things, they could be punished for things that they've done wrong. If you take a materialistic mechanistic scientific view and you say, well I am what I am because of my rules in my brain, because of the genes that made up the embryology of the brain, you could imagine defense lawyers of the future defending the accused on the grounds that they couldn't help themselves, I think it is something we're going to have to face. Are we going to continue to maintain what I think of a kind of fiction of individual human agency and responsibility, or are we going to go over to a wholly mechanistic, materialistic point of view? That's one of the things that in a thousand years' time, if we would if we could come back then, we might be surprised to find that just as if we go back a thousand years, to time of William the Conqueror, you would meet a very different kind of view of the human condition. If we go forward a thousand years, that would be my guess as to one thing that might happen is, that the status of the individual human agent as an explanatory concept might have changed a bit to say the least.

Velamoor: Professor Ed Wilson of Harvard fervently hopes for consilience in terms of multidisciplinary jumping together of disciplines such as biology, psychology, physics et al going forward in trying to really understand (1998). What are the prospects for that?

Dr. Levitt: As a large intellectual project over decades, I think it's a superb idea and one that will be realized perhaps in fits and starts and with more obstacles than we now can imagine but I think that's the way things are going in the large. In the narrow compass of the sociology of the university, of course many people profess to be shocked about Wilson's ideas, to regard them as a kind of intellectual imperialism where the scientists are going to push aside the sociologists and the psychologists and the critics. But I wouldn't worry about that too much. You can't take universities all that seriously.

Velamoor: That would cause some concern if we didn't take them seriously. What's the future of education? Generations to come.

Dr. Dawkins: I agree with what Norm Levitt has just been saying. I think that consilience is fine when the academics concerned are honestly seeking truth. What I fear is that there are some disciplines who are, as a matter of ideology, not sure what they are interested in, but I think that one could imagine consilience between scientists and historians and scholars of literature and anthropologists and psychologists, all of whom have a shared agreement that we want to understand the world in all these different aspects together. But if there are people who are willfully obscurantist who actually set out to pull the wool over the eyes of other scholars and of the general public, then I'm not interested in having a dialogue with them. I think it's a waste of time.

Velamoor: I'd like to go back to a question that was quite predominant and dominated the scene in the 60s. Is God dead?

Dr. Dawkins: Why ask a question about whether he's dead if he was never alive?

[laughter]

Levitt: I'm afraid that's going to be my answer as well.

Dr. Dawkins: If it's taken to mean, is the idea of God dead in human minds? In a way that was not true earlier? I wish that were the case, but I fear it's not and I fear as a sociological phenomenon, a psychological phenomenon, God is very much alive. Looking into the future, I would like to think that in a few hundred years' time, God really will be properly dead but I'm not that optimistic.

Velamoor: One last question. The Foundation's flagship program is *Humanity 3000* and the reason why you distinguished gentlemen are here. Would you care to speculate about humanity, not necessarily by exactly the year 3000, but in very long-term future. Any aspect, any facet.

Dr. Levitt: If I had to guess and it would be purely a guess, I think that we are going to change biologically for the simple reason that the capacity to change ourselves biologically is now pretty much within our grasp. Of course, this horrifies not only traditional believers but even the scientists who have developed the technologies to do it but I think it's going to happen. Now, what will that entail in terms of culture, in terms of the whole spectrum of values that we have? I haven't the faintest idea. I think that it merely deepens the darkness that always conceals the future from us. In this case it's not only that we don't know how people will be, but we also don't know who they will be in a thousand years. That's about the only insight I'm sure enough about that I'm willing to say it out loud.

Dr. Dawkins: There are two main ways in which humans have to change biological nature. One is to manipulate the selection part of Darwinism and the other is the mutation part. The selection part, we've been changing in domestic animals and plants for many centuries, and we've got huge differences in dogs, in cabbages, in agricultural plants, in cattle, pigs and so on. We could have done that with humans and the odd thing is that we apparently haven't. There doesn't seem to be any evidence for artificial selection having changed humans in the same period as wolves have been changed into, for example, poodles.

You could say that we've now reached the stage when technology can manipulate the mutation part of Darwinism and change the genes themselves and manipulate the genes themselves. It's not necessarily obvious that we will do that because if we had the will to change humans, we could have done it already by artificial selection.

On the other hand, the indications are that we probably are going to use that kind of technology insight. In a thousand years' time, we probably will find the results of genetic manipulation in humans. A thousand years of course is a short time by evolutionary standards. We are we still evolving. You wouldn't expect to see any major evolutionary changes, no new species of humans. That would probably take longer than a thousand years. Whether we produce new species would depend on whether subsets of humanity get isolated from each other or not. You've got to have sexual isolation for that to happen. That would come from perhaps, space travel - if there are colonies of humans sent out either into orbiting colonies or to set up great green houses on Mars or something, so that the gene flow between them shrinks to a trickle or to nothing at all. Then, there might be the possibility for speciation - for humanity to divide into different species. If that does happen, it will be a lot further in the future than a thousand years.

The sort of world in which our descendants live in a thousand years is likely to be stunningly different, even in a hundred years it's going to be stunningly different because of the advances of technology, advances of computers for example which is happening at an enormous rate now and in the end, is still exponential. If that continues for even a few more decades, it will have stunning effects. There's a similar effect in DNA technology to the famous Moore's law and in ecology, and it's very interesting to speculate about where we'll be in understanding biology, in even a hundred years let alone a thousand years.

Velamoor: Thank you so much. I wish we had a couple of more hours.

Interview sourced from the archives of the Foundation For the Future.

References

Calvin, W.H. (2004). *A Brief History of the Mind: From Apes to Intellect and Beyond.* Oxford University Press.

Levitt, N. & Gross, P.R. (1994). *Higher Superstition: The Academic Left and Its Quarrels with Science.* John Hopkins University Press.

Wilson, E. (1998). *Consilience: The Unity of Knowledge.* Knopf.

Further Readings

Dawkins, R. (1986). *The Blind Watchmaker.* Norton & Company Inc.

Dawkins, R. (1989). *The Selfish Gene.* (2nd ed.). Oxford University Press.

Dawkins, R. (1989). *The Extended Phenotype.* Oxford.

Dawkins, R. (1995) *River out of Eden.* Basic Books.

Dawkins, R. (1996) *Climbing Mount Improbable.* Norton.

An Interview with Spencer Wells (2007)

Spencer Wells

Dr. Spencer Wells is an American population geneticist, anthropologist, and author of the book and documentary on the *Journey of Man*. From 2005 to 2015 Wells was the director of "The Genographic Project" at the National Geographic Society, studying the mutations in the genome to unearth ancient human lineage. He became the youngest ever recipient of the annual Kistler Prize Award in 2007, a prize awarded to a scientist who has done original research studying the relationship between the human genome and society. Wells is also the founder and executive director of personal genomics nonprofit The Insitome Institute with which he aims to educate and promote the debate around genomics.

An Interview with
Spencer Wells

(2007)

Spencer Wells was interviewed in 2007.
The transcript of this conversation can be found on the following pages.

Seshadri Velamoor: Good afternoon. I'd like to begin by congratulating you on winning the Kistler Prize for the year 2007. As you know you're joining distinguished company at a very ripe young age of 38. Tell me how you feel about that.

Dr. Spencer Wells: It is a huge honor. To begin with, I'd like to thank the foundation, you, and Bob Citron and Walter Kistler in particular, for your faith in me as a scientist. As a young scientist it is daunting to look at the past winners of this prize including a man who served as my post-doctoral advisor at Stanford, Luca Cavalli-Sforza, for many years and to be placed in the same category as those minds, as those scientists is a little bit daunting, but I very much appreciate your faith in me and what we're doing in the Genographic Project, the work that I've done so far and the work that I'll continue to do in the future. I have a sense that part of the reason you're giving this to me at the ripe young age of 38 as you say, is that you want to encourage me in my career as I move forward. So instead of it being a reward for a lifetime of what I've already done, it's more about you think that I've achieved something and then the potential of what might still come.

Velamoor: Let's get some basic things out of the way as I'm sure you are aware, there is considerable controversy being generated by, what I will describe as indigenous populations, about the nature of the project and, if I recall basically going through what they have objected to, is having to do with the idea of not providing or getting informed consent.

The second thing that I could extract from all of the publications that I could was about some absence or a lack of quid pro quo or a benefit accruing out of this study and thirdly perhaps, shattering a sense of who they are in terms of identity background myths and so on. Why don't we get that out of the way and address these objections and how you have met them, are they substantive, and do they make any sense?

Dr. Wells: You're starting with the easy question first, good.

[laughter]

The question of indigenous participation in this project is vital. The reason we are focusing so much of our scientific work on indigenous populations is because these are people who retain a connection to their past, to the geography where they live, to a much greater extent than those of us who have moved here from somewhere else. I live in the East Coast of North America, my ancestors come from all over Northern Europe, what do my genetic patterns tell you about the prehistory of America or even one particular part of Europe? Virtually nothing. We ideally want people who have been living in the same place for a long period of time and retain that link back to the past. That's the reason why indigenous participants are so important to the project. Now, in terms of the objections we have received a few as you say. The consent issue hasn't really been a major objection. The people have raised concerns about it, but we've thought long and hard about how you go about doing these sorts of studies. Consent is slightly different for indigenous groups than it is for people in an empowered Western society. In a liberal democracy, we tend to think of consent issues as being an individual choice whereas indigenous groups often have collective ownership of many resources and that would include their genetic patrimony. So, you must go about the consent process by approaching the group initially, and we always do that.

We have an entree to the group - someone who is interested in the project, may have heard about it, they may know a researcher already, something like that. We explain to a group of elders what it is we're trying to do and often we have a group meeting and explain to everybody in the village or whatever it might be, what the project is all about, what the benefits are and what the potential risks are and after that we then ask the individuals who want to participate. If the group as a whole decides to participate, the individuals also give consent, so we go through this two-tiered process. I don't think there is any other way to do this. I don't think there is a better way. I think that we've studied this very carefully, we've learned from past mistakes that other people have made, and we've taken that into account in the design of the ethical protocol that we follow.

The other issue I guess you had, was the benefits through the quid pro quo. Well, the benefits for indigenous people, just like everybody else, would be finding out something about your history. Something about where they came from the genetic side of the story. Now, we're very clear to say that the genetic story certainly for the small piece of the genome that we're studying is not everything. And it certainly doesn't define you, so your mitochondrial DNA haplogroup is not going to tell you who you are, but it tells you a little bit about your past and who your ancestors might have been at least on that lineage. So, it's not like we're trying to replace traditional stories. We're trying to add to them. If people find that interesting and beneficial, and many of them do, 30,000 participants from the indigenous communities around the world have chosen to be a part of the project already, then, like everybody else who joins the project, will get something out of it. Are they going to get improved medical care? Are they going to get a direct monetary benefit? No but they get the same sort of benefit that all the other participants do, and as I said, many people are participating. I think it is it's a little bit condescending to say that, as some of our detractors have, that indigenous people are not as interested in learning about this stuff as the rest of the people in the world. I think a lot of them are and the numbers show that, now in terms of the final point that you make, and this is the real crux of the issue in my opinion, will something about their worldview be threatened? Potentially, yes. Potentially, that might happen. That's the point of science. We're discovering new things and people may have a perception of the way the world is. The world is flat and yet you look at the science in the world and it turns out to be round and the Sun is not revolving around us. So, that's the way science works. It's constantly pushing the boundaries. Again, we explained very carefully to all the participants that they may find out something that contradicts some long-held notion and a traditional story and ultimately it does come down to a debate about the scientific worldview. I mean do you think that science is the way we should be investigating these things, or do you think we should rely on stories that we've gotten from our elders that people have portrayed it as the Mythos versus Logos-debate where Logos is logic and science and striving to learn something about the future based on the tools of logic. And Mythos is where you basically accept the world that your parents and grandparents bequeath to you with the stories that they told you and you never question that. That is a bigger debate than we can solve in this project. I am a scientist, I use scientific methods to investigate the past and you know that the people who participate in the project think that is a valid way of doing it, but some people may choose not to participate and that's fine.

Velamoor: It's understandable though, because even living in the most advanced society, if one can describe the U.S. to be that way - this whole decentering that has taken place from the Copernican revolution to the Darwinian concepts of evolution and so on - has still not been reconciled even in this society where a lot of people don't believe in evolution.

Dr. Wells: Yes, I know. I find it appalling that in a way we seem to have regressed over the last 20 or 30 years and I cannot believe that in the year 2007, we are still having debates about whether Intelligent Design should be taught in high school Biology classes.

When I was growing up in the 1970's and early 80's, there might have been a few people who talked about that but it was accepted that evolution was a scientific fact and that's what you learned about in science classes. If you wanted to learn about creationism you took a religion class. Why are we suddenly having this debate? It's a bigger issue in society. I mean, it's something that I'm talking about in my next book *Deep Ancestry: Inside the Genographic Project* (2006). There is a kind of resurgent fundamentalism everywhere in the world. I mean, we in America think about Islamic fundamentalism but we are going through that same kind of resurgence and why is that? I think it's because a lot of people feel left out of the future that's being created. They're afraid of the pace of change. They feel and that they don't play a role in this logos-driven future, the science-rational future and they're reacting to that in saying "We need to return to the old ways, we need to go back to the ways that have comforted us", even though they didn't actually comfort people and many people were harmed by those old ways, but I think it's part of a broader pattern in society. The other night I saw the film *Inherit the Wind* (Kramer, S. 1960). I don't know if you've seen that. With Spencer Tracy, and it's basically about the Scopes Monkey Trial, but when it came out in 1960 it was also a commentary on McCarthyism and so these are larger issues that have played out in society over the last century or so and I think unfortunately it's still something that we as scientists must deal with and again, we're not trying to replace anybody's sense of self. We're not trying to take the comfort of the past away from people. What we're trying to say is science also plays a role in the understanding of who you are.

Velamoor: Perhaps it also has to do with the fact that religion or faith systems or belief systems essentially are collectivist in their nature. Therefore, if an institution such as a religion or a faith system is collectivist, power and influence is wielded by a few people at the top, whereas knowledge in a modern context is accessible to anyone based on the scientific method. And so, it poses an inherent threat to their own status and their standing *vis-à-vis* their influence over their herds. To that extent, they are likely to lead the resistance rather than saying, well let me get out of the way and let you understand what the science is.

Dr. Wells: Yeah, I think you're right. I think knowledge is democratizing by its very nature. And particularly with the access to knowledge being so democratic now, you don't have to be located at a university or in a major city with a large library. You can go on the internet and get basically most of the world's information and more and more of that is going to become available. Anybody, anywhere in the world with an internet connection, hopefully within the next decade or two, everybody will be able to get to whatever they need to know, and they can make up their own minds. What's interesting is, that a lot of these fundamentalist groups are making use of that power of the internet to spread their story, so they are in opposition to what the internet stands for.

Velamoor: But it's good. That process itself should also be evolutionary in the sense that, just like we biologically have evolved surviving by virtue of our fitness, the idea should go through the same process.

Dr. Wells: That's right, I agree.

Velamoor: Let there be Memetic evolution to see what comes out at the end. My conclusion is that they will lose, and knowledge and science will win.

Dr. Wells: I think so. I certainly hope you're right, as a scientist. At this point in time, we're at a critical juncture.

Velamoor: Along the same lines, globalization is progressing I would think, at an exponential pace right now. So, what risks do you see in terms of cultures, in terms of languages, in terms of we as societies, because of the homogenization that is taking place. For instance, in a biological sense, is globalization exacerbating the risk for instance of a genomic homogenization which would make it susceptible to a pandemic of sorts?

Dr. Wells: Well, genetic homogenization, is obviously going on, people are moving around to a much greater extent than they ever have. I don't see that as exacerbating or increasing the likelihood of a global pandemic because we'll still have genetic variation. The key for me and what I do as an anthropological geneticist, is that we will have lost the context of those patterns of genetic variation. So, what I study is human diversity. And I study basically the underlying patterns of human diversity, how we laid down the diversity we see around the world today. And that is a very long story by human lifetime standards. It's a story that began in Africa 200,000 years ago with the appearance of our species and we stuck around in Africa for a very long time. About 150,000 years. And then between 50,000 and 60,000 years ago, a small group of Africans after going through a near extinction event. So basically, there was a huge homogenization process before we ever started to leave Africa.

A small group left Africa and went out and populated the world. And today we are scattered all over the continents: 6.5 billion people speaking 6000 different languages, all different appearances and so on. How did we create those patterns of diversity? Now as you said we're now mixing and moving around to a much greater extent, as I also said in my book *The Journey of Man* (2002). That is changing. Basically, what we're trying to do is beneath the surface of that, so we know that that's something that's happened in the last couple of centuries. How did we create those initial patterns of diversity around the world? Our ability to do that is threatened by the mobility revolution of the last two centuries since the Industrial Revolution. And as people move and mix, they're going to carry their genes with them, which is why I don't think we're in greater risk for pandemic, although certainly, people moving around increases the spread of diseases, but again, we're going to lose the context of the genetic variation, so the trail that I follow is as a forensic detective if you will….

Velamoor: It's a permanent record that moves around and, in that sense, where it came about is what is lost.

Dr. Wells: Yeah, it's the context.

Velamoor: Whereas culturally and otherwise, all bets are off.

Dr. Wells: Well, culturally, it's probably a good thing sociologically speaking, for people to be more mobile and to encounter far-off lands and places and people who speak different languages and people who look different and to mix with them and to create more of a melting pot, because it breaks down the differences between different societies and it encourages communication. And as we know, people who study the history of technology, the kind of long-term history of technology, the evolution, the cultural evolution of ideas happens faster, the more exchange there is and we need new ideas. We've got a lot of major challenges facing us as you guys know very well.

Velamoor: Same thing with technology too. The rate of change of technology is far higher than our ability to adapt and use it.

Dr. Wells: Yes, yeah

Velamoor: So, for the uninitiated like myself, would you do me a big favor and explain or define the basic terms that are common currency in the kind of work you're doing? Gene, haplotype, mutation etc.

Dr. Wells: Let's step back and let's talk about the genome. So, I think the genome is something that's a common parlance. People read articles about it all the time. Craig Venter, just a couple of weeks ago, just published his own genome. So, the genome is the sum total of all the genetic material that you're carrying in your body. It is composed of DNA which is composed of four subunits; we call them A, C, G and T (Adenine Cytosine Guanine and Thymine). And it's the sequence of these in a linear order in the DNA molecule, the famous double helix, that is basically the blueprint to make another version of you. And most of the genome supposedly has no known function. It almost certainly does have a function. There have been several studies that have come out over the past year suggesting that what we previously called junk-DNA. We didn't know about its job, and it is not really junk and it's probably in some ways even more important than a lot of the genes that are sitting in there, but basically, you've got genes, which traditionally have only coded for proteins but now there are probably other gene-like regions that are important and are regulating the genome. You've got the stuff in between the genes. You've got regulatory sequences, you've got structural sequences around the ends of the chromosomes, around the centromeres in the center of the chromosomes, so that is your genome. A gene is a block of DNA, which up until quite recently, coded for a protein and the proteins were thought to be the important part of the cell. They work out in the cytoplasm. They're the machinery, so this is the blueprint. It tells you how to make a new machine, a new forklift or whatever it is out there doing, in the cytoplasm of the cell.

Now, people are not identical. You walk down the street, and you notice that people are different and most of those differences are caused by differences in DNA sequences. So, if you compare the DNA or a chromosome, one of these linear bundles of DNA from one person to another person, you'll see that there are differences between them and they're not identical. And we differ on average at about one in every thousand nucleotide positions. Again, there's new evidence coming out, suggesting that there's more complex variation, copy number variation, where you increase the number of copies of a gene and their inversions and insertions and deletions that play into this. But basically, what we studied, because we can measure the rate, are what we call, single nucleotide polymorphisms, or SNIPS, and these occur at a rate of roughly one in every thousand nucleotides as you scan down the genome.

Velamoor: So, there would be what?

Dr. Wells: So, there are 90 million potential differences between two unrelated humans. Which is actually very small level of variation. We're 99,9% identical. If you look at other species of large primates—apes, orangutans, gorillas, chimpanzees—they have between four and ten times as much variations as humans do. And the reason for this, we believe, is because of that bottleneck event, the near extinction event between 60,000 and 70,000 years ago while we were still living in Africa. We dropped down to probably only a couple of thousand people. That was a founder population. We probably had a somewhat larger population, which had been stable throughout the early part of that period, the Late Pleistocene, and then we suddenly go down to this very small population then we expand back from that to create the diversity we see today.

The big question is - We've got this low level of diversity, so why do we have so much variation on the surface? And we still don't have the answer for that. These variant forms of the gene are known as alleles. So, you can have alleles, meaning different forms of the same gene. A haplotype is basically the set of variants, the linked set of variants that you possess. So, it is effectively a scan of your genome, a continuous scan of that strand of your DNA. It's describing the state of your particular genome at these positions that are known to vary.

Velamoor: I see, and they are consistent they are consistent with everybody that would have my ancestry.

Dr. Wells: Your haplotype, if we look at enough positions in your genome, is unique to you. It is a fingerprint. That is your haplotype. But there are certain markers that link your haplotype to other haplotypes that are related, so you share certain markers with other people and these markers occur from time to time as the DNA is being passed down through the generations. They occur randomly and at a relatively low rate. 50 per genome per generation. So, the relatively rare 50 out of 6 billion is not that big, so if you share one of these markers with someone that means you share an ancestor at some point in the past and that defines you as a member of a haplogroup or an ancestral clan. A haplogroup is a collection of related haplotypes that share a particular marker.

Velamoor: And then you keep going back to isolate this marker.

Dr. Wells: Right, exactly. This allows us to draw people together, the branches on the tree into ever deeper branches and eventually we get back to the root of the tree.

Velamoor: Just to elaborate on that, for descriptive purposes, I am R1a-M17. What does that mean?

Dr. Wells: That is a lineage that most likely originated on the Russian steppes or perhaps in Central Asia.

Velamoor: Mind blowing in the sense that I was born and raised in South India.

Dr. Wells: Exactly, but it originated probably between ten and fifteen thousand years ago and it underwent a massive expansion within the last 5,000 years probably concomitant with the spread of Indo-European languages driven by the spread of domesticated horses. So, these were probably the first people living on the Steppes of Russia or, as I said, northern Kazakhstan, somewhere in that area around the Black Sea or the Caspian, who domesticated the horse, and this gave them mobility—mobility that humans have never had before—and they spread their languages, we believe, down into India, so it's the reason why the Indian languages, most of them, except for the ones in the south, are Indo-European related to the European languages, even though they're very far from Europe.

Velamoor: Something you just said leads me to the next question, about horses, about languages and a biological determination about R1a-M17. How do you go about associating the context for that biological information? Am I making sense? Because how did you suddenly say, "well okay, that was 11,000 years ago and here is how I can find that it had something to do with the language or a horse"?

Dr. Wells: Absolutely, that's a really good question and there's a bit of a leap of faith. It's an interpretation. We as geneticists uniquely are able to study biological ancestry. We can say how people are related to each other and we can say, for instance, that someone from southern India is related to someone from Norway, which is kind of odd. I mean relatively closely related. I'm not talking about going back to Africa, I'm talking about within the last five or ten thousand years. So, you have to explain that and what you do is, you look at the putative site of origin of these particular lineages so R1a again. I mentioned someone around the Caspian or Black Sea, and you look at the timing of the expansion and then you say, was there anything going on in the archaeological record for instance, around this time and you look, and you say yes - people started to domesticate horses. We see the spread of a particular culture. The Kurgan culture eastward into Central Asia, northward into Scandinavia around this time, and eventually reaching India, it's thought. You then look at things like the Vedic texts, and there's a huge debate about what happened to the Harappan civilization, which was in Pakistan: were they destroyed by invading Indo-Europeans from the Steppes? Or did they simply leave because of environmental change? Or what happened? But there is some evidence at least in the Vedic texts that there was the movement of people from North of that region, down into the Indian subcontinent, so it's consistent with the archaeological pattern that we see and the linguistic pattern, and so you start to put two and two together and you say, well we see the spread of this marker at the same time you see the spread of this culture. It's consistent that it was probably driven at least in part, by the spread of those people. Because literally you had to get people moving from point A to point B. I mean this is not the spread of just a culture, this is the spread of your particular genetic lineage. I mean you are literally cousins with some Norwegian Viking, and so we have to have an explanation for how those people moved and why they would, because that's a long way to go.

Velamoor: Right, I recently read a couple of books. I'm not exactly sure how to categorize them, by Graham Hancock. I think one of them is called Heaven's Mirror (Hancock, 1999) talking essentially about the fact, with specific reference to some Middle Eastern civilizations and perhaps some South Indian cultures that existed, actually a city-state off the west coast of India, basically pointing to the fact, that right around between 11 to 13 thousand years ago, the end of the Ice Age and perhaps quite a lot of flooding, made a lot of the cities literally disappear into the oceans. And they are now discovering that some of them do exist. And that led to a diaspora out of the Middle

East and from the parts of India out to other parts of the world. In other words, in a sense maybe even the reverse of what the genetic records seem to suggest.

Dr. Wells: I would say it's very speculative. There's certainly no evidence for proper cities anywhere in the world, even in India submerged off the coast at 11 to 13 thousand years ago. The first cities don't really appear until around 4000-5000 BC, so 6-7 thousand years ago. And they appear first, as far as we know, in the Middle East, although there were probably some very early cities in India as well. And there was probably a separate origin of agriculture in India. Rice agriculture probably originated separately from the one in China, in Northeastern India and the foothills of the Himalayas, which is where the wild ancestors of rice grow, and so there was probably an expansion driven from that side. Possibly a separate domestication event of other species in southern India. But it's quite possible that, yes very early on, there were separate autochthonous Indian cities. Did they disperse because of the rising sea levels? No, I think that that probably happened much earlier and wouldn't have driven that many people away, and if it had driven them away, that it probably would have been a slow kind of gradual move inland. They would have abandoned an old city but then rebuilt it a little bit further in. Which may happen to us over the next century or two.

Velamoor: Coming back to the technicalities of determining mutations and haplotypes. This is a question that came to me, that I was unable to answer, having to do with the fact that the Y chromosome paternally is transmitted, which forms the basis for determining the information on what mutation, what haplotype and so on. The question came up is, what does a woman do to find out the genetic lineage.

Dr. Wells: Women can look at their mother's line. So, men and women inherit something known as mitochondrial DNA from their mothers. And so, this is passed down through a purely maternal line. Men can't pass it on. It's because the mitochondria are found in the cytoplasm of the cell, and we get our cytoplasm from the egg. From our mother's egg. The sperm only donates the chromosomes that go into the nucleus. It doesn't donate as far as we know any mitochondrial DNA. If it does, it's a very rare event and basically, we're just looking at a purely maternal lineage. So, women can look at that and find out something about their mother's mother's mother's mother's mother. Men can also do that. They can find out about their mother's side by looking at their mtDNA. Only men have Y chromosomes so only men can look at that line.

Velamoor: In your Genographic studies, are you collecting only male samples?

Dr. Wells: We are focusing on men for the indigenous sampling we're doing because we get more bang for our buck if you will. Because we can sample both the Y chromosome and mitochondrial DNA from men. When we go out in the field, we try to get as many male samples as possible. Now if there are women who want to participate, we're happy to take the samples but we were particularly interested in men for the sampling expenditure. For the amount that we're spending, getting out in the field, and doing the sampling and doing the DNA and all of that, it would make more sense to get both Y and mtDNA from one individual if we could, so it's better to go after men scientifically speaking, but for social reasons and cultural reasons, sometimes we sample women as well.

Velamoor: Stepping back, based on everything you have discovered so far, how many separate migrations out of Africa have occurred so far.

Dr. Wells: We see clear evidence in the archaeological record of several migrations before we start to see genetic evidence. In all likelihood, *Homo erectus* or as it's known in Africa, *Homo ergaster*, started to leave Africa around 1.8 million years ago and so erectus was spread all over the continent of Asia, typically in the tropics and subtropics and might have existed there until very recently. If you believe that *Homo floresiensis* - the Hobbit, which was found on the island of Flores and Indonesia recently was around until 12,000 years ago and it was erectus that drove it to extinction because we were clearly living there at that time. So that was a very early migration. We don't see any genetic evidence of that because that's way back before we can start to see the genetic patterns we coalesce at a much more recent day. There was a later migration of archaic *Homo sapiens*, *Homo heidelbergensis*, as it's known in Europe, probably left Africa around 500,000 years ago and these individuals gave rise to the Neanderthals which appeared in Europe around 250,000 years ago. Again, we came into Europe later than that, around 35,000 years ago, and countered them and drove them to extinction in all likelihood.

Then there's us. We appear in the fossil record in Africa around 200,000 years ago and we don't start to leave until around 60,000 - 50,000 years ago. And the evidence is that there were two migrations, two early migrations. One right around this 60,000-year mark, 55 to 60 thousand years ago, which took a coastal route, so this would have been across the Bab Al-Mandab, down through the Arabian Peninsula, the south coast of Asia by the beaches. Moving a little bit further every week, every month, every season, in search of food primarily gathering, so gathering mollusks, doing a little bit of trapping of fish. They probably started to experiment with new fishing methods maybe, develop rudimentary fishing hooks and nets and so on, but basically people living off of the riches of the sea and they were the only hominids living there at the time, as far as we can tell. So, the riches were pretty rich, and they simply followed them a little bit further and there was probably somewhat of a population expansion effect that helped to drive this but it's not that they were setting out to conquer the world, setting out to migrate to Australia, which is where they reached by around 50 thousand years ago. Simply moving a little bit further, every season, in search of food. So, the evidence is that that's the first migration of our ancestors, modern humans, fully modern humans, out of Africa. There was probably a second one, an inland route, which came out between 45 and 50 thousand years ago. And it probably came across what is today the Sahara Desert, possibly moving down the Nile Valley, but we know that the climate of the Sahara has changed substantially over the last hundred thousand years or so. There are things called Coral Sap, in the sediments in the Eastern Mediterranean, which revealed that every 23000 years or so, the Sahara is actually pretty nice place to live.

Velamoor: I read that it was actually quite green.

Dr. Wells: Exactly, but only for a short period of time. So, we have one of these wetter phases between 45 and 50 thousand years ago. We have another one around 30,000 years ago, and we have another one at the end of the last ice age. The wettest period was probably around 8000 years ago. And so during these wet phases it's actually fairly easy for populations to expand up into the Sahara. It's grassland at that time, there are lakes everywhere, and it was during one of these wetter phases we believe, between 45 and 50 thousand years ago, that another group of Africans took off for the Middle East. Then the door was slammed shut, the Sahara became very dry, so did the Middle East, and that probably helped to force them into Central Asia. Again, they were adapted to hunting on the grasslands and that's where the grass was, so they moved into the grasslands of Central Asia, and from there they were poised to spring into Europe across the East Asia and ultimately the Americas. There were also back migrations because during the next wet phase around 30,000 years ago, it looks like some people from the Middle East moved back into North Africa, and we see genetic evidence in some of the isolated populations of the Sahara today. And then later migration during the Neolithic around 8,000 years ago. Again, it was a good place to grow food, people moving in out of the Fertile Crescent and so we see evidence of an exchange during these wetter phases.

Velamoor: Is it still the conclusion based on your studies, if I recall watching the *Journey of Man*, the Khoisan, is the tribe from which all modern humans emerged.

Dr. Wells: Well, we've modified that now. We've got a paper which we're about to submit to *Science*. Trying to get at that that big question of what was going on in Africa during that 150,000-year period before we left. So, we appear in the fossil record. Modern humans were there. And we don't start to leave for 450,000 years. What was happening? But most people kind of ignore that. They just think of Africa as being the source but that's a long period of time for things to happen. And it turns out that in all likelihood, the San were a side branch of human evolution, if you will, that became separated. The ancestors of the San became separated from the main line of human evolution probably 150,000 – 160,000 ago, isolated in southern Africa. And in effect it's the East African population that was the main line of human evolution and starting around 70,000 years ago this population started to expand. This was probably driven by advances in culture. The dawn of the late Stone Age or the Upper Paleolithic, which gave them an advantage in hunting or whatever it might have been, but we see evidence of a population expansion starting in East Africa, which then re-engulfed the San population, brought them back into the human gene pool and they also expanded into a lot of Africa. So we think about the hominid bushy tree, you've heard about this, we have lots of different species. The interpretation of this is that basically the San were on their way to becoming a separate incipient species of humanity and then they were pulled back in. So that's the reason they have such divergent genetic lineages.

Velamoor: Because Meave Leakey recently published a study, saying that this notion of a ladder-like evolution of humans from Australopithecine to Afarensis is questionable because quite a few of them existed simultaneously in Africa. That's what the evidence seems to show.

Dr. Wells: Yes, we've always known that there were lots of odd things going on between four and two million years ago. The Australopithecines and the Robust Australopithecines. So, we've accepted that that was bushy, but we've always thought that once our genus *Homo* appears, *Homo habilis*, appears around 2.3million years ago. From there on it's a straight shot. What Meave's paper showed is that, in fact, there's a period of around five hundred thousand -eight hundred thousand years, where habilis and erectus overlap with each other. Two separate species living in the same place at the same time. Which one are we descended from? It's not necessarily *habilis erectus* us, now it could be *habilis* us or it could be *erectus* us or something else us.

Velamoor: Yeah, some pieces are still missing.

Dr. Wells: Why we say, it's really important to study Paleoanthropology because it's fascinating and it presents us with possibilities about our past and our ancestry, but it doesn't give us the probabilities about who we are actually related to and that's why we resort to DNA.

Velamoor: Another study that I recently was looking at was studying dental fossils. That seemed to suggest that Asian populations had a far larger role in colonizing Europe than previously thought.

Dr. Wells: Yes, and that was again, following all the different migrations that have gone on. So, I mentioned the one at 1.8 million years ago with erectus, and then the one of Archaic *Homo sapiens* and then the modern humans. We haven't seen any genetic evidence of this but it is possible that some of these different migrations could have mixed. Again, we don't see any genetic evidence for this. We don't know the underlying genes that determine tooth morphology, so I would say it's very difficult to know how much weight to place in particular characters in the teeth. Some things can probably change quite easily, and you can get convergent evolution, other things probably require many genetic changes and they're much more important. We don't know what the underlying genetic causes are, so it's a question of how you weight the characters that you're studying. Weight them all equally and we know that's not valid necessarily, but it is possible. It is an intriguing theory and I think, this is a much more likely possibility, that when erectus left, something happened in Asia and there was a back migration of those erectus populations into Africa and those were the ones who ultimately evolved into *Homo sapiens* in Africa. And then there was another out of Africa migration. That is a possibility and that's quite difficult to test. It's a very complicated model.

Velamoor: Right. You did mention Craig Venter's name just a little while ago. Coming back to his research. They have mapped all his chromosomes completely and basically the determination is that there's far greater variability between individuals than previously thought. If that is the case, then is the genetic variability and the distance between genetic groups also greater and therefore, lead to conclusions such as, perhaps, that the notion that groups are essentially the same with minor differences within the human family, is not justified and that groups are likely to be far greater in terms of variability than we thought? Giving substance to the notion of race and groups and so on?

Dr. Wells: Craig found, as you said, that there is more variation in the human genome than we suspected. Now, what he didn't find was that there's more single nucleotide variation. Again, those are the changes we know about the rate at which they occur. He found that basically it's 0.1 percent, so one in every thousand positions.

Velamoor: If you could, when you use the expression "rate" - the rate at which they occur - for the benefit of illustrating or explaining, what is it in terms of time frames.?

Dr. Wells: It's in terms of time frames, it's also in terms of the frequency of these in the genome, so one in every thousand nucleotides positions.

Velamoor: In a time frame you associate times to it.

Dr. Wells: Right, exactly. So what we can do is we can compare humans and chimpanzees and now we have some Neanderthal sequence and we know the divergence time of these based on the fossil record and we can say, okay how many changes are there? That is the rate at which they occur. We can also do single sperm studies and that's probably the way of the future and doing this in a much more scientific way. If you scan several sperm and you look at the rate of De Novo mutations that occur in the sperm, you can calculate, literally, the rate of mutation in the human genome. So we basically know that rate, and in Craig's analysis has not changed that. 50 per genome per generation roughly. So we have a very good estimate of the rate at which these Single Nucleotide changes occur, so Craig's results are not going to change our estimates of divergence times between individuals. What they do though is, they reveal a different type of variation, so the copy number variation, where you can have a gene that's duplicated or triplicated or quadruplicated. You can have genes that are inverted, you can have insertions and deletions. The level of variation in those types of changes is much higher than we ever suspected and so that's what the analysis is really showing. We don't know that much about the rate at which it does happen. We need to study that, and we ideally would incorporate that into the analyses but clearly there is a lot more underlying variation, yes, than we suspect. Does it change the divergence estimates? No. Now, I think a much more important thing to come out of the analysis that Craig published, is that the genome is very much becoming personalized. The genie is out of the bottle and people are going to be doing this. Someone has done it now. Everyone is going to be doing this routinely within a generation. And a lot of people are going to be doing it within the next 5-10 years.

Velamoor: Are you getting yours?

Dr. Wells: No, I'm not going to copyright my genome. Would I release all the information to the public domain with the medical records? At this point no because I'm worried about discrimination. I think the healthcare system needs to change first. But eventually I think this will drive a change in the way we fund healthcare.

Velamoor: Of course, because that might be the downside. But the upside is that medicine and your healthcare is totally customized.

Dr. Wells: Exactly, and the idea that you have access to all of this information whereas it's been in the hands of physicians up until now. If you have access to your medical records and your genomic information and you can analyze it yourself and go onto the internet and look at the correlations between medical conditions in particular genetic variants, it gives you a lot of power. It can give you a sense of control over your life. You're not operating in the dark if you have a higher susceptibility to whatever might be, eg. lung cancer. Maybe you should never start smoking, I mean no one should anyways. We know that it's healthier but maybe it'll give you extra pause.

Velamoor: Right, that was going to be actually my next question. If you would care to comment on the ethical concerns that are about to arise because knowing as much as we are likely to know about our own genomes. There are possibilities in terms of intervening for health behavior and intelligence.

Dr. Wells: I think it's better to know than it is not to know. I think people should want to find out this information because it gives you, again, a sense of empowerment over your own health and your own life in the direction that you're going to take. Now genes don't determine anything except in a few rare cases. Yes, there are some rare Mendelian diseases, where if you have the gene there's a hundred percent chance, you're going to have the disorder. In general, most of these genetic variants predispose in a certain way. They increase your risk or your likelihood by a factor of two or three. So instead of having a one-percent chance of getting diabetes you might have a two percent chance of getting diabetes. What does that mean? Most people don't really understand probability. What that means is that you go from having a ninety-nine percent chance of not having it to ninety-eight percent chance. So, it's not a huge effect.

I am worried about misinterpretation. I do think that routinely, in vitro fertilization is becoming more common in our society, as women delay having children and it's hard to get pregnant. A lot of women in their early 40s are now trying to become pregnant. IVF is becoming much more common, and I think as we learn more about the genome, people are going to be more likely to want to test these genetic variants and the embryo that they decide to implant. If you've seen the film *Gattaca* (DeVito & Niccol, 1997), I think that is going to happen at some point. Are they going to choose particular variants that determine or help to determine physical appearance? Possibly, I don't know. We don't have any genes identified yet that clearly affect intelligence but there are probably genetic variants that do affect it in some way. They don't determine it, but they probably do affect those traits in some way. I think people probably will start to test for some of these things. I think it's inevitable. Should we regulate this? Probably but I don't know that it's possible in places like the United States where there are private clinics, and anything is possible if you have enough money. It does concern me that basically it will be driven by money and access to these technologies and a certain segment of society will have access to all of this stuff and it might lead to a general genetic divergence within that group from the larger group. Shades of Aldous Huxley. It's a little worrying but I think the potential benefits are far too important to kill the research. I think we need to continue learning more about the genome and how it affects all of these characteristics, both disease states and the normal range of variation.

Velamoor: Given the alternatives, insofar as such things are concerned, one is to preemptively regulate and moderate and control and circumscribe the field within which these things operate or let the market decide. Which side would you fall on?

Dr. Wells: It depends. When it's a question of the commons, I think it's been shown resoundingly, by a lot of economists that you must regulate. The government must help create a market. So, if we think about pollution and carbon credits and so on, that's one way of creating a market. That's going to help the environment which is part of the commons. In this case, these are individual decisions and it's very difficult to regulate those individual decisions. I mean you're deciding about your children. We make lots of other decisions about our children where we don't have to consult the government, including significant decisions about their entire lives. Where they're going to go to school, what they are going to study, who they can marry etc.. I don't think it's possible to really regulate that, but I do think that educating people about these genetic variants is incredibly important and that's part of the reason I spend so much time communicating science. Because we don't really understand how the genome works yet. If you read through the genetic epidemiological studies and you see a two times higher relative risk of two particular genetic variant associated with the disease. That's studying one particular effect of that gene in isolation. And in fact, most genes are Pleiotropic, so there are other effects that that gene probably has. Particularly for complex traits like intelligence. There could be knock-on effects of the genes that are being studied. So, you may find a genetic variant that is twice as likely to increase your IQ score by a factor of 10 but it might also give you a higher risk of Schizophrenia or manic depression. How do you choose which genes you want your kids to have? What are you actually bequeathing to them?

Velamoor: It's a fine line between genius and madness on the one hand, but then you tinker with either one, you could end up with leukemia or something else on the other. I'm sure you're familiar with Jared Diamond's work *Guns, Germs and Steel* (1997), *Collapse* (2005) and so on. Is there a coincidence or a variance relative to what you find, using the pathways that you are using to understand human travelers?

Dr. Wells: I think there's a clear coincidence. I actually really enjoyed *Guns Germs and Steel*, but I thought it was the elaboration of something that he had talked about in *The Third Chimpanzee* (Diamond, 1991), his first major book which I actually thought was a much better read. But basically, in *Guns Germs and Steel*, he was talking about the history of the last 10,000 years and attempting to answer this deceptively simple question that he's asked at the beginning - Why do you white guys have all the cargo? Why do you have so much more stuff than we do, why are you richer and why are you more advanced technologically? And he traces it to geography and the idea that the transmission of ideas, the speed with which transmitting of ideas across geographic zones horizontally within the same latitude, increase the rate of social change and that's why Eurasian populations tend to be better off than a lot of the tropical groups. I think that's entirely valid, and I think certainly, a lot of the things that he went through in that book that had very little to do with that core thesis, tracing the Bantu expansion and so on. There are themes that I explore in my own research and there's a clear coincidence between what he's writing about and what we find.

Velamoor: What would Spencer Wells see himself doing when he is 48 years old?

Dr. Wells: I don't know. I have been thinking about this recently. We're about midway through the Genographic Project and to be able to have a project like this at my relatively tender age is a huge honor. I don't know exactly what I'm going to be doing at the end of it. I do know that there are certain things that I want to continue doing, whether I am still a practicing scientist or not.

I want to continue to synthesize scientific ideas, to write about them, to educate the public, get people involved. I feel very strongly that science is something the public can contribute to. And that's part of the reason why we have the public participation side of our project. It's kind of science 2.0 where people can play an actual role in the science. And I think particularly in the genomics revolution with the idea that people are going to be sequencing their own genomes and compiling all this data, I think they could play a vital role in understanding the patterns of genetic variation. So, getting these stories out to people, books, films, articles and so on. In 10 years, I would like to think that the Genographic Project will be viewed as groundbreaking. A new model for doing scientific projects. I might possibly be involved in something else like the Genographic Project. Something that is looking at the interaction between genes and phenotype in a much more explicit way. That could be in the private sector, it could be working with a university possibly. But I think it will be in this whole notion of the genome having an impact on society and we're right on the cusp of where that's starting to happen and people are starting to realize it and it's starting to enter the common parlance and it's appearing in ads and television.

Velamoor: It is changing the entire field of social sciences.

Dr. Wells: I think that education is such a vital part of that. Telling people what's true and what isn't. What we know and what is speculation. It's critical because it's a very powerful technology. I mean when we were choosing the genes to put in our children, we're choosing the genes to put in every generation that comes after that and it's a kind of transgenerational power that we haven't really had access to before. We're shooting a genetic bullet way into the future, thousands of years. And where is that bullet going to come to rest? What's the ultimate possibility of response or reaction from doing that?

Velamoor: Was there a single experienced person or book that got you started on this path long ago?

Dr. Wells: It was a it was a combination of things. I actually wanted to be a historian when I was a kid. I was much more interested in history and archaeology, saw the King Tut exhibit, the tour in the states back in '77 and '78 stood in line in the rain for 12 hours in New Orleans to get my ticket and went in with my parents and I was blown away. It was like you were looking at something that was created the day before, but it was thousands of years old or 500 years old. And I just became obsessed with this idea of time travel. Can you imagine what it would have been like to be alive at the time of the ancient Egyptians are the Greeks or the Romans or whatever. Some of these other groups, the Phoenicians, vanished peoples.

And I only got interested in science secondarily when my mother went back to school to get her PhD in Biology, so she had a huge effect on me. She showed me that science can be fun and fascinating and it's about solving puzzles I mean it's not just about the guys in the white lab coat speaking a funny language doing something obscure. It's really about trying to understand the way the world works, and it is a huge intellectual challenge but it's also fun and fascinating. So, she had a huge impact on me.

My high school biology teacher, Charles Swift, had a huge impact on me for the same reason. He started to show me the wonders of biological science and how fascinating the world is and the world right under our noses. You look through a microscope and you see all these incredible things that you didn't even dream about. So, he was a huge impact.

And then my advisor in college who encouraged me to go work with Dick Lewington at Harvard. Mark Kirkpatrick, I did an independent study course with him in theoretical population genetics. I was very interested in being a theoretical geneticist, mathematical geneticist when I went off to graduate school and ended up becoming more of an experimentalist but big questions like why do we have sex, why does sex exist? Because it doesn't seem very adaptive, it seems like it would be better to reproduce your genes and they're entirely without sharing them with somebody else. And in fact, they're very important theoretical questions. If you could clone yourself, you could potentially beat out everybody else, including your spouse.

Dick Lewington obviously had huge impact on me. I really started to see the social impact of what we were doing as geneticists in his lab with the historians and philosophers of science who came through. Ed Wilson, who was on the floor just underneath us and interacting with him. And Ernst Meier. Just stellar minds. So that was a huge experience for me being up at Harvard for five years. And then of course working with Cavalli-Sforza who really got me excited about working with indigenous people and becoming more of an anthropologist. He said you need to get out and meet these people. I mean these are people and you need to learn something about their cultures and live with them and it's very important for what we do.

Velamoor: I think, Spencer, this interview shows that the Kistler prize is a very important prize in terms of precisely what you have described so far. It is important to study the relationship between genome and the phenotype, or genome in society. So, Walter Kistler actually is far ahead of his time in putting the emphasis on it and I think this interview also shows why you are very deserving of the 2007 Kistler prize. Thank you so very much.

Dr. Wells: Thank you!

Interview sourced from the archives of the Foundation For the Future.

References

DeVito, D. (Producer), Niccol, A. (Director). (1997). *Gattaca* [Motion Picture] United States: Columbia Pictures

Diamond, J. (1991). *The Third Chimpanzee*. Hutchinson Radius.

Diamond, J. (1997). *Guns, Germs and Steel*. Norton.

Diamond, J. (2005). *Collapse: How Societies Choose to Fail or Succeed*. Viking Press.

Hancock, G. (1999). *Heaven's Mirror: Quest for the Lost Civilization*. Three Rivers Press.

Kramer, S. (Producer & Director). (1960). *Inherit the Wind*. [Motion Picture] United States: Universal Studios

Wells, S. (2002). *The Journey of Man: A Genetic Odyssey*. Princeton University Press.

Wells, S. (2006). *Deep Ancestry: Inside the Genographic Project*. National Geographic

Wells, S. (2010). *Pandora's Seed: The Unforeseen Cost of Civilization*. Random House.

An Interview with Craig Venter (2008)

Craig Venter

Dr. Craig Venter is a world-renowned Genome research pioneer and Biotechnologist. Dr. Venter came to prominence in scientific circles in 1991 for his novel technique for rapid gene discovery and in 1995 for the first sequencing in history of a genome of a living species. In 2007 Venter's own complete individual genome was sequenced and published in the first-ever publication of a genome sequence of an individual, covering both chromosome pairs. He is the founder and acting CEO of the J. Craig Venter Institute where he and his team of over 200 employees study the societal implications of genomics in addition to genomics itself. Dr. Venter is thus being honored by the Foundation for the Future for a body of pioneering work in genome science.

An Interview with Craig Venter

(2008)

Craig Venter was interviewed in 2008.
The transcript of this conversation can be found on the following pages.

Seshadri Velamoor: To give you [the audience] some background, there's quite a lot of information about Dr. Venter and his work. For the past several weeks, in anticipation of this interview, I have been trying to kind of dig into it and understand as much as I could so as to make this interview interesting and meaningful. Hopefully it will turn out to be that way. If not, we still have the option where I'll give up and have Dr. Venter present himself. So, let's start there, I've been going through parts of your book which I would imagine, would be equal to a biography, an autobiography, which is *A Life Decoded* (2008). One of your colleagues states that you operate as follows, and I'd like you to react to that. "Craig likes to high dive into empty pools. He tries to time it, so the water is there by the time he hits the bottom." Have you succeeded? You're still alive and sitting here, so you must have.

Dr. Craig Venter: I haven't hit the bottom yet. I think what that was referring to was, I've been able to present my teams with what we've considered impossible challenges. I knew they weren't impossible. And soon when the team started working on things, they learned they weren't impossible. They viewed their goal was to fill the pool with water and to prove me right. But as a result, I think, people all rose to a level beyond which they thought they were capable. That's why instead of taking 15 years and five billion dollars to sequence the human genome, we did it in nine months just with a small team of people for a hundred million dollars. My team has never let me down, they keep filling the pool.

Velamoor: The analogy of the pool, and water, and diving, it's more than a coincidence because it's also a fact that Dr. Venter, in his earlier years, was a champion swimmer. Would you like to comment on that a little bit?

Dr. Venter: Recently, with watching the Olympics, I couldn't carry the water bucket for the Olympian athletes. Techniques and skills have changed very dramatically.

Velamoor: And the dress they wear.

Dr. Venter: Right, in fact I've argued, when you see people like Michael Phelps, on the genetic basis, it proves we are not all created equal. [chuckle]. The Olympics is one way we emphasize this.

Velamoor: Yeah, especially that eighth medal that he won, by one one-hundredth of a second, or even less than that I believe, and all it involved was touching that one finger to that end point. And that's how he won the eighth Gold Medal.

Dr. Venter: In fact, it's possible the other guy touched first but he touched harder.

Velamoor: In your book (2008) you have written, "I'm driven to seize life and understand it." What might be your quintessential findings in this regard?

Dr. Venter: Well, I think we're hopefully very early in that process. What we've done is, we've made a synthetic chromosome for a virus. We put the synthetic DNA into a cell and the cell was able to read this synthetic chemical that we made and start producing the virus. What we reported earlier this year, we've now made something a hundred thousand times larger. We've made a first bacterial chromosome just from four bottles of chemicals, and we're in the process of trying to boot that up in a cell. But in showing that it is the software of life, we show that we could actually take the genetic material, the chromosome from one cell, and put it in another cell. So, the original chromosome in the cell is destroyed. And with the right engineering we can completely convert one species into another. So, with the early stages of understanding how DNA is in fact the software of life, we are at the earliest stages of learning how to write that software. And when we learn to write that software intelligently and can design species from scratch, then we can claim as a species that we at least have some understanding of life.

Velamoor: When you understand the genome of something and you can synthetically recreate it, I would imagine that is possible now, if you were to do that and then, somewhere between that and life itself, is there a ghost in the machine or is there no distance between putting the genome together and life spontaneously emerging?

Dr. Venter: We're not creating life from scratch. We are doing what has happened with all life. All life comes from other living cells. That's how you and I started. That's how all life starts. We're building on top of that, three and a half million years of evolution, by learning that we can just swap out the software and go much further than anybody imagined. So, it's a totally different question of trying to create life from scratch, from basic chemicals. And I think that's important to do when understanding the origins of life. But those aren't the steps that are going to take us dramatically to the next stages. We are trying to design cells right now, as Walter Kistler earlier mentioned, to try and create new fuels from CO^2 and sunlight. Try to design new systems so that living systems that will self-replicate.

Velamoor: With regards to decoding your own genome, what I've gathered is, that there has been a gene identified that demonstrates whether you have moist ear wax or dry earwax. And in this case, you have determined that in your own genome, its moist. If I understand it correctly, what else have you found?

Dr. Venter: Well, that sort of sums up the status of our knowledge. In fact, the earwax was a particular fascination to Canadians. The Canadian press constantly talked about the earwax.

Velamoor: Really? Interesting.

Dr. Venter: But we are at the early stages of reading the genetic code, we now know how to do that, and we're scaling up to hopefully over this decade do 10,000 human genomes. The challenge is interpreting the genetic code. And so, in fact, that's the goal, we are trying to do thousands of genomes. So, not only the genetic code but we're trying to get complete Phenotypic information on all these people, so we can do one of the biggest calculations ever in history and find out, for the first time truly, what is genetic and what is environmental? What's nature and what's nurture? What part of human existence is purely genetic or mostly genetic? Those are all answerable questions. We have the technology, we have the interest to do it, and whether it takes one decade or two or three, within that time frame we will know most of these answers. That's a pretty exciting prospect. Right now, we're staring at a lot of earwax.

Velamoor: Talking about nature and nurture again, I refer to one of the statements that you have in your book:

> One of the most profound discoveries that I have made in all my research is, that you cannot define a human life or any life, based on DNA alone. Without understanding the environment in which cells or species exist, life cannot be understood. An organism's environment is ultimately as unique as its genetic code.

Is this being apologetic? Is this being politically correct or is it truly something that is the case? That the environment and the genetics are inextricably linked, and one cannot separate the other in understanding.

Dr. Venter: One thing I like about the Kistler Prize, it is not known for political correctness.

Velamoor: Right, that's the reason for the question.

Dr. Venter: Nobody has ever accused me of being politically correct or trying for it. It came from doing experiments and trying to interpret them. In 1995 we sequenced the first two genomes of living organisms and one of them had 500 genes and the other had 1,800. We just asked simple questions, could we get down to a smaller simpler genome in a simpler life form that might tell us about the origins of life. We started knocking out genes in this very small genome. In fact, it's the same one that we made synthetically earlier this year, trying to understand if the cell could live without certain genes. And what we found instead is that to get to the secret genetic code for life, the genetic code is only half of the equation, and the environment is the other half. It's a very simple experiment. The cell will live long, two sugars, glucose, and fructose. There's a gene that it codes for a cell surface transporter for each sugar. So, if you knock out the gene for the glucose transporter and you have fructose in the media, the cell happily lives because it could live off of fructose. And so, if you were coding things you would say, that glucose transporter is not an essential gene for life. But if you do the same experiment and you only have glucose in the media, you knock out the glucose transporter gene, the cell dies. And you'd say under those conditions it's essential for life. The difference is not in the genes, it's what's in the environment. So, we have to define the environment and we have to define the genes. This is for the simplest cell we know in history. Just think how complex it is for you and I with a hundred trillion cells and 23,000 genes in each cell. So, the environment is critical. It was a very humbling experiment. As a molecular biologist working on the genetic code thinking we could define life on that basis, now we know that we can't

Velamoor: I see. This is an area that not much has probably been explored, having to do with knowing what you know about genomics, even at this early stage. What are the potentials for weaponizing in terms of biological warfare, agricultural sabotage, and things like that? Is it possible?

Dr. Venter: It certainly is possible. Humanity's been using biological warfare for a long time. In the early stages of this country, where these troops would give out blankets contaminated with Smallpox to kill the Indians - that's biological warfare. We've seen it in even more recent history. You don't need to be able to engineer the genome to try and do harm to others. We saw that with the anthrax attacks. Humans, as we know, looking back in history, have a sad history in terms of violence against our fellow humans. Could this technology be used for that? Yes, but if you look at that question, there are so many different readily available things. Any farm can give you anthrax for example. But there is no need to weaponize genomics. As we can design the genetic code, as we can make it, we can bring back extinct species. So, that's now been done with the third virus that was made. The 1918 flu virus was reconstructed in the laboratory. It was almost a true Jurassic Park-scenario, where RNA was isolated from a virus of a soldier that died in 1918, whose tissues were kept in Washington and from a woman who died in 1918 and was buried in the permafrost. So, the RNA was still intact in her lungs. The RNA was isolated from the 1918 flu virus and sequenced. And looking at the sequence, none of us looking at it could tell why that virus was so virulent and why it killed so many people and even how to build a vaccine against it. So, using the synthetic probe processes, it was reconstructed at the CDC in Atlanta and now we know what parts lead to the lethal effects of it. And new vaccines are already in development that hopefully could prevent another pandemic, but that's a species that everybody thought had completely disappeared and was brought back by synthetic technique. So, science fiction scenarios that we all thought were science fiction are potentially doable.

Velamoor: If I understand correctly, I think it was Japanese scientists who were trying to do the same with the Mastodon or the Woolly Mammoth that was found buried in the Siberian ice.

Dr. Venter: DNA from woolly mammoths is being isolated. It hasn't been sequenced yet. In Germany we're getting the sequence of Neanderthals. Like we don't have enough of them in Washington already.

[laughter]

Velamoor: This is something we were discussing yesterday. Do you think Neanderthals and modern humans not only interacted but cohabited and reproduced?

Dr. Venter: You know, I got drafted and was in the Navy. My view is they coexisted after what I saw in the Navy. They certainly tried to reproduce.

[laughter]

Velamoor: That's what I was telling Walter Kistler the other day saying, "you just walk around, and you see many that resemble some mixture of both'.

Dr. Venter: But the evidence right now for the limited genetic information is, there is no evidence of crossbreeding, but it's still early with what we know.

Velamoor: What would you guess?

Dr. Venter: It's more unusual if they didn't. They coexisted in time. If they coexisted geographically, you know, it's possible that there's enough molecular differences in the sperm and egg recognition, that even if they try, they weren't able to reproduce. That's a possibility. As I said from what I saw in the military, if they coexisted, they tried.

[laughter]

Velamoor: One of your contemporaries, and I'm not sure I would describe the situation as a colleague, perhaps a competitor, in the process of doing approximately similar things, walked into a forest and saw the mind of God. What about you?

Dr. Venter: I think he found magic mushrooms.

[laughter]

Velamoor: I'm referring of course to Francis Collins who worked along in similar time frames, to do what he already did. And the race was won by Dr. Venter if I am putting it correctly.

Dr. Venter: I don't think we need religion to explain science. We may need science to explain religion.

Velamoor: I'll have to think about that. Again, in terms of going into that realm a little bit more, progressively we as humans have been de-centered and de-structured in terms of our own importance. Relative to everything else around us. How do you think we are handling it and how do you think the scenario will unfold?

Dr. Venter: I'm not sure I agree with the statement. You can't turn on television without either seeing Britney Spears or Governor Palin right now. I mean, we do just the opposite with how we treat people and trying to make them seem far more important than they actually are. I don't think we're decentered at all, as a species. We're constantly expanding the challenges. Over the next 40 years, we're going to go from roughly 6.7 billion to maybe 9 or 9.5 billion people. I was born in 1946. There's now three people alive for everybody that existed the year that I was born and soon that will be four. Humanity has never faced this kind of expansion in population, testing the limits of everything that we know about in society, and the limits of what our planet can absorb. I think those are the fundamental challenges we are facing.

Velamoor: Earlier on, you referred to the ability for humans to take over evolution. How do you think that's going to intersect *vis-à-vis* with what you just said which is, having taken over human evolution, breeding, and going to be 9 billion soon, what are we doing to the environment? If we are doing something to it? Is this a good idea taking over evolution or is it just simply a delusion that we are?

Dr. Venter: It's not clear yet how fast we can take over human evolution. In my views, we have to take over evolution if we're going to survive. We have to find alternatives to burning oil and coal. What we're taking now is probably here for over the next few decades roughly. I think that number is now roughly 4.2 billion tons of

CO_2 that remain added to the atmosphere each year. Just from burning this ancient carbon. We're not going to have enough clean water, enough food, and enough fuel for all this new humanity, unless we change what we do. I was at the meeting in Davos in January and the consensus was, there's basically nothing in the next 40 years of new technologies, wind, solar, that could have more than a few percentage differences. The only wild card is if we can harness biology to produce fuels from the sun. So, the only true game changer that we have in the near future, is biology.

Velamoor: I believe it was in the TED presentation (2007), that you had discussed the fact that in about 18 months, if I'm not mistaken, you would have an alternative in terms of energy. Would you care to elaborate on that?

Dr. Venter: Well, the important thing is, I didn't say 18 months from when.

[laughter]

Velamoor: I'm more interested in the technology so that people here can understand what the mechanics, what the biology is, how the elements come together. Walter was referring to it in terms of some chemical ingredients and photosynthesis and biology and so on. Enlighten me on that.

Dr. Venter: We have a number of different approaches we're taking at a company called Synthetic Genomics. One is, we have a major program with BP where we're looking at life deep in the earth. So, with the Sorcerer Global Ocean Sampling Expedition we found new life all around and the oceans. This time we went a mile deep in the earth, found 50- to 70-million-year-old water, and the question is "would there be life there and how much life would there be?".

Velamoor: This is in the core, not the oceans?

Dr. Venter: That's right. A mile into the core of the earth. There was more life there, a higher density, and more diversity.

Velamoor: How hot is it down there?

Dr. Venter: It's less than a hundred degrees centigrade.

Velamoor: That's it?

Dr. Venter: We know now in biology, the world's record is 116 degrees centigrade, I think. For an organism, that's its optimal temperature. So, the estimations are, there's more life beneath the crust than in the oceans. And these organisms, we have large numbers of them that live off coal, break down the coal and produce methane. But most of the methane from coal to methane, and the methane that's in coal mines, that causes all the problems, is biological. So, we're understanding these processes to see if we can speed them up quite substantially. You get about a tenfold improvement of going from mining coal and burning it, versus biologically converting it into natural gas. And that's one huge reserve but it's still taking old carbon out of the ground, and eventually adding it to the atmosphere. So, we have programs where we're changing the genetic code of different types of cells using different processes. We have some that go from sugar to gasoline or diesel fuel directly. We have others, as Walter described, we're going from sunlight and CO^2 to making chemicals that could go right into a diesel engine, right into a jet engine, without any purification or refining.

The challenge will just be the capex for building the fields to grow these in and the apparatus for doing it and harvesting these. It's an embarrassment in this country that we put a tiny fraction of the federal science budget towards any of these problems and it's only because there's private capital available to try these new things. These are obviously hot campaign issues but the government's done virtually nothing about energy. And they are then wanting to drill more oil wells. There's lots of groups with different solutions based on different biological engineering to change manufacturing in this country and around the world. This is hardly even being discussed, let alone people recognizing that this is a transformational period. Within 10 years, the equation could be totally different.

Velamoor: If the starting point of the 18-month was today, are you on track?

Dr. Venter: We're getting ready to build our first pilot facility. We will start building in January, so we hope to have something going on scale. But let's not lose track of the scale. If we built a micro refinery that could make 20,000 liters a day from sunlight or from sugar, we need a million of those refineries to replace what we do every day with oil. It's a huge challenge. Biology is scalable, which is why theoretically, it's one of the few things that could work. But coming up instantly with a million refineries that can do this, is a big challenge.

Velamoor: One of the things I've always wondered about, and I don't know about everybody else in the room, what are the tools of a geneticist? Like a biologist or somebody studying chemistry, I can walk into their lab and there's a Bunsen burner, there's pipettes and tubes and different liquids and so on. What are the basic tools of a geneticist?

Dr. Venter: There's different types of geneticists but essential is that we use the computer. We've digitized the genetic code, we're not taking the genetic code back out of the computer, and we can then, from these four bottles of chemicals, synthesize those molecules in the lab and come up with new pathways to do these processes. But if you look at a lab, they're extremely ordinary people using micro-pipettes, we have robots that do some things, we have some pretty amazing instruments, but it's mostly what happens in people's minds and using the data in the computer and transforming that in the lab.

Velamoor: So, it's mostly having to do with models and simulations.

Dr. Venter: There's no simulations.

Velamoor: Actual manipulation.

Dr. Venter: And then using Chemistry to build things. Because you can build it once at a micro scale and with the replication of biology you can make billions or trillions of copies of the same thing.

Velamoor: One of the things you have said is,

As people start to get genotyped, they'll be able to take control of their lives. Our database will allow them to know their future. Technological implications of each of us carrying a card with our genome as it relates to health behavior and intelligence.

Dr. Venter: I've said that very early on.

Velamoor: Would you like to restate that?

Dr. Venter: Well, I certainly think that we won't know the genetic code for intelligence, but what we will know is things like risk for heart disease or risk for some types of cancer. Because only about three to five percent of cancer is actually genetic in terms of what we would inherit from our parents. Most cancer is genetic in terms of genetic damage accumulated during a lifetime from smoking, radiation, chemical damage etc. One example, statins are clearly a preventive medicine. Depending on whether you know your risk from family history, eventually we'll know the real risk for each of us from our genetic code for heart disease and stroke. Some of the latest data is on prostate cancer. There's a clear genetic predictability of prostate cancer. If then there is a drug that can be given to prevent prostate cancer, it doesn't make any sense to give it to the whole population. But by doing genetic tests, you know you're in the group for that increased risk, like a statin, that could make sense for you to take that preventive medicine. The future of medicine is going to be preventing diseases, avoiding them. We have a society that, in medicine, like we respond to everything in society, wants to instantly fix problems that have occurred. We're not very good at preventing the problems and that's what we have to learn how to do. That's what the genetic code can help teach us for those components that are genetic.

Velamoor: If you were a betting man, what time frames would you assign approximately for the fact, for instance, that medicine as we know it will change radically?

Dr. Venter: Medicine is very hard to change. Recent studies have shown that less than fifty percent of physicians in this country practice the accepted standard of care. So, even if you know something, that's hard to change. That's one type of challenge. We have to teach insurance companies, governments and third-party payers that it's cheaper for them to prevent diseases than to treat them afterwards. That's a social challenge and a mathematical challenge and an argument much more than anything else. I'm part of the XPrize. We have a 10-million-dollar prize right now for whoever gets the technology for rapidly sequencing human genomes for around a thousand dollars. There are at least two companies now looking like they might have something in a couple of years. So, instead of costing 5 billion dollars in the federal program, or a hundred million at the program at Celera, we're now doing human genome sequencing for roughly one and a half million dollars. But if we get it down towards one and a half thousand, suddenly doing tens of thousands, tens of millions, will be possible and that's when medicine will start to change. Once we have that data.

Velamoor: Looking at a thousand-year time frame, do you suppose it'd be reasonable to think that humans can be understanding the genomics, can be tailored or engineered for habitation and other environments outside of the earth?

Dr. Venter: Are we talking about blue states or red states?

[laughter]

Velamoor: I'm talking about the blue yonder states up there. Typically, maybe for space.

Dr. Venter: I see. Well, some have argued, and some of those arguments we've heard tonight, humanity's only choice is to leave this planet. And many people have argued that there are two choices. Leaving the planet or changing the genetic code. I think we actually have other options, and we start adopting them quickly. For example, change how we deal with things on the planet, find alternate energy sources chemically, and make it so we can survive and so that a thousand years from now, people here can have that discussion intelligently. I think that's possible. Not at the rate we're going though.

Velamoor: Yes, if you have observed, Dr. Venter, I haven't taken the bait on any of the statements regarding blue and red or the personalities involved and the current elections. I would love to continue that conversation outside this framework. And that's primarily because the Foundation is prohibited from politically getting involved in any sort of discussion about the future. Our primary focus is on science. Is there any question that I should ask, that I didn't?

>**Dr. Venter:** Yes.

>**Velamoor:** Please. What might that be?

>**Dr. Venter:** I'm not going to tell.

>[laughter]

>**Velamoor:** Dr. Venter, thank you very much you!

Interview sourced from the archives of the Foundation For the Future.

References

Venter, J.C. (2007, May 3rd). *Craig Venter: A voyage of DNA, genes and the sea*. [Video] Youtube. https://www.youtube.com/watch?v=E5X6Qy772YU&ab_channel=TED

Venter, J. C. (2008). *A Life Decoded: My Genome: My Life*. (Reprint ed.) Penguin Books.

Further Readings

Venter, J.C. (2013). *Life at the Speed of Light: From the Double Helix to the Dawn of Digital Life*. Viking Press.

Venter J.C. & Duncan, D.E. (expected 2022). *The New Darwin: A Revolution in Our Understanding of the Natural World*. Robinson

15
CHAPTER

An Interview with Svante Pääbo (2009)

Svante Pääbo

Dr. Pääbo, a Swedish-born biologist specializing in evolutionary genetics, is the Director of the Department of Genetics at Max Planck Institute for Evolutionary Anthropology in Leipzig, Germany. Dr. Pääbo was awarded the Kistler Prize in 2009 for a body of work with ancient DNA, beginning in 1984 with the demonstration of DNA survival in a 2,400-year-old mummy. He developed and refined the techniques used to isolate and sequence ancient DNA, thus playing a key role in creating the field of Molecular Paleontology. Dr. Pääbo's work is of a pioneering nature in terms of connecting the science of genetics with human evolution at very basic levels. His work takes on the macro issues of the origins of humans and why modern humans composed an evolutionary experiment that worked while other near species did not.

An Interview with
Svante Pääbo

(2009)

Svante Pääbo was interviewed in 2008.
The transcript of this conversation can be found on the following pages.

Seshadri Velamoor: How would you characterize the main organizing principle or the framework or the paradigm of your research?

Dr. Svante Pääbo: It's a difficult question. What we would really like to do is, find a sort of biological background for unifying and universal themes in humans today, that makes us unique compared to all organisms that exist today and our closest extinct relatives. That will be sort of a biological substrate of what makes humans culture possible, not what explains human culture but something like a scaffold that made that building of human culture possible.

Velamoor: You are the director of Evolutionary Anthropology at the Max Planck Institute in Germany. In the course of your term there, you have brought together DNA experts, Linguists, Primatologists, Psychologists, essentially an interdisciplinary collaboration. In this context, what are your views on the future of scientific research? And secondly, what are you views on our current system of education and the future of conventional traditional academic disciplines like Anthropology, Sociology, Psychology?

Dr. Pääbo: It depends on the area of science and research probably but if you are interested in questions about human uniqueness, what sets humans apart, that's per definition an interdisciplinary question. It's very valuable to bring together different disciplines that are traditionally at the universities and very much kept apart, such as humanities, natural sciences and so on. The principle we found to bring them together was actually to focus on the fact that for the litmus test to be able to work, it has to be empirical, it has to be data-based because there is actually no problem for me to understand what a linguist does as long as her or his work is data-based, so you can discuss your ideas, what data should be collected and how you test it. That's how everybody in this institute works and on that level it's really possible to work in an interdisciplinary way and contribute to each other's work.

Velamoor: Studies are showing that the phenotypic differences between humans and chimpanzees are due not so much to mutation and selection but due to differential gene expression. First, what do you mean by gene expression. Also, what are the factors that affect gene expression. For instance, I've been reading about the fact that there have been studies of diets on mice that have changed gene expression.

Dr. Pääbo: This goes back to the work of Mary-Claire King and Alan Wilson at Berkeley (1975) who first pointed out few decades ago or so, that gene expression is probably a very major cause to the differences between humans and the great apes. But it's only in the last five to ten years that we've gotten the technical possibilities to investigate that. For example, you look on what genes are turned on and off, until what level are they turned on and make proteins in different tissues between humans and chimps and so on. It's actually a lot of genes, maybe ten percent, that differ significantly. That is not to be seen as some total dichotomy with nucleotide sequence changes because those expression changes actually relied to a large extent on Nucleotide changes in regulatory sequences in the genome for example. It's of course also true that much of such differences in how genes are turned on and off are due to influences from the environment. We did an experiment that you referred to, where we fed laboratory mice for different diets. The normal diet they get in the mouse house or the foods our employees get in the cafeteria.

[laughter]

Or the food that our chimpanzees get in the ape facility in the zoo in Leipzig (Germany) and the fourth one was a bit more sensitive - an exclusive McDonald's diet.

[laughter]

The interesting result of that was that the McDonald's mice became more like a tennis ball's forms after a few weeks, and they were very happy.

[laughter]

When we then compared gene expression in the liver of these mice, although the McDonald's mice were very fat and the ones on our cafeteria diet were much leaner, the two ones on a human diet differed significantly in their level and what genes had turned on. So, there's really something in this human diet that is quite different, and we don't really know what that is. It might have to do with cooking for example. Another interesting thing was also that there was an overlap of those genes that changed in those mice with the differences we see between humans and chimpanzees when they look in the liver. Much of this is also due to simply behavioral differences in what we eat for example.

Velamoor: In terms of the terminology that most of us would understand, where does that kind of research put the argument in terms of nature versus nurture? As to who we turn out to be as people or mice?

Dr. Pääbo: I think, as always, it's really a combination. There is of course a clear biological foundation for being a human. What one doesn't do today, but it was done earlier, is trying to put newborn chimpanzee children in a human family because they will learn many things, they will learn say 100 or 200 words, but they will not become fully adequate in human language or in human behavior. So, there is clearly sort of biological substrates that we are very interested in finding out for being a human but much of what we fill that substrate with is of course culture.

Velamoor: To take an example. A pregnant woman in prenatal conditions. Do differing prenatal conditions affect different gene expressions?

Dr. Pääbo: I'm no expert in that but I'm sure it will.

Velamoor: On to Neanderthals for a minute. Your research specified that Neanderthal seemed to have gone extinct between 24,000 to 30,000 years ago. Evidence in a cave in Gibraltar seems to suggest that they were far more capable than what was understood earlier. Fire, tools etc. have been found. So, what accounts for their extinction? Multiple reasons have been given but what is your take?

Dr. Pääbo: That's the million-dollar question and no one knows the answer. I sometimes try to avoid the question by saying that it says more about us and our worldview how we speculate about why Neanderthals are not there than about what really happened. You can go either way. You could say, clearly it was the first genocide, look how we behave today to each other - we must have killed them all and it can sound plausible. I can say that looking in the Middle East, the earliest fully modern humans appear there 30,000 years ago. The last Neanderthals were there around 60,000 years ago, so we have 30,000 years of peaceful coexistence back in the Middle East. That also sounds plausible. So, which of these versions are true? We really don't know. I think there is clearly an argument for that when modern humans come to an area and establish themselves, after a while at least, Neanderthals do disappear. I do think it has something to do with humans and probably competition, but what form that competition was, we probably will never really know.

Velamoor: You're referring to competition. I have read also about possible other reasons such as climate change, inbreeding and cannibalism among the Neanderthals. Is there any plausibility to those explanations?

Dr. Pääbo: I would regard them all as most implausible. The Neanderthals had survived several periods of very harsh conditions before. After all, they existed as a group in the order of 400,000 years. I think maybe we should come together in 300,000 years and see if we are as successful as the Neanderthals were.

[laughter]

Velamoor: Do we see them amongst us today? Meaning, did they interbreed?

Dr. Pääbo: That is something that we are analyzing just in these weeks. We have the first version of the Neanderthal genome. What is already known is that there is not any large contribution, specifically to Europe. One would have seen that in the variation in humans that exist today. But we can now ask much more detailed questions about this possible interaction, for example, gene mixing can go two ways of course. For the first time we can look in the Neanderthals. If there was contribution from early human ancestors in the Neanderthals. Or even very early on for example, if say, 100,000 or 200,000 years ago there were connections between early human ancestors and Neanderthal ancestors.

Velamoor: The central role that biology has taken in the last 40 to 50 years, ever since the DNA molecule was first configured by Watson and Crick (1953), when it comes to understanding ourselves, where do you think this will lead? Do you foresee a day when the human or all life will be an open book? If at all, when?

Dr. Pääbo: I do not think that life will be an open book through genomics or genetics. It's always fascinating to me. I'm old enough in this business now. 20 years ago, I had a talk with journalists about saying, wait a minute, it's not only environment and education, it's also genes that matters. Now I'm in the opposite role by telling them, wait a minute, is not only genes, it's all these other things that also matter.

Velamoor: It turns out that just accidentally, the day before yesterday I got home, and I happen to be flipping channels and PBS had a show on hand-walking humans (Harrison & Holt, 2006) - a family in Turkey where five of 17 children never got past the stage of crawling. Now between the ages of 18 and 34, they are still crawling on their fours. Then, in the same show, there was another group of youngsters in the UK where the children had difficulties with their speaking abilities. A third example was given about what they described as a micro encephalic, where the brain sizes are as small as it was in earlier primates.

I know your research has to do with Forkhead box protein P2 (FOXP2). If you would tell us a little bit more about the FOXP2 and what might that entail as it relates to those five children that have speaking disabilities. One of the speculations in the show was, a Turkish geneticist or evolutionary biologist suggested that it indicated devolution, meaning a step backwards as far as evolution was concerned, though largely discounted. Is this another example of gene expression where it is truncated at a stage that failed to evolve into the stages where one is able to talk, or one is able to walk?

Dr. Pääbo: I think it's more the situation that these diseases that you find by genetic means will point you to genes that are important for a plan. For example, in speech production at FOXP2. If there is a copy of the FOXP2 gene destroyed by a mutation, you will have a severe speech and language problem. That led Tony Monica's group to identify the scene. Now you have a gene that you know is important in this process but this mutation that destroys the gene is not a step back in evolution to some earlier stage, but it allows you to study the genome and that's important. When we then sequence it in humans and the Apes, we find two substitutions in this very conserved gene that was unique to humans.

Velamoor: Substitutions compared to a FOXP2 in what?

Dr. Pääbo: In the apes. In chimpanzees and gorillas and all the other primates. When we then engineer those two substitutions into a mouse FOXP2 gene, we can confirm that this seems to have something to do with vocalization because the mice do keep differently when you do that. But that's not the same mutations as in their family because those mutations simply knock out the gene. These are two mutations that change from one functional state to another functional state in the gene and I think for understanding evolution of some human specific traits, that would perhaps be a way to go on in the future, to construct animal models like that for some tiny aspects of them that you can then study.

Velamoor: Going back to the Neanderthals for a second. Just as they are trying to do with the Woolly Mammoth, do you suppose we would be able to reconstruct a Neanderthal with the correct substitutions in the FOXP2 so they would be amongst us talking?

Dr. Pääbo: First, the Neanderthals had the same version of FOXP2 as us. But on the more general question, of course not. I know there are people that go around and say we will clone the Neanderthals and find out what they're like, but I think it's sort of both technically and ethically totally indefensible to contemplate that. We would not create the human being purely for scientific curiosity.

Velamoor: The Nobel laureate Paul Dirac made a statement which is quite remarkable basically saying, the solution of great problems requires the giving up of great prejudices. What might be some of the prejudices in your field that you currently see that you and your discipline have to give up?

Dr. Pääbo: That is of course a hard question. That's a difficult one.

Velamoor: I think we can pass on it for you. Let's get to the last question and then we'll turn it over to the audience. You have been chasing a question for 25 years now. What makes humans human? Have you found the answer?

Dr. Pääbo: No, we have not, but we hope we are a bit closer and that we will be a lot closer with the Neanderthal genome providing a tool for the biological community at large, to ask questions. It's not so that we will stare at the Neanderthal genome and have all the answers but it's a tool for future biologists to really ask these questions in a much better way.

Velamoor: Thank you. At this point, we can get to the audience. Anybody who has a question? We have time for a few.

Audience Member 1: I'm not a geneticist by training but having listened to your talk about the pathologies of chimpanzees and early man, I wonder if you were on the Aesthetic Committee for the Kistler organization, if you would change the relative proportions of the double helix and the world conversely?

Dr. Pääbo: So, making the DNA smaller or bigger?

Audience Member 1: I think the DNA molecule much smaller and the world much bigger based on what I learned from your talked. To clarify, it's just a question about the enormous changes that have occurred, that are largely superficial in the human genome, because of the radiation environmentally across the broad time.

Dr. Pääbo: It's of course true that we don't have huge genetic changes but important ones in the origin of humans and there are probably actually rather few changes in my dream world. It is rather few changes we will identify that have allowed humans then to develop technology and culture and change the biosphere as we have. So, I do think that the genomic changes will be quite important to find. But I don't know about the proportions, maybe we can keep them.

Audience Member 2 [Dr. Charles Murray]: The book published recently for general audience by Gregory Cochran and Henry Harpending, *The 10,000 Year Explosion* (2009), essentially argues that human evolution has not stopped and that indeed there have been very important evolutionary changes in the last 10,000 years since the advent of Agriculture. Cochran and Harpending are especially well-known for their argument that Ashkenazi Jews for example, and the elevated IQ there, is a product of a matter of centuries from about 800 to 1500. I just would like to have your reaction as you read that sort of thing, and as to how it fits into the way you see the data.

Dr. Pääbo: I would really be extremely skeptic of that. I would say that, in a growing population it takes a long time for a new mutation to come to fixation or come to high frequencies. We would have to think about very high selection coefficients and a very high advantage of a new variant for it to have a chance to spread. And the few examples we have with agriculture and lactose tolerance for example, it is particularly those things where we directly interact with environment as I pointed out. Something that we eat, where we sort of have a very direct influence. So, I would really tend to think that those things are to a large extent cultural differences.

Audience Member 3 [Dr. King]: You defer a bit the question of how you would consider the biases among people in our field and what you would consider to be interesting biases in our field. I wonder if the biases of our field might include the arrogance of exceptionalism and that every culture considers itself exceptional and uniquely promised in some way, and indeed every culture may be exceptional and uniquely promised in some way, but all cultures are. The heterogeneity within the human species is so great that every culture indeed has the right to make this claim, but no culture has the right to make it uniquely on the basis of genetic heterogeneity and genotypic analysis.

Dr. Pääbo: Of course, there is a bias in our culture with the technological advances we have, to claim exceptionalism. That may be something one looks back to one day and points to us as an enormous bias in this time. That could well be. [crosstalk] But I mean, perhaps to sort of relate to this foundation too, I guess it's also true that precisely this economic and technological development that our culture produced, is what influences the biosphere to this extent today. So, it does come perhaps with a special responsibility to think about what we do.

Audience Member 4: Earlier, you commented on the experiment with rats and we know that, in terms of agricultural systems, there's a lot of emphasis over time around monocultures, particular breeds of agricultural being reinforced over and over again, so if you were to fast forward and if we continue on that trend where we're developing singular species of potatoes, that we're creating fries all around the world or we're basically narrowing down the food which we eat. Is there a possibility that we lose some of the diversity that we've gained over the last 300,000 years and does that put us at risk to become like the Neanderthals?

Dr. Pääbo: I do think that it puts a domesticated species at risk. I don't know how convinced I am that it poses a risk to us as a species because we still have a huge diversity of things that we consume and eat. But I do think it puts our cultivars at risk.

Audience Member 5: As far as the current dating for *Homo sapiens* goes, it takes it back to about 200,000 years ago. It's only three quarters the way through that period, so about 50,000 years ago, that you an effervescent creativity. Lots of tools, tiles, lots of habits and planning ahead and things like that. It's sometimes called the "creative explosion". There's the question of why the emergence of these three quarters of the way through the *Homo sapiens* period. Would you care to comment?

Dr. Pääbo: I really have no strong opinions of that. It's of course also true that the archaeological record is very imprecise. It could very well be that there was a cumulative sort of ratchet-like effect where you accumulated these things, and they appear then to suddenly come later in the record.

Audience Member 6: Do you have any hunches, empirical or otherwise, about some of the mutations that may in fact stick with our species in the future? What can we look forward to in the near term as possible mutations for adaptation?

Dr. Pääbo: In a way my bias with that would be to say that any genetic change in humans is so slow that I would really expect any response to things to be cultural. I would really think that it is fruitless to speculate about genetic change in the future when we don't know the cultural change. Sometimes I like when I talk to people about this and say, traffic accidents is a big risk to our children. But we're not waiting for mutations that make them look out for cars, we create sort of crosswalks and talk to them about looking out for cars. It's a cultural response to this cultural, technological threat. I think that's really where the future is. I think we have to live pretty much with the gene pool in the genome we have and adapt culturally

Audience Member 7: Will our modern species as we're here today and our whole civilization as we know it globally, go extinct?

Dr. Pääbo: Eventually, absolutely but why and when, I have no clue.

Interview sourced from the archives of the Foundation For the Future.

References

Cochran, G. & Harpending, H. (2009). *The 10,000 Year Explosion: How Civilization Accelerated Human Evolution*. Basic Books.

Harrison, J. & Holt, S. (Producers). (2006, November 14th). *Family that walks on all fours*. [Television Broadcast]. PBS.

Watson, J.D. & Crick, F.H.C. (1953). Molecular Structure of Nucleic Acids: A Structure for Deoxyribose Nucleic Acid. *Nature*. 171 (4356), 737–738, DOI:10.1038/171737a0

Wilson, A. C. & King, M.C. (1975). Evolution at two levels in humans and chimpanzees. *Science*, 188 (4184), 107-116. DOI: 10.1126/Science.1090005

An Interview with Leroy Hood (2010)

Leroy Hood

Dr. Hood, Co-founder and President of the Institute for Systems Biology, Seattle, is one of the world's leading scientists in Systems Biology, Biotechnology, Immunology, and Genomics. Dr. Hood received the Kistler Prize in 2010 for creating the technological foundation for the sciences of Genomics and Proteomics through the invention of five groundbreaking instruments and for explicating the potentialities of genome and proteome research into the future through his pioneering of the fields of Systems Biology and Systems Medicine. Dr. Hood's long-term passion for working at the frontiers of biology and medicine has greatly aided humankind's understanding of how genetics impacts human society, and significantly improved health and life for individuals dealing with a variety of serious illnesses. Going forward, his inventions and achievements make possible a revolution to predictive and preventive medicine specific to the individual and replace the reactive approach common today based for groups.

An Interview with
Leroy Hood

(2010)

Leroy Hood was interviewed in 2010.
The transcript of this conversation can be found on the following pages.

Seshadri Velamoor: Let us talk a little bit about consciousness. As I've heard it described, consciousness is a biological property of the brain, much like the firing of neurons or the production of neurotransmitters and biology will someday be able to explain how organic tissue can produce it. Would you agree?

Dr. Leroy Hood: I would say that consciousness is certainly the hardest biological problem that I know of by far. I would say none of the techniques we have now, that is, analytic techniques, that we have now, can probably begin to measure the critical parameters of consciousness. And I think the one hope we have is for imaging techniques that in the future, will be able to take precise and detailed pictures of the brain down to the point of seeing how individual molecules in certain cells will change themselves. If we can do that, then I think we can begin to unravel some of the issues that might be easier than consciousness, like memory and things like that. Now, we have a little bit of a biochemical handle on memory but it's at the very earliest stages. But I just do not see any techniques out there. I mean, because the brain is an incredibly complex system and because its properties are a consequence of that system, you have to study brain function in the context of the brain. So, we have to develop the tools for being able to do that. And do I think we will? Absolutely, but I have no idea what the timescale for that might be.

Velamoor: Before, you have described the disease aspects of it. What are the potentials for emotions and behavior?

Dr. Hood: I think with the kinds of tools that we've developed now, we can really begin to get at complex genetic diseases such as Schizophrenia and many others that have a big component. The problem with a disease like Schizophrenia is exactly the same as a disease like Alzheimer's, namely it is an enormously complicated mixture of different entities, and we have to be able to stratify those entities into discrete types that have defined molecular network correlates that we can do. And I think that is going to be possible and again, I think these IPS (Induced Pluripotent Stem) cells that I talked about, offer us an enormously exciting way to be able to take from any one of you, a little bit of blood and get in a test tube, whichever of your tissues we need, to be able to interrogate and to deal with complicated diseases of that tissue.

Velamoor: The reasons for your creating the Institute for Systems Biology, if I am characterizing it correctly, was based on some disillusionment with the idea of pursuing your interest in the academic disciplines in a university environment. So, what would you change if you were in charge and had a free hand to say, "you can go about re-designing academia any which way you would like"?

Dr. Hood: I think the trouble with any new idea is that it is a mismatch often from the institute in which it rises because the bureaucracies of those institutes are really formed by the past, and they're not set up to be able to deal with the future. Almost no institutions can deal very effectively with future. The one example in industry that I've read a lot on, and it's really fascinating, is some of the bigger companies have actually formed what they call skunk works, where they put together a group of people and say you can work on this new problem and we're releasing you from all of the profit and loss constraints. And what happens inevitably with those skunk works is, when they do succeed it is impossible to reintegrate them. Almost always they end up going off and being other kinds of companies. So, I think academia does things very well. I think what it can't deal with very well, is really truly new kind of innovation. And then I think the best thing to do is to split out and create a new institution. The institution we created is great for doing what we're doing now but I have no disillusions about the fact that, in 20 years, we may not be able to deal with the things that are going to come in the future. It's what I said at the beginning, I think new ideas require new organizational structures and I think it's really difficult to achieve them in old institutions.

Now, is there any chance it could be done in academia? I think there is if you had leadership that was really enlightened and was really willing to be flexible in ways most Deans and most Provosts and most Presidents are not. But those are really rare traits, so I'd say if you have really no ideas, go get something new started. But, obviously, the downside of getting something new started, it's really a lot of work and it costs money, and you have to figure out where you're going to get money and things like that. But that is the way to do it - start something new.

Velamoor: Will a reproduction by sex disappear altogether?

Dr. Hood: Gosh, I hope not.

[laughter]

Velamoor: Now the technologies that you are developing have, as you have described, the capacities for disease prevention, prediction and so on. But the capacities also exist for enhancing attributes of humans. What side of that debate would you fall on as it relates to the capacity to enhance attributes? And do you think that if that were to occur, within the time frames that you foresee, will we be creating a hierarchy of humans where some of them have it, some of them don't, and then therefore, those that have it will demand more rights? And will the concept of liberal democracy and the equality of humans disappear?

Dr. Hood: I think that's about a one-hour-answer. So let me say two things. First, we can, by selective breeding, do utterly incredible things and my favorite example of this are dogs. Dogs have been around for less than 10,000 years now and the Phenotype of the dogs has been driven almost entirely by the breeders. And contrasted, a Chihuahua which can sit in a teacup with an Irish Wolfhound, which can be seven feet tall, those are exactly the same species. Those changed from one another in 7,000 - 8,000 years. Now, that's physical appearance. What about mental appearance? Think of what they have bred into herding dogs, like Collies that can herd. You can breed really fascinating mental traits. So, the given is, if we wanted to do selective breeding with humans, we could make enormous differences. Now, I will say, for all the breeding you do with animals, you introduce a lot of negatives too. Those animals never ever could survive in the wild and a lot of them have a lot of problems as you as pet owners probably know. So, we could do these changes in human beings. Would it be a good idea to do it? That obviously is an issue that society would really have to think about and decide. My own guess is that generally, most people and myself would be very much against it for exactly the reasons that you mentioned. You could easily generate Have's and Have-not's. You might generate a culturally superior race of humans that would be hard on the rest of us. I would guess there would also be enormous approbation for selective breeding but I will say, evolution is a powerful tool for sculpting whatever the breeder would like to sculpt. And there is no question, we could make really dramatic changes. I mean, in some senses, that would be a fascinating way to study how the brain works and things like that, but my guess is, only a few people would accede to that as a reasonable kind of objective.

Velamoor: I'm sure you're familiar with Gregory Stock. He argues that the market mechanism should be allowed to function no matter what the implications of such technologies are as opposed to getting businesses and government and other elements involved in this (Neal, 2002). Do you have a position on that? Will it not actually, eventually, evolve? Parents wanting to have children that have enhanced attributes. Will there be mechanisms by which you can even stop attempts such as this?

Dr. Hood: Well, it is not that simple because you're not going to be able to breed what you want in one or two or 10 or 30 generations. You have to take a very long-term view of this, and you would have to set up a program to make sure it's insured. So, I think the market would not stand a chance in pushing those kinds of ideas at all. The market is looking for something fast and clean and I would say, in genetics, there aren't very many fast and clean kinds of things that you can do.

Velamoor: Leon Kass, the Chair of the President's Committee on Ethics, asked the following question: Is it alright to kill a creature made in God's image even before it looks like him? (Adelman, 2005)

Dr. Hood: Is it all right to kill a creature?

Velamoor: He's talking about stem cells and embryonic research and the objections that were raised.

Dr. Hood: Okay. My friend Lee Silver has written a book on this very topic (2006 & 2007) and one of the critical questions is, when does humanity come into a fertilized egg? And his argument is that takes a certain amount of time, and you have certain options prior to that time about doing things you can make arguments about. And everyone makes these arguments as it pushes them up and down, but I think on the other hand, there are getting to be other routes that are going to be really effective in dealing with these kinds of issues. For example, being able to take certain kinds of birth control pill and things like that, that hit at the root of it, even before getting egg and sperm together. So, I think they're talking about how many Angels dancing on a pin there are. And my own feeling is, I mean, one of the interesting questions is, this recent issue that's come up again about embryonic stem cells where a federal court judge said, "we're going to start restricting that again", so on the one hand, I'm firmly opposed to that. I guess I don't see much difference between using human embryos that are going to be thrown away for mankind's good than just throwing them away and getting no benefit whatsoever. It's just choosing, how you're going to use it. But the other point that is really interesting, is with the emergence of IPS (Induced Pluripotent Stem) cells. There is the possibility you can circumvent any of that kind of argument whatsoever, because here, we are taking a differentiated cell and we're converting it to a stem cell and then we can go to all the different cells you want to. There is even a recent report that you can start with one cell, and you can move it directly to another differentiated cell by putting certain kinds of factors in it. So, my own feeling is, we are going to have a lot of ways of dealing with the issues that have choked us on Embryonic Stem Cells and so forth. But in principle, I really question the judgment that it's better to throw things away than to use them to humanity's good.

Velamoor: Francis Fukuyama, the philosopher, has written the book *Our Posthuman Future* (2002) in which he points out that science and technology from which the modern world springs, themselves represent our Civilization's key vulnerabilities. Airliners, skyscrapers and biology labs, all symbols of modernity were turned into weapons in a stroke of malign ingenuity. What are the potentials for such risks? Such dangers with the kinds of technologies that you are developing? So far, we have discussed all of the positives.

Dr. Hood: I think with all technologies, they have the opportunity to do enormous good and in some cases they clearly can do bad. There's no question about that. And I think what is really critical, is to have not only proper taste and judgment about how to use them, but guidelines and laws that will not let us move in inappropriate direction. So, I think it's impossible to argue that you can't use modern biological technologies to be destructive of human beings if you so desired to do it. But I think what I would argue is, it's a question of what you wanted. If you wanted to destroy human beings, there are much easier ways than doing it with Biology. And if you wanted to create certain kinds of human beings, it's an awful lot easier than these arguments of "We can clone 10,000 Sergeant York's". That's just nonsense because that says, even if you add the right genes, you'd have exactly the same environment that made a Sergeant York and I've argued that that's going to be virtually impossible. So, a lot of the right-wing philosophers have these very narrow points of view, and they argue, I think, from a not very broad point of view. But I will say, there are technologies that you do have to be concerned about and that they don't get used in inappropriate ways and that's why we have laws and Congress to look into these things. They don't always make the right decisions but it's better than nothing.

Velamoor: I know you touched, in your talk, on the whole idea of race and genes and so on. If you could elaborate on the following comment. Is genetic determinism fact or fiction?

Dr. Hood: The reason I think you can't answer a question like that is the object of the genetic determinism isn't specified. So, what one can clearly says is, your genome gives you an envelope of potential that can be enormously modified by your environment. So, if you ask me, at the point of birth, is this embryo genetically determined to become a Hitler? I would say, not at all.

And that's the hope for being able to deal with terrorism. That if we could go to the Mideast and if we could set up schools and jobs and health care and things like that,

I think you can take away a lot of the disillusionment that exists there. It isn't that they are genetically determined to be terrorists, it's that their environment has molded them into this. So, rather than worry about genetic determinism, I am really worried about the environment and how we can optimize that for education, for all the things that we talked about.

Velamoor: Thank you!

Interview sourced from the archives of the Foundation For the Future.

References

Adelman, K. (2005, November 1st). Biotechnology & Stem-Cell Research: Interview with Dr. Leon Kass. *Washingtonian*. https://www.washingtonian.com/2005/11/01/biotechnology-stem-cell-research-interview-with-dr-leon-kass/

Conan, N. (Presenter). (2002, April 15th). Biotechnology. [Audio Podcast]. *Talk of the Nation*. Retrieved from https://www.npr.org/templates/story/story.php?storyId=1141610

Fukuyama, F. (2002). *Our Posthuman Future: Consequences of the Biotechnology Revolution*. Farrar Straus & Giroux.

Silver, L. (2006). *Challenging Nature: The Clash of Science and Spirituality at the New Frontiers of Life*. Ecco.

Silver, L. (2007). *Remaking Eden: How Genetic Engineering and Cloning Will Transform the American Family*. Ecco.

An Interview with Charles Murray (2011)

Charles Murray

Dr. Charles Murray is a political scientist and author best known for his co-authored book *The Bell Curve* in 1994. Murray received the Kistler Prize in 2011. His work has critically examined the assumption that human characteristics can be molded by the right government interventions, drawing upon a large body of evidence documenting the failures of social programs in the USA from the 1960s onward to produce their intended outcomes. He has argued that the reason for these failures is not technical defects in the design or implementation of the programs, but refusal to confront the genetic reality that people differ in their abilities for reasons that are beyond the power of policy to alter and concluding that such programs and policies will yield better results if focused on "individuals" rather than on "groups."

An Interview with Charles Murray

(2011)

Charles Murray was interviewed in 2011.
The transcript of this conversation can be found on the following pages.

Seshadri Velamoor: Dr. Murray, what in retrospect, were the most egregious, extreme misunderstandings and misinterpretations of the ideas in your book *The Bell Curve* (1994)?

Dr. Charles Murray: The obvious one was race. If you have not read *The Bell Curve* and you're old enough to remember when it was published, then what you probably took away from what you read about it was, this is a book of pseudoscience which tries to demonstrate that the blacks are genetically inferior to whites. That was pretty much the story line.

In fact, *The Bell Curve* was about the effects of IQ on the development of class structure in the United States. Which we might get into later with some of the other questions. When it came to the race question, Richard Herrnstein and I, when we wrote that chapter, and rewrote it, had in mind the fact that this was the most incendiary topic in the social sciences. And we wanted to say things very, very precisely and we also wanted to say them very un-hysterically. Because we didn't think there was anything that required you to run screaming from the room if you knew the facts. There were differences in test scores between blacks and whites, between Asians and Whites, with Asians on top, and other kinds of ethnic differences. These test score differences are not the result of bias in the tests but when it comes to the issue of genes versus Environment, Richard Herrnstein and I were explicitly agnostic, and we even put that sentence in italics, I believe. And we said, it seems to us that the jury's still out, we don't know. And we think that people who are either saying "Oh it has to be all environmental" or for that matter "It's genetic", we're both going much farther than the data permitted.

When you would have people, including quite respected social scientists, people with big names, who said Herrnstein and Murray say blacks are genetically inferior to whites. And I would go back and reread that chapter after the book came out and I'd say, "How could we have said this differently?", and the answer is "I don't think we could have". I think we are looking at a Rorschach test where people were taking a very sensitive topic and projecting their own anxieties on to that text. It was something maybe for a psychiatrist to look at.

Velamoor: Just a couple of weeks ago, two scientists, Corey Fincher and Randy Thornhill published a peer-reviewed paper. They suggest that the presence of, and the fighting off of parasites to avoid infection in the childhood years, devotes considerable energy that might otherwise go to a development of the brain which requires nearly 85% of the energy during childhood. And they go on to show that there is a direct correlation between lower IQs, geographic areas across the board, considered where parasites abound and lower IQs (Fincher & Thornhill 2014). Is this another case of an erroneous connection between correlation and causation or is there something to the idea of the plasticity of the brain, especially in the formative years?

Dr. Murray: Well, first, I'm not familiar with this specific research but it's of the same ilk as research which says, "It's the lower IQ and low socioeconomic groups because of exposure to lead at a young age", "It is the result of impoverishment in early years". And there are a variety of environmental explanations which have an element of truth insofar as, there are ways in which you can depress IQ environmentally. If you lock a child in a closet for its first couple of years of life you are going to severely damage the cognitive abilities of that child. If you have starvation, you might have some effect, although there's very interesting data from the Netherlands, where people who were pregnant in the post-war, late war of World War two, it apparently did not have long-lasting effects on IQ. But there are a variety of ways in which, you say, is it possible for the environment to really damage what would otherwise be the genetic level of IQ? Absolutely. But they have to be extreme circumstances. And by the same token, all of you out there who have had children and have gotten just the right mobile to hang above the child's crib that will stimulate its cerebral cortex and play the right music to it, I'm sorry, it didn't help if your children are brilliant, they would have been brilliant even if you hadn't done that. It's really hard to jack up IQ through the environment.

Velamoor: Except for the Flynn-effect.

Dr. Murray: Yes. When you're talking about large-scale differences in IQ among groups, these specific explanations probably have applicability in quite limited times and places. But the idea that they explain the whole thing is hard to swallow.

Velamoor: On to the next book. In *Real Education* (2008) you begin by stating as follows, "The education system is living a lie", and you identify four simple truths. What is this lie and what are the four simple truths?

Dr. Murray: This is going to be really embarrassing but I can't remember the four truths. [laughter]

Real Education came out in 2008. In the history of publishing, I doubt if there has ever been a worse publication date. That book came out in the same couple of weeks that the United States nominated his first African American candidate for President in which Sarah Palin was nominated for the Vice Presidency, and in which the world economy melted down. The book did not get all the attention I wished to have. The lie that I refer to is, that every child can be anything he or she wants to be if only that child gets the right opportunities. It sounds like I'm being hyperbolic. Come on, nobody really believes that. The fact is, no parent who has more than one child is under the impression that you can make both children the same if only you apply the right environmental influences. But that is, in fact, the premise on which American public education is founded. And that will be said quite explicitly. That if you don't have equal outcomes, if children don't advance, it's because of something in the education. The *No Child Left Behind Act*, if you think I'm exaggerating, legislated that all children would be above average. I'm quite serious. They said, by 2014 all children would become proficient and meet the standards of proficiency in Reading and Math. And in effect, that said, by 2014 all the kids are going to be above the average which we have at the time we're passing this law in 2001 or whatever it was. Absolutely insane, that was the lie.

The first of the four simple truths is, that ability varies. I said, these were simple. That from the time children are born and start to grow up, we all know, we all observe that kids have different repertoires. Whether they are cognitive, whether they are personality, or they are in their ability in sports. That was the first of the four simple truths.

The second of the four simple truths is that half of the children are below average. Now, Tom Bouchard is sitting there shaking his head saying, now half of the children are below the median but you get what I mean. The reality is that a lot of kids are not only never going to be rocket scientists, they are also going to have a hard time getting through high school in a lot of cases. But that applies to all kinds of abilities. If you take multiple intelligences of the kind that Howard Gardner (1993) is famous for promulgating, which I think have a lot of value if you think of them as multiple talents, which would make me much happier, but the idea that there are people who have very high interpersonal skills? Absolutely true. And low interpersonal skills? That's true. It's also true that some people who are very smart on verbal skills are very poor in interpersonal skills. All these different dimensions interact. The idea that you say, because someone is below average in verbal abilities, that poor kid is never going to have a fulfilling life, is nuts. You go with each child's strengths. But it is also true that there are some children who get the short end of the stick on a variety of dimensions. Well, they also do not have to live miserable lives. This idea that somehow, we have to have all the kids be above average in these various ways is not only technically wrong, it gives an inflated importance to the kinds of things that the people in this room tend to value in our own lives, because of our own experiences. And it ignores the ways in which everybody should be able to lead a fulfilling life.

The third of the simple truth is, too many people are going to college. Way too many people are going to college. Part of that means that a genuine college education requires skills that are possessed by only 10-15% of the population if you're talking about really doing well. You have a very hard time making that case if you're talking about verbal abilities because after all, everybody can read. But if you go to look at the items that are missed by 70-80% of students in high school on the National Assessment of Educational Progress and then go look at your old college textbooks in terms of what you're expected to be able to understand, verbal abilities sufficient to master college-level material have to be in the top two deciles. And of course, it's obvious with Math. We have lots of Engineers in this room, I bet, and I'm convinced that lots of us who are not Engineers and majored in the social sciences or in Literature or so forth, could never have gotten BAs in engineering, let alone physics. So, there are way too many people going to college in that sense, but the real problem here is the way college is structured. The BA is the work of the devil insofar as it says, we have established an educational criterion, called the BA, which if you do not possess it, you are a second-class citizen in this country now. In some important sense, you are looked down upon in many circles if you were "just" a high school graduate. We've established that and we've said, okay it's going to take four years to get this thing no matter what you're studying. And the way that people are supposed to ordinarily do it is, go off to a residential facility which will cost a lot of money and oftentimes put them into debt, and so we will lure lots of people into trying to get this, a magic thing called the BA, and then when they fail, we will stigmatize them. It's just crazy. My problem is not with almost everybody getting education after high school. My problem is with the artificial, constraining, unresponsive thing called a BA and the program that leads to that. And that's where I want reform to be focused.

The last of the four simple truths is that the future of the country depends on the gifted. And I hurry very rapidly, very rapidly to disabuse people. I am not saying, we have the gifted, these little darlings that we must pamper and hold up, so they can go off and run the country. I'm saying, look, whether we like it or not, this country is organized so that the people who rise to positions of influence are drawn in fact, from the cognitively most talented. They are all going to college and while they're there they need to have their feet held to the fire in several important ways. I'm not going to go through those now because I've already taken more time on this question than I intended but we need to take those people who are going to run the country, whether we like it or not, and we need to instill in them a sense of rigor. In thinking and in critical thinking, in judgments and we also need to instill in them a sense of humility because we have way too many kids now going off to elite colleges finishing their degrees and they have never ever failed at anything. They have never been pushed to a point where they have to say to themselves "I can't do this". Every other student in this country hits that wall. Sometimes they hit in the second grade sometimes it's in high school, sometimes it's trying to go to college, but they all hit such a point. People who are in Mathematics hit that wall. In the social sciences and humanities, you don't necessarily hit it and it's very important that the most able students, the ones with the most promise, reach maturity having realized a sense of their own limits and being able to empathize with everyone else.

Velamoor: In the same book you articulate the motion of a funnel as a framework for solutions.

Dr. Murray: The funnel is in terms of thinking about education, which is to say that we've poured all of these resources into trying to improve the education of the bottom half. The *No Child Left Behind Act* was kind of the apotheosis of that but that's what we've been doing since the 1960s. And the social science on this is quite clear. I'm not talking about a controversial body of evidence. The attempts to jack up the performance of the lower half have had results ranging from very minor to zero, and occasionally negative. And it's not so hard to explain. Forget about academics. Suppose you took me at the age of eight and said, we are going to take Charles and we are going to make him into as good a basketball player as he can become. You could have pumped all the resources into that you wanted and I would have still been a rotten basketball player because I didn't have the inherent kind of ability. Suppose you take a Kobe Bryant at the age of eight and say how much can we improve his basketball performance. You can improve it a whole lot because there's so much ability there that you can deal with. And in the case of academics, it's the same thing. There's a very narrow limit of how we know to raise the cognitive functioning or even the academic performance, of those in the lower half. For really smart kids, it's pretty much open ended in terms of what you could do to improve their education. And there are the ones we pay no attention to.

Velamoor: Moving on to the next book, *Losing Ground* (1984). You point to:

[E]lite wisdom overwhelming popular wisdom, shifting the debate from what in your view, is the American system, has been benign and self-correcting to the pervasive assumption that if something is wrong, the structure in the system is to blame and not the individual.

Would you maintain that given today's circumstances? 14 million unemployed, 50 million without insurance and an equal number below the poverty line are a result of absence of personal responsibility and accountability or, perhaps, some structural and systemic issues?

Dr. Murray: *Losing Ground* was published in 1984. Do you have any idea how scary it is when somebody says, I'm going to ask you a question about a book you wrote in almost 30 years?

[laughter] I'd say, "can I remember what I said in that book?".

Velamoor: To do my job, I had to go through everything you've ever written.

[laughter]

Dr. Murray: In terms of what we're looking at today, in terms of unemployment and the rest of it, of course at this point we are looking at the effects of a severely damaged economy. It's one of these cases you can go out there and try as hard as you want to get a job and you aren't going to be able to find one in a lot of areas because of the economic situation. That goes without saying but in trying to analyze what's been going on, you shouldn't focus on the last couple of years. I have a book coming out at the end of January 2012 (Murray, 2012) which goes from 1960 to 2010 and I deliberately stopped all the numbers involving employment and things like that in 2008. They say look, the important thing is not what's happened to the trend line in 2009-2010. The important thing is what's going on before. Let me give you an example of something that has not evolved the economy. Let's take the case of males on full-time disability. They've gotten the government to say they are physically unable to work. Let's limit it to white males ages 30 to 49 so I've now pared it down to a group of people who don't have any excuses. Either by age or ethnicity or anything else. Let's take the percentage of those white males, ages 30 to 49, who are on disability in 1960 and 2010. Now, we know for a fact that that percentage has to go down. I mean, if you think about all the ways in which you were physically disabled in 1960, which can now be cured medically. That's one thing. The ones that can't be cured. Think of all the ways in which aids have been developed to enable you to do jobs, whether they are Prosthesis or whether they are other kinds of assistance. Think of all the ways in which jobs have changed, so that digging ditches does no longer require you to be wielding a shovel, but you are now sitting behind the controls of a machine. Obviously, the percentage of white males, ages 30 to 49, who were physically disabled, went down from 1960 to 2010. Except that among those with a high school education or less, working in blue collar or service jobs, the percentage of those that were physically disabled in 1960 was two percent. The percentage of the disabled in 2010 is ten percent. What's going on there is not the result of a bad economy. What's going on there is a fundamental change in behavior which we must look to other causes for and the kind of elite wisdom to which you referred, that people are not responsible for the consequences of their actions. Now, at this point I could say, we are looking at a change in the industriousness of a certain category of the population, which is very worrisome, and to me reflects the results of a lot of the kinds of changes that occurred in the 1960s.

Velamoor: You postulate, what I think, were three beautifully articulated laws as it relates to social policy - the law of imperfect selection, the law of unintended rewards and the law of net harm. Can you please elaborate?

Dr. Murray: This is what I meant about remembering.

[laughter]

Now, what did I say in it? I used a smoking experiment. I said, suppose that we have a certain amount of money, a couple of billion dollars, and we are going to use that to induce people not to smoke and we will provide rewards to people who stop smoking. And I went through the logic of it and thought, there is no way to use that money to reduce smoking because of the three laws. Without going into great detail, it means that you cannot increase the rewards for stopping smoking without increasing the incentives to start smoking or to continue smoking. I went through an elaborate set of exercises where I tried to tweak the incentive structure so that you can make it work right and you'll get fewer people smoking than you had before. And I attempt to prove you can't do it. That built into the logic of interventions that are intended to change behavior through incentives. It is a kind of moral hazard.

Velamoor: It creates the opposite. The laws indicate they create the opposite consequences.

Dr. Murray: Yes, and so it's not the case that people were stupid in the way that they did incentives. Whether there are incentives to get off welfare or incentives not to commit crimes and so on. The fact is that incentives backfire. There's a classic example of that. They had a controlled experiment in Germany where they had a superior form of breaks that they put on one half of the taxi fleet and did not put them on the other half of the taxi fleet and then they measured the subsequent accidents. It turned out that the accidents went up among the ones of the better brakes because they took more chances. There's an argument that can be made, if we're trying to get people to drive more carefully, prohibit the use of seat belts. It goes by the same logic.

That was the essence of the laws of unintended consequences. They are not going to be fixed by getting clever or social scientists to design the programs.

Velamoor: On to another book. *In Human Accomplishment* (2003) which I found to be very interesting, you have identified 4002 individuals who would constitute the sum and substance of accomplishment between 800 BC to 1950. I think it's too detailed to go into the methodology and the identification of the names and so on, but your conclusion was very interesting, and I'd like to like to challenge you on an aspect of that. You conclude that the nature of accomplishment in a given time and place can be predicted with reasonable accuracy, given information about cultural status with regard to four dimensions. Purpose, autonomy, organizing structure, and transcendental goods. Not goods in terms of material things but the truth, goodness, and beauty, as I recall you articulating them to be. Please predict, what do you think with regard to the US *vis-à-vis* the BRIC countries, for instance, over the next 20 to 30 or 40 years.

Dr. Murray: I don't think that the picture looks very good for any of them. I'm talking about human accomplishments in the Arts and sciences right now. Now, what do I mean by purpose, autonomy, organizing structure and transcendental goods?

If you have a society in which people grow up with a sense of purpose. That they were put on this earth for a purpose. That will provide nourishment for an environment of achievement in the arts and sciences.

If you are growing up in a culture in which familial relations are paramount and your own druthers and preferences are secondary, it can be a very rich wonderful culture in terms of the family structure. By the way, this is not good versus bad. I'm saying that if you have that, as East Asia had for example, your sense of autonomy, the sense that you're going to walk away from your family and you're going to do what you're going to do, and that you have the power individually by your own actions to affect your life, all that's going to be diminished. Whereas if you do have a culture in which children grow up thinking they have a lot of power over their own destiny, that also tends to nurture accomplishment in the arts and sciences.

Organizing structure is one of the most interesting of those. Think of the development of music in the West. You've got the idea of polyphony back in the late Middle Ages, but to make really wonderful music with that, you had to have better instruments. The invention of the Violin, the invention of the Harpsichord and other technical improvements in the organizing structure just opened up the capacity for an explosion of great achievement in music. In Art, the rediscovery of perspective in the 15th century and the invention of oil paints just provided an organizing structure that they hadn't had before. And this led to an explosion of great art.

And finally, transcendental goods. I keep science aside for the moment. You've got truth, beauty and the good. Those are the three classic transcendental goods. The good in the Aristotelian sense. If you have a coherent sense of those transcendental goods in the culture, I think it's prerequisite for great art and great literature. I don't think you produce great art without the artists having a sense of what they are trying to achieve. That goes way beyond expressing themselves. Beethoven expressed himself, but he did so within the context of an incredibly coherent concept of beauty as a transcendental good.

If you look at that, I don't know of any culture in the world which is looking good on all four of those dimensions. The United States and Western societies still look strong in terms of autonomy. If anything, autonomy, the sense of we can be whatever we want to be, is at least as strong as it has ever been. Purpose, that's probably diminished here along with religiosity. Because, to say "I was put in this world for a purpose", Christianity was especially effective at fostering that sense of purpose. And to a degree Christianity is attenuated. And in terms of transcendental good's, it says if modern art and literature try to deny that such things can exist and that's been true now for almost a century.

My challenge that I give to people, with respect to the arts and literature is, think about the fact that there are still works from the past that are part of our culture. Jane Austen is a part of our culture as you can buy her books in almost any airport bookstore, let alone all the movies that have been made of her novels. Vivaldi, Beethoven, Mozart, Bach are all live forces that we still listen to. Tell me, what art, music or literature produced since 1950 will still be part of the culture two hundred years from now in the same way that Jane Austen and Vivaldi are of ours?

I've heard that answer before. If I could go back and tell you about popular artists who were every bit as overwhelmingly popular in 1900 or 1910 or 1870, in the context as the Beatles were and we don't even know who they are now, it's really hard to come up with nominations that you can be fairly confident, will not be timed out and will still stand. That's a challenge. I think that art and literature are in a kind of dormant phase and it's going to take a very basic kind of cultural revitalization to bring them back.

Velamoor: I promise you, this would be the last of the books that you've written.

[laughter]

Dr. Murray: I wondered how many more you have left.

[laughter]

Velamoor: To me, this was the most interesting because it gets into the realm of political philosophy. You wrote *What it Means to be a Libertarian* (1997). You describe yourself as a lower-case libertarian, as in, l in the lowercase. Can you please elaborate with respect to the differences between yourself and a libertarian with a capital L?

Dr. Murray: The "capital L" libertarians argue deep into the night about whether it's okay to have laws prohibiting child pornography. They have a very pure philosophy about a complete absence of any kind of government except to prohibit the use of force and fraud. Lowercase libertarians don't argue about that kind of stuff. Lower-case libertarians basically believe the same things that Thomas Jefferson, James Madison, and George Washington believe. They say, what we need is a society and a government which does protect people from each other and otherwise leaves people alone. Not so they can go out as individuals and live in their own separate little castles but so that you can have a society in which people can live their own lives as they see fit and come together voluntarily to solve the community's problems that are around them. There was one glaring terrible exception to that. It's almost like a Greek tragedy, the tragic flaw, and that is that the United States countenanced slavery.

Granted, it is a big exception, but if you look at the northern states during the 19th century and the western states as expansion group and you look at the way the society functioned, it was one of steady progress toward that kind of society. It was a vibrant society. One which did an incredible job of solving its problems as compared especially to any other society throughout history, solving problems at the local level. As time went on it got better and better. By the end of the 19th century, the beginning of the 20th century, once again I'm putting aside the south and the huge problems associated with slavery, but the deep inequities that persisted at that time in the society were founded on force and fraud. When you had company towns who exploited their workers, they were using goons or paid off police to maintain the company town. Whenever their competition existed, whenever the market was able to enter, the United States provided wonderful examples of the power of freedom to solve problems over the long term. That includes community problems as well as problems of living in an individual life. For people like me, lower-case libertarians, we had a wonderful thing going for us and it continued going for us up through the midcentury constantly making progress. Starting around the 1960s we continued to make progress on a couple of very important fronts. We've made progress on the racial front, and we made progress on equal opportunity for women. Those are not trivial achievements. They are achievements which I am utterly convinced would have happened in the absence of the Civil Rights Act of 1964 or other kinds of title 9 legislation. What has happened since the 1960s has undermined that civic culture to such a degree that it is in some segments of the society virtually dysfunctional. That is also going to be a major theme of the book that's coming out in January (Murray, 2012).

Velamoor: Staying on the subject of libertarianism, it seems to me that clarity and cleanliness, as it relates to the notions of the public good and the tragedies of the commons, are the two most problematic issues when it comes to libertarianism. Are these notions adequately accounted for? I'm referring of course to the biologist Garrett James Hardin (1968) as an example of people buying more cattle.

Dr. Murray: They're problematic for you in what sense, Sesh?

Velamoor: In that libertarianism does not adequately account for the commons. Or the notion of the public good is hazy at best. Along the lines of Ayn Rand or to say the public good is accounted for by virtue of an approach to libertarianism.

Dr. Murray: Let's talk about what a classic public good is. The phrase has become so corrupted that it now essentially means whatever a majority of people think is good for the public. In the classic sense, a public good had a couple of characteristics which set it apart from other kinds of things. One was that it is indivisible. Take National Defense as an example. There's no way you can protect Cleveland without protecting Detroit and if you're going to provide national defense, everybody is going to participate in it. And it is appropriate for people to pay for that because it is something that people cannot provide for themselves. Similarly, a criminal justice system or a court system, administering and ministering civil law. That is a public good that is not eligible for solution at an individual level. Street lighting is an example of a public good that's sort of getting at the boundaries. It gets some people saying that actually people could light. Yes, but if you do have street lighting it does sort of light everything, and people can share it. Roads are an example. A capital L libertarian will say, no you could have toll roads, and everybody could pay according to how much they use them, and they could be privately owned toll roads. Lowercase libertarians are willing to treat roads as a public good. This means that my use of that public good does not prevent you from using it, so it's not a zero-sum game whereby if I drive on the highway from Frederick to Washington DC, the other guy can't drive on the highway.

Regarding public goods, the classic tradition says that there are certain things that it's okay for the government to do and even essential for the government to do. For example, a legal system and a national defense. But as soon as you get to something where the government has decided that Sesh can give his money to another specific person because the other person needs it more than Sesh does, that is no longer public good. That is a transfer and that does not fall within the rubric of classic public goods. I wouldn't say that's a defect of libertarianism. I don't think that the argument for income transfers holds water in terms of a governmental policy. You have to distinguish two questions. One is should we do things to help the disadvantaged and the other one is, who can best provide assistance? When it comes to things like income transfers, I would argue that the reduction in poverty in this country prior to the 1960s was phenomenal. We have calculated what the poverty line was and how many people would have been little below the poverty line going back to the 1940 census. At that time it was more than half the population but I think the more telling statistic here is that in the 1950 census it was still 41 percent of the population. In the somnolent Eisenhower years, when supposedly nothing was happening, that poverty rate went from 41 percent down to about 20 percent in 1961 when JFK came to office. A stunning achievement. It was not done through income transfers. It was done by a dynamic growing economy combined with America's traditional civic culture. And I would argue that the subsequent flattening out of our progress against poverty is sort of a practical illustration where libertarians like me can say, if you want to help the poor, we were doing a lot better before the government decided to take over this function.

Velamoor: This is a more personal question coming from my own understanding of things based on conferences and seminars over the last 15 years. Is it not the case that ultimately what can be broadly described as cultural or memetic evolution as an ongoing process, is what dictates the emergence of political economic social and cultural norms for human societies? That it is a work in progress? That there is no such thing as a perfect prescription as a starting point?

Dr. Murray: I guess that I affiliate myself with William F. Buckley who once said that he wanted to stand athwart history yelling "Stop!" (Buckley, 1955). I am hesitating here because I recognize cultural differences. If I were to go to India and be given godlike power to install an absolutely perfect set of libertarian laws, do I think they would necessarily work in India? The answer is no. But I will talk about the United States and by extension eventually in broader chunks of the world. I think human beings have very common needs. I think Abraham Maslow's needs hierarchy is a really good way of thinking about those.

It starts out with at the most primitive level. You got to have food and shelter. And then human beings need safety. Once you get beyond food and shelter and safety, then you move into needs such as need for self-respect and the need for self-actualization, in Maslow's terms. I think those are pretty much universal.

In wealthy societies, where you can deal with the food and shelter and the safety needs easily, in a variety of different ways, the question then becomes, what is the way that you can deal with those, that both fosters the self-respect that people need and the chance to feel that they are being all they can be. I would say that the great defect of contemporary systems, especially the vast welfare states of Europe, is that they have treated these needs as if they can be segmented. Give people food and shelter and then we will let them go out and work out their own ways of achieving self-respect and self-actualization. But it doesn't work that way. If you're one of the lucky few who is, let's say, a great composer, it doesn't make any much difference how you get your food and shelter. You're creating great music and you're getting gratification from that, you're getting respect for them. But most of us are not great composers. Most of us work at humdrum jobs and we never become rich or famous. Then, a great deal of self-respect comes from earning a living and supporting a family. It's authentic self-respect, it's not fake, but in order for it to be real you have to earn a living and support them. A great many of us get a lot of self-actualization from the jobs we do, not because they make us rich or famous but because we are exercising our realized capabilities under a condition of challenge and we find this gratifying, we find it satisfying and we take pride in what we do, but that also depends crucially on the ways in which we have responsibility for the consequences of our actions. And things that undercut responsibility for the consequences of our actions inherently get in the way of those.

So, I'm saying, these human needs are not separable and that maybe in times of great scarcity you have more constraints on how you can do it but to me, it is precisely the wealthy societies that ought to be looking most carefully at the way these things are linked and the universal importance of making sure that people are living lives filled with meaning. And lives are only filled with meaning when you feel you actually and literally are an actor who is making choices, taking responsibility for the consequences of choices, trying to think ahead, trying to be the best thoughtful persevering human being you can be. The regime that fosters that in my view, is the system that the founders gave us here in this country.

Velamoor: On that high note I will end my session with Dr. Murray. We'll open it up for questions and answers for a limited period of time.

Audience Member 1: Dr. Murray, in this political climate where we have this election coming up [referring to 2012], can you give us an idea of where you see it going and what you think would be best for the country in terms of what you're looking at, for us to really move ahead? And who would you vote for?

[laughter]

Dr. Murray: I'm writing in Mitch Daniels' name. What's happening right now is potentially of historic proportions.

[Cut]

I read the tea party as being very interestingly and overwhelmingly a very wide-ranging group of people who are feeling an allegiance toward the kind of American system I just described. Of one of limited government in which people are left alone to live their lives and it's not the government's job to solve all our problems for us, but it is the government's job to get out of the way. It's a much clearer set of alternatives than we have tended to have in this country in presidential elections. The problem is that it would be nice if the Republicans could come up with a standard-bearer appropriate to their side of the debate.

When I said Mitch Daniels, I think he was precisely that kind of guy. I think he is a very principled limited government advocate but he's also an effective executive. I do not think Mitt Romney is that person in terms of his principles. I'm going to alienate just about everybody in the room with this answer because I'm going to dump on all of it.

[laughter]

I don't think Rick Perry has demonstrated that he has sufficient grasp of what's going on here. It's going to be a potentially historic election. Whether it will actually end up being that way is another question

Audience Member 2: Dr. Murray, we're here with the Foundation for the Future, I was wondering if you could talk a little bit about your thoughts on the future of the United States, or whether it has one. I'll just throw out a few items that might start the conversation - first is the demographic transformation of not only United States but all Western societies and how in many ways the bell curve-argument has been transformed in the new demographic reality that we're living and experiencing.

Dr. Murray: Specifically, what transition are you're talking about?

Audience Member 2: In terms of mass immigration into western countries.

Dr. Murray: Well, that's not the one that worries me. The new book has as a subtitle. The main title is Coming apart. The subtitle is The State of White America 1960 – 2010 and the reason I have that subtitle is because I limit the analysis to non-Latino whites. The reason I limit the analysis to non-Latino whites is that one of my main arguments is that we have seen the development of a new lower class in this country - unlike anything we have ever known before. We've also seen the development of a new upper class unlike anything we've ever seen before. What I wanted to do was to make this case and putting the issues of immigration completely aside. Putting issues of race completely aside. I'd say, this is going on with non-Latino whites and it goes to the core of the way the nation is functioning. In that sense, I don't see massive immigration as having a huge effect. I am one of these people who believes that, even as a libertarian, one of the things governments are supposed to do is to have control of their borders. In that sense, I am wholeheartedly against countenancing the illegal immigration that has gone on. I think that is very bad public policy. On the other hand, I am a great believer in immigration as having been the thing which has kept this country fresh and vital all this time and I think that continues to be the case. I'm not an open borders person who says, "We ought to let anybody come here who wants to come here", but I am just not exercised about immigration.

I've got to tell this anecdote because it happened so recently, and it was so much fun. I like to play poker and there is a there is a casino that is only 17 miles away from us. So, I go over there and play poker and it is an extremely heterogeneous, socioeconomically, racially and ethnically, social situation in the United States. There is never a time I'm at the table where there aren't at least a couple of Asians, a couple of African Americans and so on. One day, I'm sitting there and at my end of the table was an Afghani American, a Serbo-Croatian American, me and an Indian American, all of them speaking completely unaccented, perfect English. We got to talking about my daughter. She had as a fiancée an Italian and all of them are saying, "Well do you trust him?"

[laughter]

Because they were probably all reacting to the stereotype. I said to myself, we are all Americans, they're all talking exactly like Americans, are acting like Americans and I just loved that situation.

I want to get rid of illegal immigration. As far as legal immigration is concerned, I think thank God for it.

Dr. Murray: Do you think the country can survive the stratification that you were talking about?

[crosstalk]

A creation of the massive underclass and a upper order that, in many ways, is hostile towards the values that you put forth.

Dr. Murray: Yes, that's a completely different question. The answer here is that the founders, when they talked about the Constitution, unanimously and explicitly and repeatedly said "This will not work without certain virtues in the people". Four of those virtues are marriage, industriousness, honesty, and religiosity.

Religiosity by the way, was emphasized by all the founders including Jefferson, including those that were most clearly deists. Most of the founders were not very devout in traditional terms but they all said the religiosity was essential to a self-governing nation because self-government first of all means, governing oneself. One of the things that I'm talking about in the book, looking at the new lower class, is the extent to which we've seen a working class in the 1960s, which basically was very similar to the upper middle class. Now, we see huge divergence on all four of those measures and that's very problematic for their functioning in a free society. At the upper end, the weird thing about the upper end, is that what they do is actually pretty good. Marriage and industriousness and honesty are still alive and well in the upper class. The problem is, they don't preach what they practice. They do not feel that the fact that marriage is important in their lives and in raising their children and that industriousness is important in their lives. They don't feel that it's okay to propagandize the rest of the nation to share those virtues and those values. If you are a fan of Arnold Toynbee, you know he said something along the lines of: "If you want to see a civilization on the downslide, take a look at one in which, what he called the creative minority, has simply become a dominant minority and has lost confidence in its own values" (Toynbee, 1934-1961). I think in many regards his analysis fits what we were looking at in the United States. I am not necessarily predicting disaster in this regard, I think there's a pessimistic scenario and there's an optimistic scenario, I won't go into, but that's a real issue right now.

Audience Member 3: I want to shift the focus to Europe a little bit. You talked about the USA educational system that makes going to college very freely available. I'm not talking about monetary terms. But Europe, as I understand it, has long had a system that does have a process of selection and that 10-15 percent of high school graduates go to college. That infrastructure is supplemented by a network of vocational institutes that also provide respectable and self-sufficient careers for people. How do you evaluate that? Would that ever be considered here at all?

The second question is: You've talked about the migration of at least one political element in the US towards the European, if you will, the structure of social welfare etc. Yet the evidence right now is that in Europe economic circumstances are causing enormous dislocations in both welfare states and they are migrating very quickly away from those situations into being able to pay for what you can really afford?

Dr. Murray: In fact, we have about half of all high school graduates try to go to a four-year college. When I said 15-20 percent, that's the percentage who actually can do well intellectually in a traditional college setting. But I also was saying, everybody needs post-high school education. So the answer is that the vocational kinds of technical training are great and wonderful and I wish they would expand. What I want to get rid of is the invidious distinction between getting a technical degree and getting this magic thing called a BA - because all of you in the room who are employers know that when somebody sits down in front of you and says I got a BA, you don't know a thing. It's a certain crude screen for a degree of IQ and a degree of perseverance but until you know what school the person went to and what major they had, you don't know anything and even then, you don't necessarily know more than that. So, I want to get rid of that distinction and I want to substitute the concept of certification. If you have a young person who really wants to go into business and they have certain specific marketing courses they want to take and they have certain kinds of accounting courses they want to take and business organization courses and if they want to take four years to do that, that's up to them, if they want to do those in two years that's up to them, but there will be a really good certification test. By good I mean defined by the users of the test as indicative of whether they mastered that material. I want something they can take to an employer which proves what they know as opposed to where they learned it and how long it took them. It would lead toward a situation which would be fundamentally different from the one we have now. Instead of the BA having this artificial value, we would look upon all young people's education as having the goal of arriving at adulthood having learned something that they like to do and having learned how to do it very well. And we would do another thing as well. I would like to have an understanding that whether you are a physicist or you are a English literature professor or whether you are a plumber, all of our careers go through the same phases. We all start out as apprentices, we all become journeyman if we get confident in our craft and the very best ones become master craftsmen. I am tired of kids graduating from college very pleased with having gotten the BA from Swarthmore or Harvard or Stanford or whatever and not seeing that they basically are engaged in the same kind of process as someone who became the plumber. I want that the way they will measure their success in life is measured by the same kinds of career pattern I just described. I want to have more of a sense of kinship across classes in this country to recognize the real things that unite us.

Regarding Europe, my optimistic scenario for the United States is predicated in the fact that over the next 10 or 15 years we will be watching what happens in Europe and it will not be pretty. That Europe, and that means Germany, Netherlands, Scandinavia, and the whole bunch, will find itself unable to sustain the welfare state as they have created it. They will be unable to sustain it partly because of the ineluctable dynamics whereby the welfare state creates more and more people who depend on it. That's just the way the system works and fewer and fewer people who contribute to the system.

Interview sourced from the archives of the Foundation For the Future.

References

Buckley, W. F. (1955, November 19th). Our Mission Statement. *National Review*. https://www.nationalreview.com/1955/11/our-mission-statement-william-f-buckley-jr/

Fincher, C. & Thornhill R. (2014). *The Parasite-Stress Theory of Values and Sociality*. Springer.

Gardner, H. (1993). *Multiple Intelligences: The Theory in Practice*. Basic Books.

Hardin, G. J. (1968). The Tragedy of the Commons. *Science*, 162 (3859), 1243–1248. DOI:10.1126/science.162.3859.1243. PMID 5699198.

Murray, C. (1984). *Losing Ground: American Social Policy, 1950–1980*. Basic Books.

Murray, C. & Herrnstein, R.J. (1994). *The Bell Curve: Intelligence and Class Structure in American Life*. The Free Press.

Murray, C. (1997). *What It Means to Be a Libertarian*. Broadway Books.

Murray, C. (2003). *Human Accomplishment: The Pursuit of Excellence in the Arts and Sciences, 800 B.C. to 1950*. HarperCollins.

Murray, C. (2008). *Real Education: Four Simple Truths for Bringing America's Schools Back to Reality*. Crown Forum.

Murray, C. (2012). *Coming Apart: The State of White America, 1960–2010*. Crown Forum.

Toynbee, A. (1934-1961). *A Study of History*. Oxford University Press.

About the Author

Sesh Velamoor, recognized as a Fellow of the World Academy of Art and Science, has had a unique and distinguished career in three different fields spanning over nearly 45 years:

- in business, as a member of boards, chief executive and consultant in the electromechanical manufacturing industry;

- as a lecturer in business administration at university level; and

- as a trustee and director of programs at the non-profit Foundation For the Future with responsibility for planning, designing, and conducting conferences, seminars, workshops and onstage interviews involving several hundred scholars of world renown, exploring the long term future of humanity on a wide array of themes such as climate change, energy, water, cultural evolution, future of humans in space, demographics, genetics and society, future humans, education etc.

He is a regularly invited panelist in global seminars and conferences, as a speaker at numerous global forums on aspects of the future. He has also published articles and essays in several different journals of Future Studies.

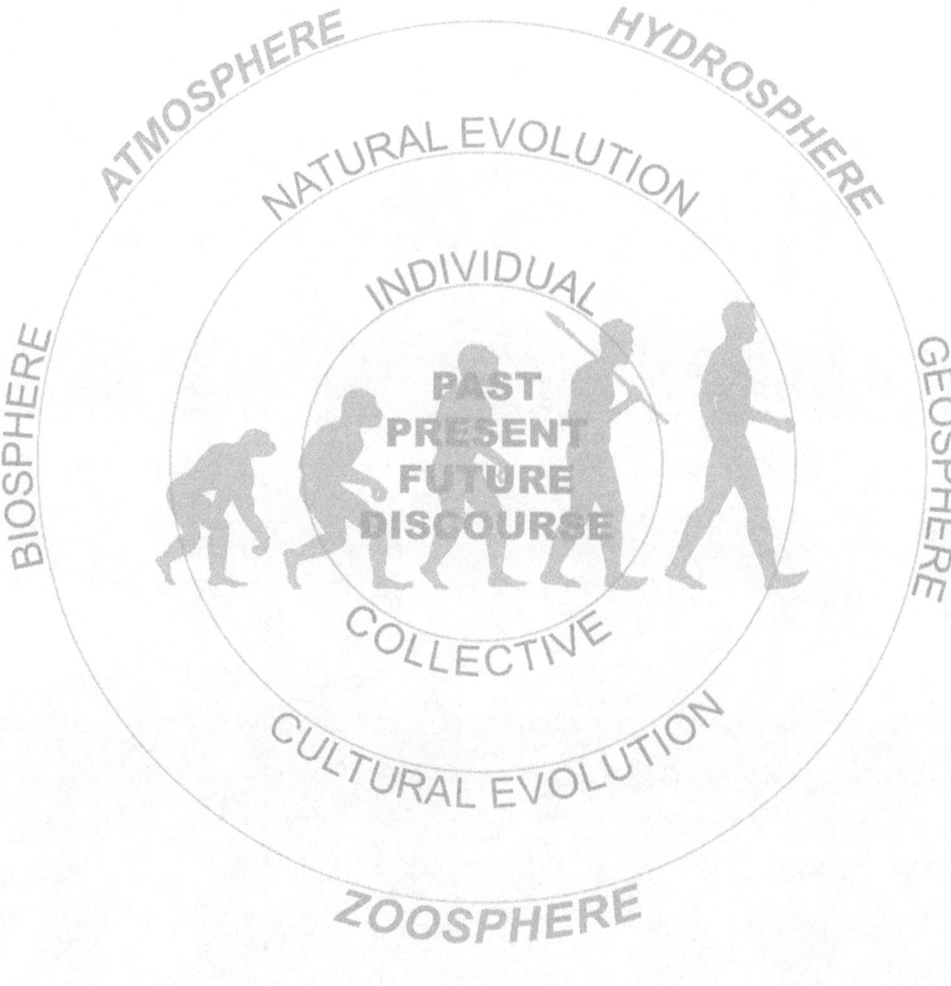

ATMOSPHERE
HYDROSPHERE
NATURAL EVOLUTION
INDIVIDUAL
BIOSPHERE
GEOSPHERE
PAST
PRESENT
FUTURE
DISCOURSE
COLLECTIVE
CULTURAL EVOLUTION
ZOOSPHERE